EXPLORING THE

BLUE MOUNTAIN PLATEAU

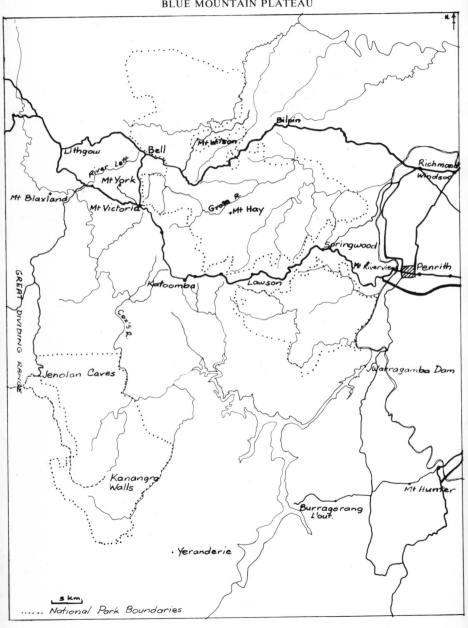

5 km.

...... National Park Boundaries

A HERITAGE FIELD GUIDE

Exploring
The Blue Mountains

SECOND EDITION

Meredyth Hungerford
and J. Kay Donald

Kangaroo Press

Acknowledgements

The authors wish to acknowledge the assistance given to them by the Springwood Historical Society, the Blue Mountains Historical Society, the Mount Victoria and District Historical Society and the Lithgow District Historical Society, and to thank Dr John Pickett for his advice concerning the geology of the Blue Mountains, Leslie V. Barnet for help with photographic printing, and the Blue Mountains City Council and the National Trust of Australia (N.S.W.) for the use of their registers.

Quotations from the journals of Gregory Blaxland, George Evans, William Cox, Governor Macquarie, Major Antill, Mrs Elizabeth Hawkins and James Backhouse have been taken from *Fourteen Journeys Over The Blue Mountains of New South Wales 1813-1841* collected and edited by George Mackaness O.B.E., M.A., Litt.D. (Melb.), M.A., D.Litt., D.Sc. (Syd.), F.R.A.H.S. and published by Horwitz-Grahame, 1965.

Warning

The authors wish to stress that many of the places mentioned in this book are PRIVATE PROPERTY and are not open to the public. They hereby disclaim responsibility for any person who may incur the law of trespass or violate rights of privacy.

This second edition published in 1992
Reprinted in 1986 and 1990
Reprinted with corrections 1983 and 1984
First published in 1982 by Kangaroo Press
3 Whitehall Road (P.O. Box 75), Kenthurst 2156
Printed in Singapore by Singapore National Printers Limited

ISBN 0 86417 505 1

Contents

Cliffs of the Grose Gorge showing the landslide at Burramoko Head as viewed from Rigby Hill. The Grose River is visible at the foot of the talus slope.

Introduction

1 A Personal Perspective

The Blue Mountains are part of the romance of childhood for me. My personal introduction to the beauties of nature, to bushwalking and poetry, to history and geography, and to the rudiments of botany and geology.

Some of my earliest and most beautiful memories are here: late August snow falling on a roadside bank of thick white clematis, then the warmth of my grandmother's big log fire; a sunny morning high on a swampy mountainside, where my father showed me the first sundews in my world — and it seems to me now that their sticky 'dew' was composed of tiny rainbows; the great warm grey fallen tree that was my rocking horse and climbing frame; and a rush circled pond full of tadpoles.

Later I led expeditions of younger cousins into the bush to find places our parents had loved when they were our age. Our mothers were not afraid to let us wander, for this had been their playground too, and they had instructed us in the first law of the Blue Mountains. 'Stick to the ridges', they said. Of course we found out for ourselves that between these ridges the shortest distance is not necessarily a straight line. We found out why it was easier and quicker to walk three kilometers round the head of a creek than to clamber down and up again through a steep-sided sandstone gully, often full of almost impenetrable scrub. After one such scramble I wrote my first 'poem', entitled simply

'1813' — I was sure I knew how Blaxland, Wentworth and Lawson really felt.

Many years later I read the journals of earlier explorers in the mountains, Barrallier and Caley and others who had not found the secret of 'sticking to the ridges'. Although I did not know their names till later, I began to know the geography that defeated them. An uplifted dissected peneplain: a vast area of sandstone, laid down under ancient waters: a plateau which had risen as the streams of the new land wore downwards. The almost level tops and the great chasms were visible from almost any high point. In places landslides demonstrated the processes forming cliffs and talus slopes. I could almost imagine I saw the waterfalls at work. More puzzling were the group of knob shaped mountains with basalt caps — igneous rocks on top of the sedimentary. Where had the basalt, which provided rich deep soil for my grandmother's bulb garden, come from? Though I searched about for likely volcanoes my efforts were doomed; the basalt was remnants of ancient lava flows from long-gone unmarked sources.

The plant life was another wonder. Sandy ridges could suddenly burst into scent and colour with seas of pink boronia, or carpet themselves with flannel flowers. Lower on the hillsides waratahs bloomed, and deep in the gullies another world existed, cool and green with treeferns, mosses and liverworts. I collected the names of plants, collected and pressed little flowers; but there is no way to retain the joys by collecting anything but memories. Now every walk in these mountains carries the richness of many memories, and also the awareness of others' experiences. I have felt the struggle of the newcomers who tried to force a way through the mountains and found them bitter enemies. I have felt the cold and warmth, the fierce winds and scented breezes, the exposure and shelter, the fear and joy of the place. The Aborigines who rubbed their axeheads on the sandstone ridges must have feared and respected, as well as loved, these mountains. Although sometimes gentle they are never tame. I have fought a bushfire; and fallen as a rock broke under me; and wondered if I'd make it back to the top of a ridge. Respect and fear are part of my love too.

The Blue Mountains, as I've known them from childhood, as the explorers found them, as the Aborigines knew them, are preserved by a National Park, but also by their own nature. The urban sprawl reaches out, the roads are widened; but from the end of any ridge — beyond the tarred surface, beyond the car track, beyond the foot track — are scarcely trodden labyrinths of gullies and ridges, cliffs and canyons to beckon and defy any wilderness seeker. From the tamed accessible places one can look into the wild parts, or pit oneself against them, and enter a timeless world where the difficulties of past men are real and where the future must contain these rocks and trees, these streams and ferns, this pure air and untouched beauty.

The division into two sections for the present book is based on two lines of exploration, which became the two roads over the mountains — the Great Western Highway through Katoomba and Bell's Line of Road from Richmond to Lithgow. Both roads follow the high ground, on the principle of 'sticking to the ridges', of the watersheds between the Grose and the Cox's — Warragamba system to the south, and the Grose and Capertee — Colo system to the north. The Grose Gap appeared as the most tempting way 'through' the mountains to Europeans who thought of river valleys as leading to mountain passes. This deeply dissected plateau with its tortuous streams was beyond their experience, and the Grose led to some early disappointments. It is in fact the only one of the river systems mentioned which is contained wholly within the sandstone area; which does not rise on the watershed of the main dividing range beyond.

The mountains were first named by Governor Phillip — Carmarthen Hills to the north of Grose Gap and Lansdowne Hills to the south, with Richmond Hill, between the two. Phillip was on an exploratory journey and fifteen miles inland from Narrabeen Lake, in April 1788 (3 months after settlement), when he recorded these names. The settlers ignored them and soon referred to the range as the Blue Mountains. The pattern of the range may be seen from any high point in Sydney on a clear day; and the barrier does not appear formidable.

But formidable it was. Reports from a succession of governors and the journals of explorers show a growing pessimism. But each journey contributed to the final solution; arrived at under economic pressures by a process of elimination. Straight compass courses led to cliffs and ravines — impossible; rivers led to rapids and high waterfalls — impossible. Blaxland, with an eye on the limited extent of pasture land on the Sydney Plain, was the man who saw the solution and managed to implement it. So we remember 1813, Blaxland, Wentworth and Lawson; the date of achievement and the heroes who gave names to present towns on the Great Western Highway. Evans, who surveyed their route then went on to cross the Great Divide and discover the Bathurst Plains has less praise. Cox, who completed the road to Bathurst in six months with a party of 28 convict workmen, and half a dozen soldier guards, has a river named for him. But all this rested to a large extent on the earlier, often forgotten, 'failed' attempts of Dawes, Tench, Paterson, Hacking, Bass, Barrallier, Caley.

The 'shades' of all who conquered, and tried to conquer, by European force, this inhospitable area are present when one walks on these ridges, in these gullies. And here too are older 'shades', of soft-footed Aborigines who trod their trade routes in a land of peace and plenty, where food and shelter were sufficient, and no boots wore out. Follow some of the well-worn tracks, or those that have grown over since the 30s. And as you walk, silently, you'll hear and see and breathe what all these heard and saw and breathed. And in imagination you may feel the frustrations of the aliens, as well as their courage and endurance; but you may also perceive the 'home' that has sheltered and provided for people over thousands of years.

J. Kay Donald

2 Geological Story

The sandstones that form the dominant features of Blue Mountains scenery are part of an enormous geological structure called the Sydney Basin, stretching from Newcastle to Ulladulla and west to Lithgow. These rocks, still for the most part in their original horizontal positions, were laid down after the ocean gradually invaded a land surface formed 460 to 360 million years ago. After this the sea in its turn was pushed back by the development of huge deltas. Here lush vegetation grew and accumulated, to form in time, the coal measures of the Sydney Basin. Rivers deposited more silt and sand and erosion material over the deltas and the sandstone of the Narrabeen and the Hawkesbury strata were laid down on a gigantic flood plain. At a somewhat later time, in an extensive fresh water lake, Wianamatta shale was formed on top of the sandstones.

A very long period of about 150 million years followed when there was very little earth movement and the surface rocks were slowly eroded. Then, about 18 to 15 million years ago, basalt lava flows covered the old land surfaces. Forces of erosion continued their slow work, wearing away the basalt down to the sedimentary rocks beneath, leaving a few basalt caps in some places, to be seen today on Mounts Hay, Banks, Tomah, Wilson and Tootie, and in pockets here and there.

Only a few million years ago were the rocks of the Blue Mountains lifted up to make the plateau. The Lapstone Monocline and the Kurrajong Fault were produced during this uplift. Streams formerly flowing slowly seawards along a gradual gradient now plunged dramatically over the edge of the mountains. The erosion rate at the point of fall was drastically increased, so that the rivers now cut back along their old courses. The spectacular gorges were carved out of the plateau leaving basalt residuals standing higher than the general level of the tableland.

The shape of each river valley is determined by the rock structure through which the streams have to cut their way. In the upper Grose, for example, the water of Govett's Leap falls 159 metres in one drop and the scenery is dominated by sheer sandstone cliffs. The coal measures wear away first, being softer, and this undermines the sandstone, which then breaks off at vertical cracks, or joints, and falls to make the talus slopes stretching down to the stream at the bottom of the valley.

Near the edge of the plateau in the east, at the Lapstone Monocline, the coal measures are further beneath the surface, and are below the level of the streams. Without the soft shales beneath the sandstones, the valleys are narrower and V-shaped.

West of Mount Victoria, the Cox's River and its tributaries have cut rounded valleys through the granite and the hills have been worn to rounded shapes, whilst the cliffs of Shipley and Narrow Neck Plateau are the result of their 'sandstone above coal measure' structure.

The limestone at Jenolan accumulated on the sea floor about 400 million years ago. The caves, however, are much younger, being formed only in the last million years or so, after the earth movements had pushed the limestone to the surface. Its marine origin is evidenced by the fossils of corals, shells and crustaceans which are sometimes found in it. The caves themselves are the result of erosion processes that are still going on.

3 The First Inhabitants

As we explored the Blue Mountain Plateau, we discovered much evidence of the presence of Aboriginal People in times past. Tool sharpening grooves are plentiful and there are also rock engravings and stencils.

The tribe which inhabited the ridges about the Grose is believed to have been the Daruk, part of the larger Kamilaroi grouping. The Gundungura dwelt in the valleys to the west and south west.

Radio carbon dating from sites excavated in the Blue Mountains has revealed that certain caves were occupied as long ago as 22,000 years

Bands of softer darker shale underlie sandstone in a road cutting. These are the strata basic to cliff formation in the Blue Mountains.

'The Cave Hotel', Bell's Line of Road. 'Emu foot' markings are visible on the inner walls of the cave.

Rubbing grooves, Du Faur's Rocks, Mount Wilson

B.P. It is thought that the climate then was probably drier than it is now, sufficiently dry to make mountain dwelling tolerable for part of the time.

Blaxland records finding a few abandoned huts at Springwood and mentions two occasions when they thought 'natives' were near. In the valleys to the west he saw the camping fires of several groups.

It would appear from the archaeological evidence that there had not been any considerable population on the mountains for perhaps several hundred years. Other reasons for few encounters with Aboriginal People being recorded here by early explorers, travellers and settlers could be that their numbers had been reduced by the spread of diseases brought by the colonists; that the mountains were inhabited only in summer, the month of May when Blaxland and party were there, being too cold; or that they were in caves below the tops of the ridges; or that they were just avoiding the white men.

The Gundungura tribe was reported by later settlers as travelling regularly through the Kanimbla Valley.

All Aboriginal relics are protected by law, legislation passed in 1970 making the National Parks and Wildlife Service responsible for their protection and preservation.

4 Defining the Area — The Blue Mountains Region

One question we asked ourselves concerned the size of the Blue Mountains area.

Taking a limited view, only the eastern side of the mountains seen from Sydney might be understood; only the relatively small area of the 'Blue Mountain Towns', from Glenbrook to Mount Victoria would be included. Yet when we followed the explorers, we found that their attacks had been made both north and south of this 'main' ridge.

Our special interest is the area the early explorers penetrated and the developments occurring later in that region. Consequently 'our' Blue Mountains stretch from the edge of the Wollemi National Park on the north side of the Grose to the southern border of the Burragorang National Park. To the west we have followed Blaxland, Wentworth and Lawson to the mountains named for them, and there we stop. We feel that Evans' crossing of the divide and the settlement of Bathurst belong to the story of the western slopes and plains, and is outside our present scope. We have included Kanangra Walls because this plateau over-looks the country reached by Barrallier, part of whose track is now out of reach under the waters of Lake Burragorang.

5 Walking Tracks

Our information comes from personal experience and a variety of other sources. It is not comprehensive; we have left room for you to do your own exploring. As this sort of information gets out of date fairly quickly, we would advise a visit to any of the following:

The National Parks and Wildlife Service Visitors' Centre at Blackheath, at the end of Govett's Leap Road near the falls; open daily.

The Information Centre at the entrance to the Blue Mountains National Park, Bruce Road, Glenbrook; open weekends.

Information Centre and Tearoom, Fletcher Street, Wentworth Falls.

Tourist Information or Visitors' Centres run by Councils are located on the Great Western Highway, Glenbrook; at Echo Point, Katoomba; and at 285 Main Street, Lithgow.

A wide variety of subjects is covered by these services.

6 Organisation

The order of our materials is geographic rather than chronological. All items relating to a particular place have been grouped together and treated in the order in which the traveller comes to them on that particular route.

The tours follow a pattern convenient for driving; where possible we have organised the routes to minimise crossings of the busy Great Western Highway.

Items located in each chapter are too many to be visited in any one day. We assume that the student of history, the conservationist, the tourist or whoever finds our book interesting and useful, will make a selection from our material to make up his or her own excursion.

Words in the text **in bold type** indicate that an historical note will follow. Places given IN CAPITALS are also of historical interest. Scenic features and places of interest to tourists are shown *in italic*.

Blue Mountains City Council has an *Historical Register Catalogue*. Items listed in it are indicated thus: BMCC HR followed by the suburb letter and a number. Buildings and other features classified or recorded by the National Trust of New South Wales are indicated thus: Nat. Tr.

Items listed in *The Heritage of Australia* are indicated thus: Her. Aus.

The authors wish to stress that many of the places mentioned in this book are PRIVATE PROPERTY and are not open to the public. They hereby disclaim responsibility for any person who may incur the law of trespass or violate rights of privacy.

On the maps **F** indicates the location of 'Footsteps in Time' monuments, which commemorate George William Evans' 1813–14 survey.

1 To the Foot of the Lansdowne Hills Prospect to Emu Plains

1 Prospect

The Great Western Highway leads over the mountains to the inland plains of New South Wales. Eight km west of Parramatta, turn left (use Blacktown exit) to *Prospect Reservoir Park*. The picnic area and the two lookouts are open daily from 10 a.m. to 5 p.m. About a km from the gate, at the end of an avenue of Norfolk Island pines on the left, a monument marks the site of William Lawson's 'Veterans Hall'.

Many of the early explorers, Dawes, Tench, Caley, to name a few, took their bearings on the **Blue Mountains** from this high ground, named **Prospect Hill**. The three successful explorers, **Gregory Blaxland**, **William Lawson** and **William Charles Wentworth** had land grants in the area and would have been familiar with this view.

The Blue Mountains

In his *Account of the English Colony in New South Wales* David Collins says that the name 'Blue Mountains' was commonly used by 1793. Its first official use has been attributed to Captain William Paterson, of the New South Wales Corps, in his despatch describing his attempted crossing of the mountains through the Grose River Valley in that year.

Prospect Hill

The history of the Blue Mountains begins before the traveller reaches the foothills. The mountains may be seen from many of the higher hills round Sydney, one of the best places being Prospect Hill.

From the soft appearance given by the blue shadows, Governor Phillip and many others thought that crossing these hills, for that is all they appeared to men of European background, would be achieved quite quickly. Yet the colony was twenty-five years old before the first white man saw the western plains.

From the journeys of Watkin Tench, William Dawes, George Bass, Wiliam Paterson, Francis Barrallier, Henry Hacking, George Caley and the ex-convict John Wilson, the nature of the Blue Mountains plateau began to come clear. Eventually the idea emerged that use should be made of the watershed ridges, that this might be the most practical means of travelling through the deeply dissected tableland. Blaxland, Lawson and Wentworth made use of this idea in 1813.

Between Parramatta and Prospect lies the tract of land granted to Dr D'Arcy Wentworth. The grant made by Governor Macquarie in 1812 to William Charles Wentworth is further to the west on the bank of the Nepean. Prospect Hill itself was part of a grant to William Lawson, and a large area between South Creek and the Nepean had been granted to Gregory Blaxland. The mountains were part of everyday scenery when they were on their properties and, as they farmed their land, they became increasingly familiar with the topography of the area.

Gregory Blaxland (1778-1853)

Gregory Blaxland was born of a landowning family at Fordwich Kent, England. He and his brother John were friends of Sir Joseph Banks, and when their Kent estates did not seem large enough to provide sufficiently well for their families, they decided to emigrate to New South Wales.

In the time of Governor King (1800 to 1806) it was thought expedient to encourage a certain number of settlers of responsibility and capital to go out to the colony. In accordance with this policy, the Blaxland brothers were promised grants of land, convict servants and free passages in return for their investment. Gregory arrived in 1806 in the *William Pitt* and after first establishing himself at Brush Farm, near Eastwood, he expanded his cattle raising projects in the Penrith area near the Nepean River and on land grants at South Creek. The Blaxlands preferred cattle-raising to grain-growing as the way to greater profits. The governors failed to appreciate that they were contributing fresh meat, a commodity just as valuable as grain. The Blaxlands were doing for the cattle industry and the wine industry what Macarthur and Marsden did for the sheep industry.

The Governors would not grant the large areas needed for cattle from the limited land available on the narrow coastal plain, and so the Blaxlands and others were stimulated to look elsewhere.

Gregory Blaxland had accompanied Governor Macquarie on an excursion to the Warragamba River in 1810, but they had not been able to go very far up its rugged course. He had also explored the western bank of the Nepean and had then found that following the watershed ridges had been profitable, although that particular ridge had not led him across the mountains. Blaxland decided that a route might be found between the Warragamba and the Grose Rivers, and with permission given by Governor Macquarie, set out in company with his neighbours, Lieutenant William Lawson and William Wentworth, Esq., on 11 May 1813, his party including four servants, four horses and five dogs. By keeping to the ridge and avoiding the valleys, they came, after much arduous travelling through the bush, to Mount York and on 31 May to a further mountain later called Mount Blaxland by Surveyor George Evans. They arrived back at South Creek on 6 June.

Each explorer was promised a grant of 1000 acres (equivalent to a little more than 400 hectares today) in the newly discovered territory, but Blaxland sold his grant. In his later years he spent his time at Brush Farm, experimenting with grasses and crops, the most successful being buffalo grass and vines. He won a silver medal for his wines in London in 1822.

William Lawson (1774-1850)

William Lawson was born at Finchley in Middlesex, England, of Scottish parents from Kirkpatrick. He was trained as a surveyor, but in 1799 he bought a commission in the New South Wales Corps. Ensign Lawson arrived in Sydney in the *Royal Admiral* in 1800. He spent a period in the garrison at Norfolk Island, where he married Sarah Leadbeater, a beautiful and vivacious woman. They had eleven children, four of them dying in infancy. On his return to Sydney he was promoted to lieutenant and was commandant at Newcastle for a time, a position he again occupied in 1809. He later joined the New South Wales Veterans' Corps.

He received several grants of land, among them 500 acres (approximately 202 hectares) at Prospect. Most of this land is covered by the reservoir. His home, 'Veterans Hall', was built on higher ground.

Lawson's knowledge of surveying made him a particularly valuable member of the expedition of 1813. His journal gives a detailed record of times and distances, and enables the route to be traced fairly accurately.

Lawson selected his reward grant on the Campbell River near Bathurst, and from 1819 to 1824 was commandant of the new settlement at Bathurst. He discovered 'coal' (really kerosene shale, then unknown) in the Hartley Valley and helped to open up the Mudgee district. He bred sheep and cattle and his horses were famous in coaching days. His nickname was 'Old Ironbark'.

William Charles Wentworth (1790-1872)

William Charles Wentworth was the son of Catherine Crowley, convicted at the Staffordshire Assizes in 1788 for feloniously stealing wearing apparel and sentenced to transporta-

tion for seven years. Dr D'Arcy Wentworth, who sailed in the same ships, the *Neptune* to Sydney and the *Surprize* to Norfolk Island, acknowledged William as his son. William was in Sydney and Parramatta from 1796 to 1803, when he was sent to school in England. Cookney, his father's agent, advised against the boy being trained as a surgeon, as he had a cast in one eye. Failing to gain a place in the military academy at Woolwich or in the East India Company, William returned to Sydney in 1810. In 1811 Macquarie appointed him Acting Provost-Marshal, and granted him 1750 acres (708 hectares) on the Nepean.

Tall and robust, young and energetic, with an adventurous spirit, he was invited to accompany Gregory Blaxland and William Lawson on the journey of discovery across the Blue Mountains in 1813. His journal contains many scientific observations of the geological formations, the climate and the vegetation of the country they passed through, and is an important record of that first traverse of the mountains.

As a result of exposure to the elements on this trip, Wentworth developed a severe cough, and his father sent him on a sea voyage to the Pacific islands. He was nearly killed by natives on the Cook Islands. His father next sent him to England and, as the Napoleonic Wars were then over, and a military career was not available, Wentworth studied law.

He wrote a book about the colony which ran into three editions. While at Cambridge he won second prize for a poem on Australasia, much of it inspired by his journey over the Blue Mountains.

Wentworth returned to New South

Wales to become one of the first Australian-born men in public life and one of the greatest. Chiefly by his influence, the jury panel, the unfettered press, the unrestricted public meeting, the free speech of the legislator, the establishment of a democracy and of an enlightened university became part of the Australian scene, for twentieth century descendants to build on.

William Charles Wentworth spent his last years in England and died there, but at his request his body was brought to Australia and buried at Vaucluse near his much loved home 'Vaucluse House'. He was given the first State funeral in Australia.

2   South Creek

Continue west along the highway to St Mary's (do not take the freeway). Turn left into Mamre Road and about 2 km along turn right into Luddenham Road and cross South Creek. Just beyond the bridge, on the right (western side of road) is a **Memorial to the Explorers**. In this **Blaxland, Lawson and Wentworth** were a team. For a closer look at this memorial, pull over at the end of the double lines and walk back.

Return via Luddenham and Mamre Roads and turn left onto the highway.

Memorial at South Creek

The citizens of St Mary's erected this memorial in 1938. On the plaque is inscribed:

> Here on the South Creek was Gregory Blaxland's farm. From it, on May 11, 1813, he set out with William Lawson and W. C. Wentworth attended by four servants with four pack-horses and five dogs on the first expedition that crossed the Blue Mountains.

Blaxland, Lawson and Wentworth — A Team

In 1813 Gregory Blaxland was aged 35, William Lawson turned 39 on the trip, and William Wentworth was about 23. Of diverse character and personality, but united in the common purpose of finding a way across mountains thought to be unconquerable, these three men pooled their economic resources and their separate talents to make a winning team. Their individuality is clearly revealed in the diary which each kept. Blaxland's is a practical record; from his journal we know how it was done. Lawson's surveyor's training enabled him to indicate the track they followed in considerable detail. Wentworth describes and evaluates the country they travelled and the results they obtained.

PROSPECT RESERVOIR

ST MARY'S

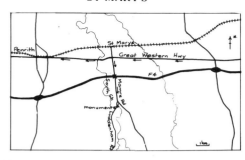

PARRAMATTA TO THE NEPEAN RIVER

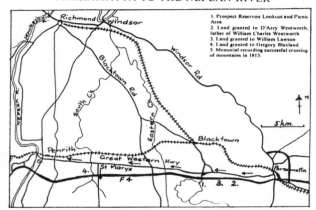

1. Prospect Reservoir Lookout and Picnic Area
2. Land granted to D'Arcy Wentworth, father of William Charles Wentworth
3. Land granted to William Lawson
4. Land granted to Gregory Blaxland
5. Memorial recording successful crossing of mountains in 1813.

EMU PLAINS

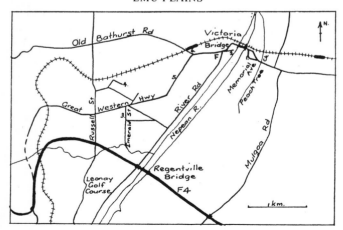

1. Memorial
2. Punt Road
3. Methodist Church
4. St Paul's C. of E.
5. Arms of Australia Inn
6. Emu Plains Railway Station

3 The Nepean River

Continue along the Great Western Highway through Penrith and turn right into Castlereagh Road for the MUSEUM OF FIRE, on the right just past the railway underpass.

Return to the highway and turn right. The next memorial of interest is by the Nepean River. Cross Peach Tree Creek and turn left into Memorial Avenue. Stop at THE EXPLORERS' MEMORIAL, PENRITH. This commemorates the crossing by Blaxland, Lawson and Wentworth, the journeys of **G. W. Evans** and the road building work of **William Cox**.

The motel nearby stands on the site of Old Ferry Road, which led to one of the **Early River Crossings. The Nepean River,** named by Governor Phillip, was discovered in 1789 by **Captain Watkin Tench** and **Surgeon Arndell.** Also of interest are **Victoria Bridge** and its builder, **John Whitton.** Return to the highway and cross the Victoria Bridge to Emu Plains.

George Evans (1780-1852)

George William Evans was born in Westminster, England. He served a short apprenticeship with an engineer and architect and gained some elementary training in surveying. He arrived at Port Jackson in *H.M.S. Buffalo* in October 1802.

Between 1802 and 1813 Evans was occupied as store-keeper, as a farmer for a time, as acting Surveyor-General and as an assistant-surveyor in Sydney and Van Diemen's Land. Macquarie appeared impressed with work he had done in the Appin region south of Sydney and, when a surveyor was needed to follow up the path of the mountain crossing, he recalled Evans from Van Diemen's Land.

Evans left the Nepean on 30 November 1813 with five chosen men and with horses, guns, ammunition and provisions for two months. In six days' travelling his party gained the most westerly point reached by the three discoverers of the route. Evans suggested that three peaks there should be named Mount Blaxland, Wentworth's Sugarloaf and Lawson's Sugarloaf. He continued to the west and in three weeks had made his way to Mount Pleasant near Bathurst and named the Fish, Campbell and Macquarie Rivers. In another week he was back at the foot of Mount York, and found his cache of hidden provisions safe. There had been bushfires on the mountains while they were away west and the last week of their expedition was spent in measuring the distance travelled over the mountains and re-marking the trees where they had been burnt. They arrived back at the Nepean River on 8 January 1814. Evans wrote a most enthusiastic account of the Bathurst plains and of the ease with which a road could be made there. This obviously influenced Governor Macquarie to engage William Cox to build that road.

Evans took part in three other expeditions under Macquarie; first as guide of the 1815 official tour; as second in command of Oxley's first excursion to explore the western plains in 1817; and again with Oxley on the second journey in 1818.

William Cox (1764-1837)

William Cox was born at Wimbourne

in Dorset, England, and was educated at the local grammar school. He joined the army in 1797 and was commissioned lieutenant in the New South Wales Corps.

Accompanied by his wife and four of his six small sons, he travelled in the *Minerva* in charge of a detachment of the corps and a consignment of Irish convicts and Irish political exiles, arriving in Port Jackson in 1800. He became pay-master of the corps and acquired Brush Farm at Dundas from John Macarthur. As a result of financial difficulties he was sent to England in 1807 to face possible charges and was out of the colony at the time of the rebellion against Bligh.

When Cox returned to Sydney in 1810, Governor Macquarie made him a magistrate. Cox took contracts for public buildings in the Windsor area, including the Windsor Court-house, built to the specifications of Francis Greenway. He had gained a reputation over the years as a humane employer. When Macquarie's decision to build a road over the mountains became known, Cox volunteered. He chose a gang of thirty convicts who looked robust and able to work hard. They were to be rewarded with their freedom at the conclusion of the project. Tools and provisions were to be provided from government stores.

Detailed specifications for the road were given. It was to be made twenty feet (6.10 m) wide, to allow two carriages to pass, with stumps removed and holes filled in to make it safe for four-wheeled vehicles. In thick brush the width of the road could be reduced to twelve feet (3.66 m) but preferably sixteen feet (4.89 m) with the scrub cleared to a width of twenty feet. Bridges were to be at least twelve feet wide. He was to

follow the track marked by Surveyor Evans and the first explorers, unless he could find a better route.

Cox and his men began work on 17 July 1814 and had progressed as far as Mount York by the end of October, when he sent a party of men to scout about for a better way down the mountain than Blaxland, Lawson, Wentworth and Evans had found. They failed in this, and Cox decided to make a descent usable by an empty cart. The sheep would have to walk up the mountain to be shorn at the top. The 101 miles (162 km) to Bathurst were completed on 14 January 1815.

Cox was rewarded with 2000 acres (810 hectares) in the Bathurst area. The Cox family ran sheep there.

Early Nepean River Crossing Places

The first crossings of the Nepean River were made at the ford onto what was then an island, Emu Island, near the place where the old weir is, about 1½ km downstream from the bridge. Blaxland and his party crossed there, as did Surveyor Evans; William Cox improved the approaches and measured the length of his road from the ford.

Boats were used as well. When Governor Macquarie made his journey to Bathurst in 1815, he and his party breakfasted with Sir John Jamison at Regentville, on the east bank of the Nepean near where the Regentville Freeway Bridge now is. The horses and carriage were sent round by the ford and the party crossed the river in the Government boat *Pheasant*.

In 1824 two boats secured together with a decking made a punt and were advertised in the *Sydney Gazette.* Wharves at Old Ferry Road and Punt Road were used.

Punt and ferry crossing continued in general use until the Nepean was bridged in the middle of the nineteenth century, and even then had to be called back into service when the bridge was damaged by floods.

Nepean River — Its Discovery and Naming

On 26 June 1789 Captain Watkin Tench, with Surgeon Arndell, a surgeon's mate from the *Sirius,* two marines and a convict, tramped to the west from Rose Hill, where Tench was stationed. They first looked over the land they proposed to explore from Prospect Hill. On the second day they reached a river flowing from south to north at the foot of the mountain range. Acording to Tench's map, they first came upon the river somewhere in the vicinity of Penrith.

They followed its course a few miles upstream, where they found bark 'huts', bird traps and marks on trees which had been climbed, all made by Aborigines. They returned to Rose Hill on the third day.

Governor Phillip named this river for Sir. Evan Nepean, Under-Secretary of State for the Home Department, and as such largely responsible for arrangements for the settlement.

The country adjacent to the river was called Evan, but later this name was changed to Penrith, after a town on the edge of the Lakes District in Cumberland, England.

Captain Watkin Tench (1759-1833)

Watkin Tench joined the Marine Corps in 1776, aged about 17, as a second lieutenant. After serving in the American War of Independence, he was placed on half pay, and so was available to volunteer for service in Botany Bay in 1786. He arrived with the First Fleet as a Captain of Marines. Tench made a number of expeditions to explore the new country in which he found himself, and as well as discovering the Nepean River, he was able to identify the Nepean and Hawkesbury as being one and the same river. His companion on these trips was often Lieutenant William Dawes.

Tench wrote two journals recording events while in the colony; they have been published in one volume, under the title *Sydney's First Four Years.* He was a man of considerable education and his lively curiosity and unfailing interest in new experiences make his journals of great importance to historians and fascinating to the general reader.

On his return to England in 1792, he served in the wars against the French, rising steadily in rank, and eventually retiring from the army as a Lieutenant-General.

Thomas Arndell

Arndell arrived with the First Fleet as an assistant surgeon on the *Friendship.* He was in charge of the hospital at Parramatta for about five years. In 1794 he retired and, choosing to remain in the colony, took up land north of Parramatta and later at the junction of Cattai Creek and the Hawkesbury River. Arndell was the first magistrate at the Hawkesbury, and a supporter of Governor Bligh. He assisted in the building of the Presbyterian church at Ebenezer. He is buried at St Matthew's, Windsor.

Victoria Bridge

The first bridge was a wooden structure built by the Nepean Bridge Company, and opened by Governor Fitzroy in 1855. The bridge was 700 feet (about 214 m) long and 30 feet (9 metres) wide and made of local ironbark. It had only been used for about eighteen months when it was swept away by a flood in August 1857. It was rebuilt, but was swept away again in 1860. A further series of floods interfered with contract work and the ferry was again brought into use, and the government provided two punts.

By the mid-eighteen-sixties the railway had stretched out to Penrith and an extension was begun to the Lower Blue Mountains. Engineer-in-Chief for Railways, John Whitton, observing the heights of recent floods, decided to raise the general level of the bridge by 6 feet 6 inches (2 metres), thus making the rails 89 feet (27 metres) above sea level and above flood level. It was completed in 1867, and was also known as Victoria Bridge. Floods in 1867 damaged the western approach and swept away the ferry. In 1869 a new pier was added to the western side.

The bridge carried a single railway track and a single lane of road traffic. An electric bell rang when the road was occupied and this often terrified the horses, as also did the trains.

In 1907 a new railway bridge was built and the old Victoria Bridge was given over to road traffic. It is still evident from its structure that it was originally designed as a railway bridge. The iron sides gave rise to the nickname 'The Sardine Tin'.

John Whitton (1820-1898)

Born in Yorkshire, England, John Whitton was articled for seven years to John Billington of Wakefield, a relative of his mother. He gained engineering and architectural experience preparing plans and tenders for railway construction and waterworks. In 1847 he was engineer for the Manchester, Sheffield and Lincoln railway and in 1852-6 supervised the building of the Oxford, Worcester and Wolverhampton line. In 1854 he was elected a member of the Institution of Civil Engineers, London. In 1856 he was appointed engineer-in-chief to lay out and superintend the construction of railways in New South Wales.

The new engineer-in-chief was a man of considerable experience. Before his arrival, several men had held the post, and confusion had arisen over gauges. After persuading Victoria and South Australia to adopt the 5ft 3in gauge, the commissioners of New South Wales reverted to the 4ft 8½in gauge, in use in England. Whitton thought that the wider gauge would have been better, but could not persuade the railway commissioners to change back.

With the aid of E. C. Cracknell, Superintendent of Telegraphs in New South Wales, Whitton overcame the engineering problems of the railway over the Blue Mountains, which required the construction of two zigzags, at Lapstone and Lithgow. Victoria Bridge over the Nepean is his work.

Whitton's last work was the Hawkesbury River Railway Bridge, opened in May 1889. He retired in 1890. He had supervised the laying of 2171 miles (3377 km) of track on which no accident had occurred attributable to defective design or construction.

4 Emu Plains

Cross the river via Victoria Bridge to the township of **Emu Plains. The Explorers** crossed at the ford to the north of the bridge. **Cox's Road to Bathurst** began there. The village developed to serve travellers and some early buildings still exist. Turn left to PUNT ROAD for a view of the river and of Victoria Bridge.

Return to the highway, turn left and left again into River Road. A short distance along, turn right into Regatta Park to look at the FOOT-STEPS IN TIME MARKER. George William Evans surveyed through this area on 8 January 1814.

Return to the highway and turn left. Drive through the shopping centre of Emu Plains, along the highway for 2 km and turn left into Emerald Street. On the right is the **Uniting Church of Australia, Emu Plains,** now used as a chapel for the Edinglassie Retirement Village.

Turn left into Stanbury Street, right into Cary Street and cross Nepean Street into Hunter Street. Turn right at the T-intersection into River Road. A few houses along on the right is THE LEWERS BEQUEST AND PENRITH REGIONAL ART GALLERY, open Tuesday to Sunday, 11 a.m. to 5 p.m. Admission is charged.

Continue along River Road under the expressway. Over the Nepean River on your left is the spot from which Governor Macquarie and party crossed for their journey along Cox's Road, 26 April 1815. From the end of River Road the entrance to the Nepean Gorge may be seen.

Return along River Road to the highway. Turn left, then right at the lights onto Old Bathurst Road. Stop after the underpass to look at **Emu Plains Railway Station.** Continuing on, turn left at the Russell Street roundabout, then left again at Pyramid Street.

Follow the signs from Mundy Street which direct you to **St Paul's Anglican Church** and the **Site of Emu Stockade.**

Return via Mundy Street and a left turn at Pyramid Street to the highway. Turn left and in about 1 km you come to **The Arms of Australia Inn.** The Museum is run by the members of the Nepean Historical Society. open Sundays: 1 p.m. to 5 p.m. Admission by donation.

Emu Plains

The area was at first known as Emu, from the number of birds observed there. The shallow gravelly part of the river downstream of the bridge was Emu Island, then being actually separated from the banks. Over the years numerous floods have altered the river bed, and it is an island no longer.

The name of Emu Plains was used in the 1832 N.S.W. Calendar and Post Office Directory and was in general use later in the century.

The Explorers, 11 May 1813

'...They crossed the Nepean River at the ford on to Emu Island at four o'clock in the afternoon and proceeded by their calculations two Miles through forest land and good grass, encamped at 5 o'clock at the foot of the first ridge of the mountains . . . The Bearing of their Course this day by Compass was South West 2 Miles.' Thus Blaxland recorded the movements of the party on that first day.

Blaxland added a note to the entry: 'The distance travelled each day was regulated by a watch and computed at about two miles per hour.'

Cox's Road to Bathurst

Cox measured his road from the ford (entry 27 July) so it is reasonable to suppose the road began there. He improved the approaches to it. His road then crossed Emu Plains, with a bridge over Jamison Creek and another at the foot of his ascent — so his journal records: 'July 25 . . . Finished a crossing-place over the creek, and worked from the creek to the crossing-place where you ascend the mountain...'

Earthworks for the freeway and housing developments have left no traces of the old road.

Uniting Church in Australia, Emu Plains (Nat. Tr.)

This was formerly the Methodist Church. The plaque on the church states that it was built in 1863. It was constructed of stone said to have been quarried close to the church, on 'Edinglassie', the estate of Mr (later Sir) Francis Forbes, Chief Justice of the Colony in the 1830s.

St Paul's Anglican Church Short Street, Emu Plains (Nat. Tr.)

On 8 November 1848 St Paul's Church School was licensed, the first resident Rector was appointed in 1856, and the church was consecrated on 16 August 1872. The chancel was built about 1887. Bushfires destroyed the original rectory and early church records in 1929.

Site of Emu Stockade

On the part of the churchyard facing Nixon Street is the site of the Emu Stockade, also known as the Government Agricultural Establishment. It was formed by Governor Macquarie in 1820 to create employment for the large number of convicts arriving in the colony. In six months 15 ships conveying 2 559 convicts had arrived in Sydney.

The superintendent was Robert

St Paul's Anglican Church, Short St, Emu Plains

Fitzgerald; by the end of 1821, 300 convicts were growing wheat, maize and tobacco. Later Mitchell's road gangs were housed there. The site of the stockade was sold in 1845.

Arms of Australia Inn (Nat. Tr.)

This inn is thought to have been built about 1833, but part of it may be as early as 1826. The first licence was issued to John Mortimer in 1841, when it was called Mortimer House. For a time it was known as the Australian Arms. The inn flourished in the 1850s and 1860s along with the six others then open at Emu Plains. It was a popular stopping place for Cobb and Co. Coaches on the Sydney to Bathurst run and was well patronised when floods held up the coaches.

The Nepean Historical Society has restored the building with the help of the Penrith City Council.

Emu Plains Railway Station (Nat. Tr.)

When the railway line was opened in 1867, the station was known as Emu, but was renamed Emu Plains in 1869. The two-storey building, with station-master's residence in the upper section, was built in 1884.

Victoria Bridge over the Nepean River. View from Punt Road, Emu Plains.

2 Lapstone Hill and Glenbrook

1 Routes over Lapstone Hill

The sudden ascent of the Blue Mountains at Lapstone Hill has always caused problems with transport. Four of the six routes are easy to follow, but the first, Cox's Road, in use only from 1815 to about 1824, a mere eight or nine years, and the first railway route and deviation, have been obliterated or overlaid by the later ones. We had to criss-cross over the terrain to find them.

The story of these routes begins with **Lapstone Hill.** In order of making, the different roads are: **Cox's Road to Bathurst** 1814-1815, **Lawson's Road** about 1824, **Mitchell's Pass** opened 1834, **Railway Line 1** 1867, **Railway Deviation** 1891, **Railway Line 2** opened 1913, **Great Western Highway** 1926.

Lapstone Hill

This name, first recorded in 1832, was given to the ascent into the Blue Mountains allegedly because of the number of waterworn stones found there. The stones resembled those cobblers held between their knees to beat the leather against.

The hill is short and steep, rising about 200 metres. The distance travelled today by the winding highway, to climb from the western edge of Emu Plains to Blaxland is approximately 8 km. Early road builders and travellers experienced difficulty with the hill and over the years four different lines have been used. The railway builders had great problems in finding suitable locations and two main routes and a deviation have been constructed.

Cox's Road Completed 1815 — Road 1

The road built by William Cox between July 1814 and January 1815 and in regular use for only a few years has been swept away by developments in the area.

The route of the first Bathurst Road marked on our map comes from the study of historical writings. Some historians think, however, that Cox attacked Lapstone Hill near the present Lapstone railway station and followed Explorers Road in the direction of Glenbrook Park. From that point on there is substantial agreement. The storage depot near Glenbrook Lagoon is well documented.

This road was very steep, although praised by Governor Macquarie. It was difficult to negotiate in wet weather and traffic was often stopped at Jamison Creek, the wooden bridge there being swept away by flood water or destroyed by fire.

Lawson's Road about 1824 — Road 2

An attempt to bypass the problems of

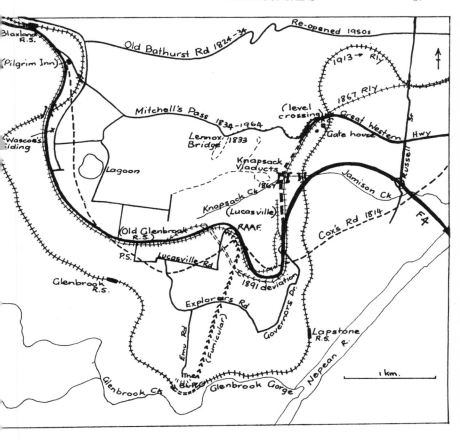

Cox's ascent had been made quite early, perhaps by Lieutenant William Lawson when he was commandant at Bathurst. This road, repaired after a hundred years of neglect in the 1950s and later tar-sealed to carry modern motor traffic, leaves Emu Plains near the railway station and winds up the hill very steeply. It is called the Old Bathurst Road today, but was once the 'Zig Zag Road'. The sharp curves of this road meant that it, too, was always less than satisfactory.

Mitchell's Pass opened 1834 — Road 3

By the 1830s the inadequacies of the first two roads were very apparent, and Major Thomas Mitchell, the newly appointed Surveyor-General and Superintendent of Roads, set about looking for another line.

Mitchell had been instructed by Governor Darling to lay out the town of Emu. He thought that the line of the western road up Lapstone Hill must be fixed first and, while looking over the area from the 'Zig Zag' Road in May 1830, he saw a gully between the two existing roads which might, he considered, provide a better route.

Work began in 1832 with convict labour. Lennox Bridge spanned Brookside Creek and the pass intersected the old lines at the top of the hill, near the Pilgrim Inn in today's Layton Avenue. Governor Sir Richard Bourke opened the road in 1834.

In 1846 Lieutenant-Colonel Mundy wrote of the Pass: 'The Highway is absolutely carved out of the living rock. Huge slices of the hillside have been blown off by blasting, hurled by convict crowds into the gulph below or pounded by them into material now called Macadam.'

Location of Railway — Line 1

In 1863 the railway line from Sydney reached Penrith which then became the starting point for coaches over the Blue Mountains. In Bradshaw's Guide of that year Cobb and Co advertised two coaches a day to Bathurst.

Lapstone Hill was thought to be impassable to trains, but as developments continued, engines became more powerful and it was decided to build a railway over the mountains, with a zigzag on Lapstone Hill. The builder was John Whitton, Engineer-in-Chief for the New South Wales Railways.

Victoria Bridge, across the Nepean, was built in 1867 to carry both rail and road traffic. From it the line took a westerly direction and curved round to the south over a level crossing at Mitchell's Pass, near the present day highway bridge across today's line. Here may be seen the ruins of No. 1 Gatekeeper's cottage. Knapsack Gully was bridged by Knapsack Viaduct.

The bottom points of the Zig Zag were situated near the intersection of Governors Drive with the highway. Trains continued round to a safety siding and dead end and then reversed across the hill on a grade of 1 in 33, to the precipice of Knapsack Creek. There the train went forward along the top track, circling in a wide curve to the west of Glenbrook Lagoon, to join the road on the narrow ridge at the top near the Pilgrim Inn.

The 1891 Deviation — Glenbrook Tunnel

By 1890 locomotives were becoming more powerful and could pull longer trains than could be accommodated within the zigzag dead ends. It was decided to build a tunnel under part of Lapstone Hill and avoid the old switchback. This deviation was used until 1913. For a while the old Glenbrook station and the Glenbrook tunnel were used for trains travelling to Sydney, and the new Glenbrook station on the Glenbrook Creek route was used by trains to the mountains.

Railway Line Built 1911-1913 — Line 2

Increased traffic on the railway required the duplication of the track. For this the second Victoria Bridge over the Nepean was built in 1907 and the first Victoria Bridge was converted to carry two lanes of road traffic, though still retaining the iron sides of its railway days.

By 1911 double track was provided all the way from Sydney to Bowenfels except for the section Emu Plains to Blaxland. To avoid the old Glenbrook Tunnel, with its problems for single track engine running, a new line, with a viaduct spanning Jamison Creek,

curved to the south, making use of Glenbrook Creek Gorge. A tunnel was built under the Bluff; during construction a spurline took materials from east of the Glenbrook Tunnel to a funicular at the cliff.

Great Western Highway 1926 — Road 4

By the 1920s the increasing volume of traffic using Mitchell's Pass was causing concern and the Department of Main Roads acquired the location abandoned by the Railways Department in 1913. When the road opened in 1926, it followed the old railway track from the former level crossing at Emu Plains to Blaxland, except for the zig zag and some deep cuttings too narrow for road use.

Although this track had been steep for a railway, early motor vehicles could easily use it. It is continually being up-graded today.

2 Lawson's and Mitchell's Roads

Cross the Nepean River at Penrith and follow the Great Western Highway for about 500 metres. Turn right at the lights into the OLD BATHURST ROAD, Lawson's 1824 road. Cross Russell Street and keep on up the steep, winding road; the surface is good.

At the top of the hill, at Blaxland, turn left into Wilson Way, then left at the roundabout into MITCHELL'S PASS, the third line of road over this hill. The road is two-lane to **Lennox Bridge** but one-lane down to the highway at the foot of Lapstone Hill. The bridge spans Brookside Creek

and is the work of **David Lennox**. On the rock face of a cutting near the bridge is a plaque to commemorate the work of **Thomas Livingstone Mitchell**. A second plaque was erected by the Road Traffic Authority and the National Roads and Motorists' Association to mark the Australian Bicentenary in 1988. There is much interesting information about this *Historic Bridge of N.S.W.*

From the uphill side of the bridge there is a walking track to the quarry where the stone was excavated; this continues up the hill to *Marge's*

Lookout; for access from Glenbrook Road, see below.

The lower end of the pass may be traversed on foot from the bridge or from the Great Western Highway at the foot of Lapstone Hill.

Return to the top of the pass and cross Wilson Way into Layton Avenue, which passes under the railway line. Built at the junction of Layton Avenue with the highway was the **Pilgrim Inn**. Remnants of it may be seen in McDonald's carpark. All the three early roads, Cox's, Lawson's and Mitchell's, converged here at the Inn. Turn left into the highway.

Lennox Bridge (Nat. Tr.)

The bridge spans Brookside Creek, which has gouged out the gully up which Mitchell built his pass. The services of an engineer/stonemason were required to bridge it. For this work Mitchell appointed David Lennox.

Lennox Bridge is the oldest stone arch bridge on the Australian mainland, an older one still existing in Tasmania. David Lennox, newly appointed to the position of Superintendent of Bridges, began work in November 1832, and the bridge was completed in July 1833. The work force was twenty convicts to whom Lennox had to teach the stonemason's art. The stone was hewn from a quarry upstream about 450 metres.

The bridge is carried on a single semi-circular stone arch of 10 feet (3.05 m) radius, the roadway being thirty feet (9.14 m) wide at the crown of the arch and the same height over the bed of the gully. Lennox also built retaining walls for the approaches, which curve up to the bridge.

On the instructions of Governor Bourke, the inscription 'David Lennox' was carved into the keystone on the upstream side of the bridge. Now this is badly weathered. The inscription 'A.D. 1833' on the downstream side has fared better.

Not long after the bridge went into service, the Colonial Architect reported a crack, and advised further work. David Lennox inspected the crack, said it was not serious and that the work recommended by the Colonial Architect would indeed damage the bridge. Mitchell accepted Lennox's advice.

Mitchell's Pass and the Lennox Bridge (sometimes called the Horseshoe Bridge) carried all traffic westwards until 1926, when a new deviation was built along the abandoned railway line. Mitchell's Pass remained open for limited use until 1964, when a serious crack did appear in the bridge. It was then closed to traffic.

David Lennox's confidence in his handiwork has been vindicated by its continuous use for 130 years, into the era of the motor car, a kind of test which Lennox could hardly have envisaged.

David Lennox (1788-1873)

David Lennox was born in Ayr, Scotland, and emigrated to Australia in 1832. He was a master mason who had worked on the building of bridges for twenty years, being associated with projects of the great English bridge builder, Thomas Telford, such as the construction of the Menai Suspension bridge, connecting the Island of Anglesea to the mainland, and of the Gloucester Bridge.

After the death of his wife in 1828 and finding some unemployment among stonemasons, Lennox decided to try his luck in the colonies.

Major Thomas Mitchell had re-surveyed the system of main roads and needed an engineer for the re-building and re-designing of bridges to replace those built in the early days of the colony. One day in 1832, Mitchell noticed a stonemason at work on the dwarf wall in front of the Legislative Council Chambers and enquired of him about his previous experience. This man was David Lennox, who was presented to the Governor with his credentials, and then was appointed a Sub-Inspector of Roads, and shortly afterwards to the post of Superintendent of Bridges.

The first bridge built by Lennox was that over Lapstone Creek to join the two parts of Mitchell's Pass, then under construction to replace Lawson's zigzag. Other notable bridges designed and built by Lennox include Lansdowne Bridge over Prospect Creek and the Lennox Bridge across the Parramatta River.

From 1844 till his retirement in 1853 Lennox held the post of Super-intendent of Bridges at Port Phillip. There, amongst other works, he built the Prince's Bridge over the Yarra River, Melbourne.

Major Sir Thomas Livingstone Mitchell (1792-1855)

Thomas Livingstone Mitchell was born at Craigend, Scotland. His education included several languages and sciences. He served in the Peninsular War as a second lieutenant in the 95th Regiment, mainly with the Intelligence Staff on topographical work. Sir George Murray, quarter-master-general, engaged him to draw plans of important battlefields of that war.

Through Sir George Murray's influence Mitchell became assistant Surveyor-General of New South Wales.

In 1827 Mitchell and his family arrived in Sydney where he found the organisation and working methods of the Survey Department unsatisfactory. He began at once on a general survey which he regarded as of first priority. He often had to use insufficient and makeshift equipment.

After John Oxley's death in 1828, Mitchell became Surveyor-General and later was made responsible for the survey of roads and bridges. Mitchell's general survey and his consequent knowledge of the country led to his making many improvements in the routes taken by major roads. Mitchell's determination and confidence in his own abilities are evident in the way he managed to put through his radical changes to the line of descent from the mountains in the Mount York/Mount Victoria area.

Mitchell's life was active, colourful and tempestuous. He made a number of major explorations. The first expeditions filled in the details of the Murray-Darling river system, proving in effect that the Darling joined the Murray, although Mitchell himself was not able to follow the river along its entire course. In the third expedition he continued south and traversed the state of Victoria, which he called *Australia Felix,* surveying as he went and thereby opening up a large area of country. He later attempted to cross Australia to Port Essington in the Northern Territory, near where Darwin was later built, but only reached the Barcoo River in Central Australia.

Pilgrim Inn, Blaxland

This inn stood at the top of Lapstone Hill at the strategic spot where the ridge narrows, and the licensee could take advantage of the custom of all passers-by. Here Mitchell's Pass and the Old Zig Zag Road joined Cox's Road. From Blaxland to Mount York the road follows the top of the ridge with few deviations.

Remnants of the inn have been restored in the redevelopment of the site. The inn is often mentioned in the early literature, sometimes as 'Wascoe's'. The accommodation was said to be very good.

The inn was built partly of sandstone and partly of weatherboard by Barnet Levey, who was granted 960 acres (388.5 hectares) at the top of Lapstone Hill in 1825. He named the estate Mount Sion. Licensees of the inn were James Evans and John Outrim Wascoe. The inn was closed in 1869 when the railway took away much of the custom. The inn then became a private residence for 99 years until destroyed by the 1968 bushfire.

3   Glenbrook — North Side

From the Pilgrim Inn follow the highway south across the railway line and take the first road on the left, Kidman Street. Turn left into Murphy Street, left into Haymet Street and right into Grahame Street, to **Wascoe Siding Miniature Railway**. The Blue Mountains Railway Society has its Running Day on the first Sunday of each month. Rides are charged for.

Turn right into Murphy Street, left into Haymet Street and right at the T-intersection with Glenbrook Road. On your right is **Glenbrook Lagoon**. Continue past the lagoon and turn left at Levy Street, left again at the T-intersection with Barnet Street and follow it for about 400 metres.

The track to the right leads to views over the Sydney plain. Where the track forks, *Marge's Lookout* is on the left. The view is north across the Nepean River, with Brookside and Lapstone Creeks below.

The right-hand track leads to *Eliza-beth Lookout*; there is an extensive view over the Sydney plain, with the Nepean River and the Regentville bridge in the foreground. Immediately below are the two viaducts over Knapsack and Jamison Creeks, somewhat obscured by trees. There is a walking track to Knapsack Viaduct (1 hour return). Tracks connecting the two lookouts with Lennox Bridge were made as part of the Commonwealth Employment Program by the Blue Mountains City Council.

Return to Barnet Street and turn left, then right into Levy Street, left into Hare Street and right into Moore Street. Beyond the Bowling Club is WHITTON PARK, a reminder of the railway builder. The nearby highway occupies the line of the first railway at this point. (BMCC HR G10).

Return to Hare Street and turn left into the highway, which widens into *Garlick Parade*. Of historical interest here are: **Old Glenbrook Railway**

Station and some brick piers from a watertank, **The Great Western Highway, The Route Taken by Blaxland, Lawson and Wentworth.**

Nearby is *Glenbrook Native Plant Reserve*. This interesting and unusual garden and nursery is run by the Society for the Propagation of Australian Native Plants.

One block down the highway is Barnet Street on the left. A short distance across the ford is a track on the right leading to A RAILWAY CUTTING, part of the Glenbrook Tunnel Deviation, built in 1891. The track and cutting are narrow and more suited to walking than to vehicles. The mushroom farm nearby utilises the old tunnel but the owners do not allow the public to enter it. GLENBROOK TUNNEL is recorded BMCC HR G 8. (Parking difficult.) Keep left down the highway. At the RAAF Base turn left into Knapsack Street.

Wascoe Siding Miniature Railway

In 1874 a crossing loop to facilitate single line train working was built near the Watertank stop. A platform was built there, and it acquired the name of Wascoe's Siding from the licensee of the Pilgrim Inn.

The name board and other railway materials are being preserved by the Blue Mountains Railway Society at the Miniature Railway site. There is a model gatekeeper's cottage on display.

Glenbrook Lagoon

Blaxland, Lawson and Wentworth passed by this lagoon on 12 May 1813. Blaxland described it as 'a large lagoon of good water full of very coarse rushes'.

William Cox put up a storeroom to the west of it when he was building the first road and Governor Macquarie later established a military depot there to prevent unauthorised persons from crossing the mountains. This depot was moved to Springwood soon afterwards.

Major Henry Antill, A.D.C. to Governor Macquarie, accompanied the Governor on his journey over the mountains in 1815 and described this spot; 'WEDNESDAY, April 26, . . . came to the first depot established by Mr Cox, when making the road, as a place of safety for his provisions for his working party. A small guard of soldiers are stationed here in a good log hut with two rooms, one of which answers as a store. It is placed about 100 yards on the right of the road, near a small lagoon of fresh water. The soldiers have enclosed a small piece of ground for a garden, and one of them had displayed some taste in laying it out in little arbours and seats formed from the surrounding shrubbery, which gave the place an appearance of comfort and simplicity.'

(Quoted from *Fourteen Journeys over the Blue Mountains* ed. George Mackaness)

Old Glenbrook Railway Station (BMCC HR G13)

The highway now covers the site of the old station, which was first known as Watertank. The three brick piers, survivors of six, were foundations for a railway watertank erected in 1892 when the tunnel was built. They were moved from the opposite side of the line after the road widening in 1981-2. Water for the tanks was piped from Glenbrook Lagoon; it was needed in this location as engines working up the Zig Zag used extra water.

In 1874, a crossing loop was built and the stop became known as Wascoe's Siding, from the inn further up the line. In 1877 a passenger platform was erected and the following year the name was changed to Brookdale. In 1879 the name was again changed, this time to Glenbrook. The remains of the original Station Master's Residence are part of the garage on the opposite side of the road.

This old station was closed in 1913 when the new line was built through Glenbrook Creek Gorge and the present station opened on that line. For a time during construction of the new line, both stations operated, trains on the 'up' line to Sydney stopping at the old station, and the 'down' trains to the mountains using the new one.

The Great Western Highway

The section of the highway between the old Glenbrook Railway Station and Blaxland has been much used as a roadway. Cox's Bathurst Road ran somewhere in this area, but when superseded by Lawson's Road and Mitchell's Pass, it fell into disuse.

The railway followed this route between 1867 and 1913, but it was again abandoned when the duplicated Glenbrook Gorge route was constructed.

In 1926 the Main Roads Board took it over and used its gentler curves to replace the sharp bends and steep grades of Mitchell's Pass. The easy grade here has allowed the road to be widened for today's traffic.

A tablet commemorating the opening of the road is to be seen in Garlick Parade.

Blaxland, Lawson and Wentworth — Their Route

The track followed by the explorers and their party came up through Glenbrook Park, crossed the present highway at about this spot and followed the ridge to the west of Glenbrook Lagoon.

A memorial stands in Garlick Parade to commemorate this event.

4 The Lapstone Zig Zag

Turn into Knapsack Street near the RAAF Base and drive downhill to the parking area. This hill is a possible route for the explorers and of Cox's Road. Zig Zag Street leads you to the Department of Lands walking track along the **Zig Zag Railway.** Points of interest are: **Lucasville Platform, Knapsack Bridge, The 1913 Railway Viaduct.** This viaduct crossed Jamison Creek, named for **Sir John Jamison.**

Return to the highway via Zig Zag and Knapsack Streets, turning left to return to Emu Plains to tour the south side of Glenbrook.

Lapstone Zig Zag Railway

The Lapstone Zig Zag was constructed in the form of a simple Z. The train was pulled in along the 'Bottom Road' over the bottom points until the entire train was contained within the wing leading to the 'dead end', then the train reversed and the engine pushed it along the 'Middle Road' over the top points into the wing and dead end there. Then the engine was able to pull forward again along the 'Top Road'. At Lapstone the grade was 1 in 30-33, the lines following the contour of the hill. In this way the train could be got up a height which would have been impossible in an up-and-down line.

There were certain disadvantages. It took time to move the trains over the zigzag. There were no passing loops, there being no available space for them on the Lapstone hillside. The zigzag was built because it was cheaper than a tunnel. Improved technology and a wealthier economy enabled tunnels to be built in 1891 and 1911-1913.

The Lands Department Walking Track goes along the 'Top Road' of the zigzag. Individual features are well sign-posted. The cuttings are impressive and the cross-bedding in them of interest to the geologist. A side-track leads to a view of the quarry. The workmanship of the sandstone culverts is worth seeing.

The 'Middle Road' leads through a very deep cutting. The walk goes part of the way to the bottom wing which is now on the opposite side of the highway.

Near the Lucasville Platform is a re-graded siding constructed in 1886 after there was an accident on the zigzag. The new wing was made with a slight slope upwards at the end to make it easier to stop the train on its downward journey.

A short distance past Lucasville Platform is a lookout from which the very beautiful Knapsack Bridge and the 1913 Viaduct may be seen; a splendid climax to an interesting walk.

The Knapsack Viaduct and the Lapstone Zig Zag, both wonderful engineering feats, were the work of Engineer-in-Chief of Railways of New South Wales, John Whitton, whose memorial obelisk is fittingly placed at the foot of Lapstone Hill.

Lucasville Platform (BMCC HR G1)

This platform was built in 1878 especially to serve Mr John Lucas, M.L.A., Minister for Mines, who had a property and holiday home called Lucasville above the Zig Zag near the top of Lapstone Hill. Note the flight of steps cut in the sandstone.

The platform was abandoned in 1892 when the Glenbrook Tunnel deviation was built.

Knapsack Bridge (BMCC HK G6)

Knapsack Creek, a tributary of Jamison Creek, the waterway that caused constant trouble for travellers over Cox's Road, had to be bridged for the railway. For this deep gully John Whitton designed Knapsack Viaduct; it is an extremely handsome bridge.

Built of sandstone quarried in nearby areas and at Mitchell's Pass, and set in Portland cement, there are five fifty foot (16 metre) and two twenty foot (6 metre) semi-circular arches. Its length is approximately 385 feet (118 metres) and its maximum height above the bed of the creek is 126 feet (38 metres). Its width was 16 feet (4.87 metres) when it carried the single line of the standard gauge railway.

The first railway line was abandoned in 1913 and the location was acquired by the Department of Main Roads in the 1920s. Knapsack Viaduct then became a road bridge. A tablet to John Whitton was placed on the north east end and was unveiled in 1926 when the bridge was opened. The carriageway was later widened to carry two lanes of motor traffic. Department engineers are to be commended on the skill with which they made the alteration without spoiling the appearance of the bridge.

1913 Viaduct

This viaduct crosses the junction of Knapsack Creek with Jamison Creek.

The viaduct is built of brick and is a worthy companion to Whitton's Knapsack Bridge.

Sir John Jamison (1776-1844)

Sir John Jamison was the son of Thomas Jamison, who came with the First Fleet as surgeon's mate in the *Sirius*. Thomas Jamison was granted 1000 acres (404.69 hectares) on the Nepean in 1805. When he returned to England, he signed over his property in New South Wales to his son.

Sir John Jamison came to New South Wales in 1814 to take up his property. He was a surgeon in the Royal Navy, was decorated by the King of Sweden for his treatment of scurvy in the Swedish navy and made a Knight Bachelor by the Prince Regent in England. From his arrival he was associated with public and official affairs in the colony. In 1815 he accompanied Governor Macquarie on his journey across Cox's Road to Bathurst. Jamison Creek and Jamison Valley are named after him.

Sir John built 'Regentville', an impressive mansion, on his Nepean property; hence 'Regentville Bridge' which carries the F4 freeway over the river adjacent to the Jamison estate. The site of 'Regentville' has been excavated by historical archaeologists and has provided much interesting information about the life style of the time.

5 Glenbrook — South Side

Follow the former highway west from Emu Plains across the railway bridge. On the left is a rather neglected park. The first of the **Gatekeeper's Cottages** (see pages 40-1), now a ruin, is situated here at the foot of Lapstone Hill beside the **Memorial to John Whitton**, builder of railways.

Return down the old highway, turning right into Russell Street to rejoin the main highway westward for a short distance. Turn left at Governor's Drive and stop near the watertank in Skarrat Park. The way into TWO RAILWAY CUTTINGS begins behind the tank. The outer cutting was part of the bottom road of Lapstone Zig Zag, going to the dead end. The inner cutting was part of the 1892 deviation and leads to the eastern portal of Glenbrook Tunnel. The western end of the tunnel is accessible from Barnet Street (see above).

Continue along Governors Drive and turn right into EXPLORERS ROAD. Near the tennis courts, on the left, is the walking track via Dark's Common and THE SPURLINE which in 1911-13 carried materials to the workers on the BLUFF TUNNEL. Still to be seen are the embankments and cuttings and the foundations of the winding house for the railway at the cliff into Glenbrook Gorge.

After passing Lapstone Primary School, turn left into Emu Road, which leads to the **Bluff Reserve**. Magnificent views can be seen from several lookouts. (BMCC HR G 12). Return along Emu Road and turn left

into Explorers Road. Follow its windings to turn right at the T-intersection with LUCASVILLE ROAD. Part of this road was possibly crossed by the explorers' route and by Cox's Road. Turn left into MOUNT STREET. Glenbrook Tunnel, in use 1892 to 1913, is beneath Mount Street. An abandoned cutting, too narrow for road use, is beside the highway.

Turn left onto the highway and after about 1 km pull into the Information Bay on the left. *Glenbrook Visitors' Centre* has books and leaflets about the Blue Mountains. as well as souvenirs. Glenbrook Park has a pleasant picnic area. Walk through the parking area nearby to look across Ross Street to the back of the service station which faces the highway. The rear portion is what remains of the GLENBROOK STATIONMASTER'S RESIDENCE. Note the rounded roof of the original privy. (BMCC HR G 3).

Return to your car and turn left into Ross Street. On your right is **Glenbrook Primary School**. Cross Park Street at the shopping centre, turn left into Burfitt Parade and follow it to Bruce Road, which leads to the entrance to the **Blue Mountains National Park**. At the park gates is the National Parks and Wildlife Service *Visitors' Centre*, open at weekends. The service provides leaflets and maps on walks, etc in the park. When the centre is closed, the wall maps are helpful.

Two places of particular interest are the **Red Hands Cave** and the

PORTAL LOOKOUT for its interesting view of the *Bluff Tunnel* and *Glenbrook Creek Gorge*.
Retrace your route to the Great Western Highway.

Glenbrook Primary School

The school was established in 1892 largely to cater for the children of railway workers who at that time were building the deviation and tunnel required to replace the old zigzag.

Blue Mountains National Park

This park is the second-largest National Park in New South Wales, covering an area of 100 865 hectares. A number of well-graded roads lead to picnic areas and lookouts at interesting and scenic spots; many walking tracks take the more active to less accessible and secluded areas.

The explorers expressed little but horror at the precipitous nature of the country and the only vegetation they were interested in was grass for their horses.

Early botanists, such as Caley, Cunningham and Brown, studied the detail of vegetation and scenery and left early records against which we can compare the changes made by European settlement. As the number of settlers born in Australia increased, so also increased the number of those with an eye to see the beauties of native bushland and scenery. Such a one was Louisa Atkinson, writer of the series of articles, *A Voice from the Country*.

Towards the end of the century the writings of John Ruskin and Henry Thoreau expressed an appreciative view of nature and their influence extended to Australia. This may be seen in the dedication of some large areas for parks and in the sudden interest of Australians in bushwalking. In the Blue Mountains evidence of the trend is clear from the large number of summer residences built by the well-to-do, taking advantage of the railway line which had extended as far as Bowenfels (Lithgow) by 1869.

A leader in this movement was Eccleston Du Faur (see Mount Wilson), who was instrumental in having the Kuringai Chase National Park declared. Homes built as summer residences still stand at Mount Victoria and Mount Wilson; unfortunately many which dotted the central and lower mountains no longer exist. The surrounding bushland was thought to be an extension of their gardens and paths and trails were constructed to give easy access for enjoyment of it. From this beginning many of the trails to be followed today were marked out.

With the coming of the motorcar, members of bushwalking clubs and others came to realise that areas for recreation must be set aside before such areas disappeared for ever before the increasing pressures of population. The idea of the wilderness area was born. Parks where the natural environment could be preserved should be saved as resorts for bushwalking and similar activities.

Large areas of the mountains were marked out as suitable for a park and after much publicity over the years and long discussion with planning authorities in government, the Blue Mountains National Park was established in 1959. It remained under the control of six trustees until its management was transferred to the National Parks and Wildlife Service in 1971.

The park is cut into two sections by the Great Western Highway. Bell's Line of Road passes through it in the area of Mount Wilson.

The southern zone of the park is accessible from Glenbrook, Woodford and Wentworth Falls; the northern sector may be reached from Blackheath, Mount Victoria and Bell's Line of Road.

Red Hands Cave

The Aboriginal inhabitants of this area decorated the walls of this cave with hand prints and hand stencils, using natural ochres found along Campfire Creek. This art represents a culture dating back possibly 20 000 years.

Beside the track are a number of narrow grooves worn into the flat rock surface near a shallow pothole in the creek. The Aborigines sharpened their spear heads and stone axes in these grooves. Other grinding groove sites are to be found in this area.

These evidences of an ancient culture are fragile; much as one would wish to put out a hand in all reverence to feel and admire this work, it is well to remember that touching will hasten the natural process of erosion. Good photographs of grooves and rock art may be obtained in early morning or late afternoon when the shadows are long and the sun low enough to accentuate the hollows.

The Bluff (BMCC HR G 12)

The Bluff overlooks Glenbrook Creek and Glenbrook Gorge. The present railway line, built in 1913, hugs the side of the gorge, and passes through a tunnel under the Bluff. Three lookouts, Ross, Williams and Chalmers, show three different views of this rugged and beautiful scenery.

The site of the funicular, used to lower materials for building the tunnel, is nearby, but the machinery has been dismantled.

John Whitton Memorial

This obelisk of blue-grey stone, fittingly placed at the foot of his Knapsack Viaduct and his Lapstone Zig Zag, has a steam engine with tender drawn above the words:

JOHN WHITTON BUILT RAILWAYS PENRITH TO BATHURST, SYDNEY TO ALBURY, SYDNEY TO QUEENSLAND.

No 1 Gatekeeper's Cottage

This cottage was burnt in the 1968 bushfire. It guarded the level crossing where the first railway line crossed Mitchell's Pass. The road ran between the cottage and the John Whitton Memorial, while the railway slanted across the present railway line to join the location now occupied by the Great Western Highway.

There were twelve gatekeeper's cottages built to the same pattern along the first railway line to Mount Victoria. The high pitched gable roof, usually painted green with decorative barge boards, was most attractive. This cottage was known as 'Green Gables'. There are only a few surviving cottages.

3 Springwood — Faulconbridge

1 Blaxland to Valley Heights

Follow the Great Western Highway to Blaxland. On the left, near the overbridge, in Station Street Mall, is the 'Footsteps in Time' marker, recording the traverse made by surveyor George William Evans on 7 January 1814, between overnight camps at Springwood and Glenbrook. Evans was returning from crossing the Great Dividing Range. Continue through Warrimoo and Valley Heights to Springwood. Much history has flowed along this section of the main ridge. Little remains to be seen, although the literature is rich. As you drive along, think of the explorers and settlers connected with **Blaxland Railway Station, The Gatekeeper's Cottages, Dawes' Line of March, 1789, Warrimoo Railway Station, The Explorers' Camp 12 May 1813, Valley Heights Railway Station.**

About 4 km beyond Warrimoo Railway Station, turn left to cross the railway line through the underpass, then right into Green Parade. A few metres along on the right is No 4 Gatekeeper's Cottage.

Continue to Springwood either by returning to the highway or by driving along Green Parade and Tusculum Road. The latter route takes you past the No 6 Gatekeeper's Cottage on the right opposite Burns Road. Near Valley Heights railway station is the former LOCOMOTOVE DEPOT, an interesting round building which may also be seen from the highway.

Blaxland Railway Station

A platform was built on this spot to serve the Pilgrim Inn, then called 'Wascoe's' after the proprietor. The railway station had the same name. It was renamed Blaxland in 1879.

Gatekeeper's Cottages

When the railway was built in 1867, there were six level crossings between Blaxland and Springwood, five of them with gatekeeper's cottages beside them.

The site of No. 2 is at Blaxland, about 1 km west of the railway station, where an overbridge carries Wilson Way across the line. The site of No. 3 is at Warrimoo, about 1 km west of the station, near the overbridge.

No. 4 at Valley Heights, 1 km east of the station in Green Parade, has been restored. The site of No. 5 is at Valley Heights on the road ramp leading up from the highway to the overbridge near the Valley Heights signal box.

No. 6 is at Springwood opposite Burns Road. It is a beautifully kept private home. A good view may be had across the railway line from Railway Parade.

When the line was duplicated and up-graded in 1902, these level crossings were eliminated.

Dawes' Line of March

Somewhere along this section of the ridge between Blaxland and Valley Heights you will cross the line of march taken by William Dawes and his party in 1789. He was attempting to follow a direct compass course from the ford across the Nepean to Mount Hay. This line took him up Mount Riverview and over the ridge the road follows.

In the Springwood area he may have travelled along the ridge or perhaps just south of it across the headwaters of Glenbrook Creek, to cross the main ridge somewhere between Springwood and Faulcon-

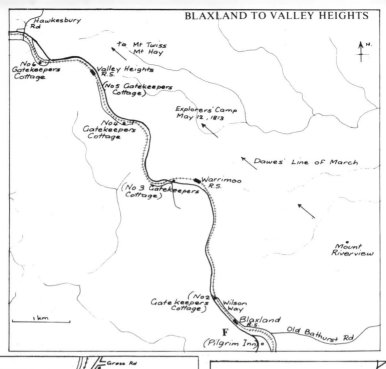

BLAXLAND TO VALLEY HEIGHTS

N

Hawkesbury Rd

to Mt Twiss
Mt Hay

No 6 Gatekeepers Cottage

Valley Heights R.S.
(No 5 Gatekeepers Cottage)

Explorers' Camp
May 12, 1813

No 4 Gatekeepers Cottage

Dawes' Line of March

Warrimoo R.S.

(No 3 Gatekeepers Cottage)

Mount Riverview

(No 2 Gatekeepers Cottage)

Wilson Way

Blaxland R.S.

F
(Pilgrim Inn)

Old Bathurst Rd

1 km

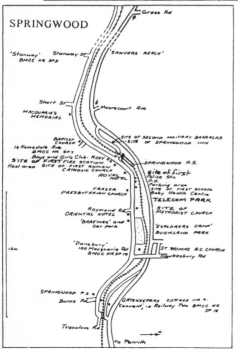

SPRINGWOOD

Grose Rd

'Stanway' Stanway St BMCC HR 5P5

'SAWYERS REACH'

Short St

Moorecourt Ave

MACQUARIE'S MEMORIAL

Baptist Church

SITE OF SECOND MILITARY BARRACKS
SITE OF SPRINGWOOD INN

14 Homedale Ave BMCC HR 5P7

Boys and Girls Club - ROXY 53

SITE OF FIRST FIRE STATION

Rest area   SITE OF FIRST ROMAN CATHOLIC CHURCH

SPRINGWOOD R.S.

ROYAL HOTEL

Site of first Police Stn
P.O.
Parking area
Site of first school
Baby Health Centre

FRAZER PRESBYTERIAN CHURCH

TELECOM PARK

Raymond Rd

ORIENTAL HOTEL

'BRAEMAR' and Car park

SITE OF METHODIST CHURCH

'Danesbury' 100 Macquarie Rd BMCC HR SP 19

'Explorers' Camp'
BUCKLAND PARK

ST THOMAS R.C. CHURCH

Hawkesbury Rd

1 km

SPRINGWOOD P.S.

Burns Rd

GATEKEEPERS COTTAGE NO 6
Convent, 16 Railway Pde BMCC HR SP 18

Tusculum Rd

to Penrith

N

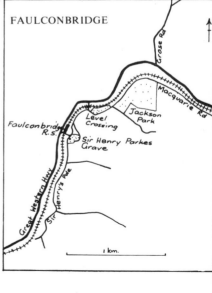

FAULCONBRIDGE

N

Grose Rd

Macquarie Rd

Faulconbridge R.S.

Level Crossing

Jackson Park

Sir Henry Parkes Grave

Great Western Hwy

Sir Henry's Ave

1 km.

bridge. Again, his compass course may have taken him across the deep gullies to the north.

Dawes' experience showed that following a direct compass course was not the way to cross the Blue Mountains, but of course this lesson was not understood for another twenty years.

The story of Dawes' journey is told in greater detail in another chapter.

Warrimoo Railway Station

In 1881 a small wooden platform named Karabar was erected about 1 km west of the present station. It was not used much and was closed in 1897.

In 1918 a station was built on the present site and named Warrimoo, an Aboriginal word for 'eagle'. Blaxland, writing on May 12th, 1813, '...when they stopped they found a Kangaroo just killed by an eagle at the Hole of Water...' As their camp for that night may have been in the area, perhaps that is the reason for the choice of name.

The 1918 station was burnt down in the bushfires of December 1951 and rebuilt in 1957.

Explorers' Camp, 12 May 1813

The Warrimoo — Valley Heights area is thought to have been the place where Blaxland, Lawson and Wentworth camped that night, their first actually on the mountains. It is difficult to establish the exact spot, as the distances travelled, as given by Blaxland and Lawson in their diaries, differ by as much as three or four miles (5 or 6 km).

Blaxland writes: '...in the evening they encamped at the Head of a deep gully which they had to descend for Water found but just enough for the Night in a hole in the rock...'

Suitable flat and sheltered spots which fulfil these conditions may be found in several places.

Valley Heights Railway Station

On Sir Thomas Mitchell's survey map of 1834, this area was marked 'The Valley'. The good soil of the region to the north of the railway line, in Fitzgerald's Gully, comes from old volcanic rock.

The Valley Inn was established by Alexander Fraser in 1832 on what is now the commuter car park. About 1835 it was known as *The Woolpack* and the Quaker, James Backhouse described it as 'a plain country inn, having moderate accommodation.' It was later called *The Welcome Inn*. Its nearest neighbour was the Pilgrim Inn at Blaxland. In the 1870s, when bought by the Hon. Geoffrey Eagar, Colonial Treasurer, it became *The Valley* and later *Wyoming* when he used it as a private residence. Before it was demolished in 1937, it had again been an inn and also a boarding house.

In 1875 a railway platform was built near his house, and called Eagar's Platform. In 1877 the name was changed to The Valley, and to Valley Heights in 1890.

Valley Heights to Katoomba covers twenty miles (32 km) of the steepest and the fastest climbing railway line anywhere in Australia, there being a rise in altitude between the two stations of 2280 feet (695 metres). Two engines were coupled in front and a 'pusher' worked at the rear. Prior to 1913 these extra engines operated from Penrith Loco Depot, but following the re-grading of the line and the construction of the Glenbrook Gorge deviation, a locomotive yard, a 10-bay 'roundhouse' (this may still be seen), an 18 metre (60 foot) turntable and an elevated coal loading stage (since demolished) were put in at Valley Heights. The Penrith depot was closed and Valley Heights took its place until electrification in March 1957, when the steam depot was closed; electric locomotives were stationed there till the mid 1980s.

2   Springwood

Turn off the Great Western Highway to the Springwood shopping centre, about 2 km past Valley Heights Railway Station. There are parking areas near the railway station and the Community Centre. Stop and take a walk along Macquarie Road. We began our walk from the western end of the township and noted the sites of buildings of historical significance, many of them being listed for preservation by the Blue Mountains City Council, the National Trust and the Heritage Council of Australia. The diagram shows the location of these places.

Bushland is easy to reach from Springwood. In Springwood Avenue, opposite the car park running through to Macquarie Road, is the start of a walking track to *Fairy Dell*, restored and reopened in April, 1990.

There are several walking tracks into Upper Glenbrook Creek.

Turn down Burns Road and left into Farm Road, which soon becomes a gravel track and more suitable for walking than for vehicles. The track leads to *Martin's Lookout, Martin's Falls, Magdala Falls* and the *Blue Pool*. A track starts also from the corner of Homedale Street and Valley Road, and another from Sassafras Gully Road, which turns left from Valley Road.

Wiggins Track is reached by following Beefarm Road to Yondell Avenue. It is wise to seek local information as to the condition of the tracks from the National Parks and Wildlife Service or the Blue Mountains City Council beforehand. Both Macquarie Road and the highway lead to Faulconbridge, the next township in our journey up the mountains.

Macquarie Memorial, Second Barracks, Chinese Camp and Springwood Inn

The memorial reads: 'Governor Macquarie and his party camped here on their journey to Bathurst on April 27, 1815, and named the place "Springwood". William Cox erected here a military depot early 1816.' (BMCC HR SP 12)

This monument, erected by the Royal Australian Historical Society in 1938, marks the site of the earliest named town on the Blue Mountains. Governor Macquarie observed the forest of tall trees and the stream of good water and named it accordingly. Cox's depot was established while he made the road through the area between 14 and 18 August 1814.

Macquarie ordered the military depot moved from Glenbrook Lagoon to Springwood and Cox built the barracks, with a fence enclosing a garden, near the site of the monument, in 1816. In 1833 the barracks needed renovation and was re-built on a site north of the railway line near Ferguson Avenue, as it is today. Part of the old site was sold in 1879 to the Church of England, and although never used for building a church, the land became known as the 'Church Acre'. It was sold in 1901.

The military depot operated from Springwood until 1845. Because of its presence, Springwood was regarded as a safe place to camp.

In the 1860s the Chinese who travelled to the western goldfields often camped on the opposite side of the road from Macquarie's camp. As many as two hundred Chinese are said to have camped there at one time. They would travel more slowly than other gold seekers, with wares and handicrafts to sell.

After the military depot was closed, Thomas Boland established the Springwood Inn on the site, using timber from the barracks. It was sometimes known as Boland's Inn and was last licensed in 1870. The building was demolished in 1939. Boland Avenue is not far from the site.

'Sawyer's Reach'

William Cox made the following entry in his diary in 1814: 'August 17; ...The timber in the forest ... is both tall and large and thick on the ground ... There is some good stringy bark

here, and having dug a sawpit I named it Sawyer's Reach.' The stretch of timber lay between Burns Road and Grose Road, the area covered by our diagram. The site of the sawpit is unknown; there may have been several to serve different stands of trees.

Baptist Church

Mr J. B. Hoare built a two-storey brick residence named 'Homedale' on this land in 1881. Between 1918 and 1960 it housed the Blue Mountains Grammar School. It was then used as a home for the elderly until demolished.

The small wooden church built in 1957 was replaced in 1965.

Springwood Boys' and Girls' Club — The Roxy Theatre

This building started life as an open air picture theatre. Later it was roofed over and a foyer added. It was closed from the mid 1950s, like many other picture theatres, until put to its present use in 1963.

Fire Station

The railway station master's residence which originally stood here was acquired as a fire station in 1957. It has been rebuilt.

Royal Hotel (BMCC HR SP 13)

Thomas Boland, of the Springwood Inn, on the other side of the railway, built the Royal Hotel in 1881 and his son Thomas was the first licensee.

Many alterations and additions make it difficult to identify the original parts of this building.

Springwood Railway Station (BMCC HR SP 16, Nat. Tr., Her. Aus.)

This small but elaborate brick station building (now renovated) was erected on the railway platform in 1884, under the direction of John Whitton, Chief Engineer of the N.S.W. Government Railways. Originally symmetrical, it has been extended at one end. The high pitched iron roof is formed behind two gabled parapets. A small central gablet carries a sandstone date plaque. There are sandstone cap mouldings to parapet, quoins, door ventilator and window surrounds.

This building makes an important contribution to the local townscape, and has been classified as essential to the heritage of Australia.

An earlier platform was built shortly after the line was opened in 1867 to which a waiting shed was added in 1877. In 1878 a crossing loop was put in to enable trains to pass at Springwood and the following year a ticket and telegraph office was erected.

When the platform was built, the single line ran on the northern side and it was possible to walk straight onto the station from the street. On duplication of the line in 1902, the platform became an island and an overhead footbridge was put up.

Police Station

The land was part of the original school block and was handed over to the Police Department in 1877.

The only part of the first police station built in 1881 which still exists is the original brick lock-up. The weatherboard section was demolished in the 1950s to make way for the present station.

Post Office

Mr Frank Raymond conducted a post office at his store in the Springwood Hotel in 1877. In 1879 the mail service was transferred to the railway station and the railway telegraph operator was appointed postmaster. This situation continued until 1891.

The present post office, opened in 1901, was built on part of the land originally acquired from the school. A manual telephone exchange was installed in 1912; when switched to an automatic system, the equipment was placed in a new building further east.

Springwood railway station

Site of the First School

The school stood where the Baby Health Centre now is and the car park is on the old playground area. On 23rd October 1876 a committee of five residents, William Henderson, warehouseman, Charles Moore, merchant, Frank Raymond, storekeeper, John Ellison, farmer, and Cornelius Lee, farmer, applied to the Council of Education for the establishment of a public school at Springwood. Their request was granted and the same five men were appointed as a board of managers to supervise its operation. When opened in 1878, the population of Springwood was about 200, mostly railway workers and farmers. The nearest schools at that time were at Emu Plains and Mount Victoria.

Frazer Memorial Presbyterian Church (BMCC HR SP 11)

The sandstone for this elegant and beautifully decorated church, built in 1895, was quarried locally. Eleven years previously the Hon. John Frazer, M.L.C., had bequeathed £5000 for the erection of a church at Springwood.

John Frazer was born in Ireland in 1826, arrived in Australia in 1841, found the low wages and long working hours of country jobs unsatisfactory, went into business in Sydney and was successful there. He was appointed to the Legislative Council in 1874 and remained a member till his death in 1884 at his residence, 'Quairang', Woollahra, at the age of 58.

A few years before his death Frazer had bought land at Springwood and built a large weatherboard mansion named 'Silva Plana' on the northern side of the railway and west of the Hawkesbury Road in 1882. Demolished in the 1940s, its name is retained in Silva Street, connecting Hawkesbury Road with the highway.

Monuments in Telecom Park

The Footsteps in Time marker was unveiled as part of Springwood's 175th birthday celebrations in April 1990. George William Evans surveyed through this location on 7 January 1814 between his camps at Springwood and Glenbrook.

A plaque nearby records Governor Lachlan Macquarie's naming of Springwood in 1815.

Oriental Hotel (BMCC HR SP 10)

James Lawson, Snr, built the Oriental Hotel in 1892, the first licensee being F. Brandon. Alterations and additions have changed its appearance considerably.

An earlier building on this site was the *Springwood Hotel* opened in the 1870s by Frank Raymond and also used as a store, post office and newsagency. The adjacent side road bears his name.

Braemar Art Gallery (BMCC HR SP 14, Nat. Tr.)

This house was built for James Lawson Snr, of the family of James R. Lawson Pty. Ltd., auctioneers. The date on the plans is 1892. The Blue Mountains City Council purchased the property in 1975. This pleasant

'Braemar', Macquarie Rd, Springwood

Christ Church of England, Great Western Highway, Springwood

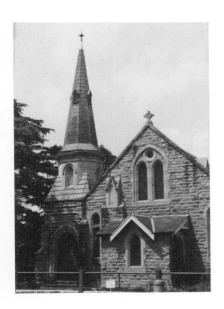

Frazer memorial Presbyterian Church, Macquarie Rd, Springwood

Door, Frazer Memorial Presbyterian Church, Macquarie Rd, Springwood

colonial-style cottage with encircling verandah is now an art gallery, open Friday to Sunday, 10 a.m. to 4 p.m.

A modern library block has been built behind it.

Explorers' Camp, Springwood

It is difficult to establish the exact spot where the party of explorers camped on 13 May, their second mountain camp. They returned to the same camp on the next three nights. It was probably somewhere between the Hawkesbury Road and Springwood Railway Station. They found water in a gully and the forest provided shelter. They decided to leave their horses and baggage in camp under guard while they cut a path for their laden horses.

They had difficulty in deciding which was the main ridge, as Lawson's compass directions show that they tried the Hawkesbury Road ridge till it turned eastwards. From Springwood on, they marked their track by blazing both sides of trees, enabling them to take only three days back to Springwood on their return journey. Then they used their old camp on 4 June, and had some difficulty in finding their way back down the unmarked Lapstone Hill. We can only assume they had not marked the track from the river to prevent run-away convicts from following them.

An interesting note in Blaxland's journal: 'May 13 they found . . . several native huts at different places . . .'

Buckland Park

The park was named after Sir Thomas Buckland, a former president of the Bank of New South Wales, whose representations to the former Blue Mountains Shire Council obtained a reticulated water supply for Springwood in the 1930s. He later built the Buckland Convalescent Hospital for Women on Hawkesbury Road.

St Thomas's Roman Catholic Church

This church was built in 1919. The wooden building adjacent was the first Roman Catholic Church, built in 1892 and originally standing opposite the railway station, on land now the rest area. It was moved to its present site in 1921.

Springwood Primary School

The present school in Burns Road was opened in 1954 by Mr R. J. Heffron, M.L.A., Minister of Education. Until that time the school was beside the railway line.

No. 6 Gatekeeper's Cottage (BMCC HR SP 4)

This is one of the few cottages still in use. It is private property and very well preserved.

Tusculum Road

This is one of the road names that is the only reminder of an early residence. The house was built by the Hon. Geoffrey Eagar, M.L.A., Colonial Treasurer, Secretary for

Public Works and Under-Secretary for Finance and Trade, opposite his home 'Wyoming', at Valley Heights.

'Tusculum' was later acquired by Mr Justice Foster.

Wiggins Track

This walking track into Upper Glenbrook Creek was built in the 1940s by F. T., Jack and J. J. Wiggins, who were the Honorary Secretary, Captain and Vice-Captain of the Miniature Rifle Range Club.

3   Faulconbridge

Travel to Faulconbridge either by Macquarie Road or by leaving Springwood via the underpass and Ferguson Avenue to the highway. Follow the highway for 3 km and turn left over the level crossing. Keep left to **Jackson Park and the Avenue of Oaks**. Wander under the trees and look for the names of the Prime Ministers who planted them.

Faulconbridge was the scene of some **Early Traverses of the Ridge.**

From Sir Henry's Parade, near Clarinda Avenue, is the start of *Victory Track*, one of the walking tracks down into *Glenbrook Creek* and *Sassafras Gully.*

Continue west along Sir Henry's Parade. On your right is **Faulconbridge Railway Station**. In Faulconbridge cemetery opposite is **Sir Henry Parkes' Grave.**

Prime Ministers' Avenue of Oaks, Jackson Park

Joseph Jackson, O.B.E., M.L.A., representative of the electorate of Nepean for 33 years, gave the land to the council of the day for a public park in 1933.

It was Jackson's idea that all Prime Ministers of Australia or their nearest surviving relative should plant an oak tree to form the Prime Ministers' Avenue of Oaks in the park. In this way future generations would be reminded of the work of Sir Henry Parkes in bringing together the states of Australia into a Federation, symbolised by this long line of Prime Ministers. A great admirer of Sir Henry Parkes and a collector of memorabilia concerning him, Joseph Jackson thought that an extension of the tree planting which had already taken place on Parkes' property would be an appropriate memorial to him. In 1881 the Royal Princes, George (later King George V) and Edward (later Duke of Clarence), planted trees at Faulconbridge; it is uncertain whether the Hoop Pine (*Araucaria cunninghami*) and Laurel Magnolia (*Magnolia grandiflora*) are the original trees, as reports at the time state that peach trees were planted.

Early Traverses of the Ridge

William Dawes is thought by some to have crossed this ridge in 1789.

Blaxland, Lawson and Wentworth worked along this narrow ridge cutting a track for their horses while they camped each night at Springwood from 13 to 15 May 1813.

Cox and his gang made the first road along the ridge in late August, 1814.

Faulconbridge Railway Station

The original platform, built of wood in 1877 to serve the residence of Sir Henry Parkes, then Prime Minister of New South Wales, was near the level crossing. The present station was constructed further west when the line was duplicated in 1902.

Its name was taken from Parkes' residence, Faulconbridge House; Parkes' mother had been Martha Faulconbridge.

Before the station was built, the guard would throw out a bag of mail for Prime Minister Parkes and his employees living there.

Sir Henry Parkes' Grave

In Faulconbridge cemetery is the burial plot of the Parkes Family. On the iron railing surrounding it a plaque has been placed by the Blue Mountains City Council, inscribed thus:

'Sir Henry Parkes, Father of Australian Federation, Five times Prime Minister of New South Wales, arrived in Australia July 25, 1839, worked as station-hand, Customs Officer, bone and ivory turner. In 1850 became proprietor of Empire Newspaper. Member of New South Wales Parliament from 1854-1894, Sir Henry Parkes is especially remembered for his efforts to develop New South Wales Education and Railways and his work for Federation earned him his title of Father of Federation'

Sir Henry Parkes (1815-1896)

Born in Warwickshire, England, the youngest son of Thomas Parkes and Martha Faulconbridge, Henry Parkes married Clarinda Varney and emigrated to Australia in 1836. A self-educated man, Parkes worked at a variety of occupations and made his mark as a member of the New South Wales Parliament. First in office as Colonial Secretary in James Martin's cabinet in 1866, he later became Prime Minister, as the title was then, on five occasions, his period in that office totalling twelve and a half years. The legislation of 1866 and 1880 concerning education was largely his work, as was that making the administration of the railways independent of political influence. Parkes is mostly remembered for the enthusiasm and energy he applied to the campaign for the federation of the Australian states, the fruition of which he did not live to see.

Parkes went to live at Faulconbridge in 1877 and it was his main home for several years. He acquired 600 acres (243 hectares) and over the years he built four houses. The first was *Stonehurst*, the name being associated with his birthplace, Stoneleigh, in England. The second house and main place of abode was *Faulconbridge House*. He also built

Moseley Cottage for his sister, Maria, and *Fern Dell* as an employee's cottage. The estate, with its garden and paths winding between trees and statues to views of the mountains, has now been subdivided and Faulconbridge House is private property.

4   Faulconbridge to Springwood — Northern Side

There are some interesting houses between Springwood and Faulconbridge. **Danville** (private property) is on the south side of the Great Western Highway, and **Everton House,** now a restaurant, is opposite, on the corner of Everton Road.

Turn north into Grose Road. Another interesting old home, PHOENIX LODGE (BMCC HR 11, private property) is on the left.

Grose Road will take you, in about 12 km of rough track (keeping left where the track forks) to *Faulconbridge Point Lookout.* There is a barbecue area here; the lookout is unfenced. You will see a very beautiful and unusual view of the Grose River, and hear the murmur of the cascades immediately below. The skyline view includes Mounts Banks, Tomah with Wilson behind it, Irvine and Tootie, Kurrajong Heights and Grose Head South. The junction of Wentworth Creek with the Grose is just out of sight to the north of the reach of the river you can see. This was the point at which William Paterson (Vale Lookout chapter) and his party turned back when their boats were damaged and the water level rose.

A walking track starts a short way back from the parking area and leads down into the Grose River valley. It is an all-day trip and rather steep. Return via Grose Road to Chapman Parade and turn left. About 2 km along is **The Norman Lindsay Gallery and Museum** (Nat. Tr.), 128 Chapman Parade. Open Friday, Saturday, Sunday and public holidays from 11 a.m. to 5 p.m. Admission is charged. Light refreshments are available.

From the end of Chapel Parade you may look down into Springwood Creek, but there are 2 km of very rough track. Return along Chapman Parade and Grose Road. Turn left onto the highway. A short distance along stop at **Buttenshaw Park.** Notice the gate posts from 'Moorecourt'. The wisteria walk is a delight in the spring. Further along the highway is **Southall,** 353 Great Western Highway, (private property) and **Christ Church of England**. Continue along the highway to Springwood and turn left towards Richmond.

Everton (BMCC HR FB 3)

Local stonemason Paddy Ryan built this summer home for the Hon. John

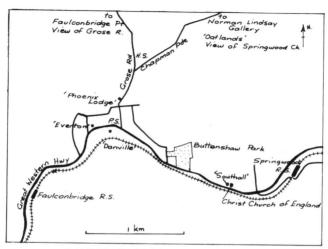

FAULCONBRIDGE TO SPRINGWOOD

Meeks, M.L.A., in 1870. He named it after the ship which brought him to Australia.

Norman Lindsay lived here for a time before he acquired 'Maryville' in Chapman Parade.

Danville (BMCC HR FB 7)

This weatherboard cottage was originally sited halfway between Faulconbridge and Linden and had been owned by Sir Alfred Stephen, Chief Justice of New South Wales from 1845 to 1873 and also a Privy Councillor.

The house was moved to its present position near Grose Road in 1921 and re-named after a town in Illinois, U.S.A.

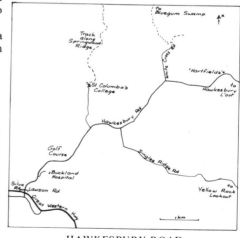

HAWKESBURY ROAD

Norman Lindsay Gallery and Museum

This interesting house and its beautiful grounds belongs to the National Trust. In it are displayed the oil paintings, etchings, watercolours, model ships, books and memorabilia which Norman Lindsay bequeathed on condition that the Trust bought the property. Other items have been added to the collection over the years.

Norman Lindsay's wife, Rose, bought the house in 1912. It had been built for Francis Foy, a brother of Mark Foy, at the end of the last century by local stonemason Paddy Ryan. The house was very run down when the Lindsays went to live there and in the process of renovation, the artist extended and changed it, replacing the roof with impressive red terracotta tiles. Lindsay widened the enclosed verandah and added Grecian pillars to the studio porch. This style became characteristic of Springwood. He laid out the grounds with statuary, fountains, a courtyard and walls and paths among the trees and gardens. His studio is set up with the artist's materials put out as if in use. Magnificent views of the mountains may be seen from a path through the bush at the rear of the grounds. His etching studio at the back of the house is now a tea-room.

Norman Alfred Lindsay (1879-1969) was born at Creswick in Victoria, one of a talented family of artists and authors. He was chief cartoonist of *The Bulletin* for many years. His etchings, oils and watercolours caused much controversy when first shown. Some of his novels were banned in Australia. Then his figures of Pan, satyrs and nude women were regarded as scandalous. He illustrated some of his own works, including *The Magic Pudding*. Among his novels are *Saturdee* and *The Age of Consent*.

Lindsay's versatility is well demonstrated in the gallery and museum, where the fruits of his labours are displayed. Many of these were produced in the fifty years he lived at Springwood.

Buttenshaw Park — Moorecourt

This park was named for a former Minister for Lands, the Hon. E. A. Buttenshaw.

When nearby *Moorecourt* was demolished, the gateposts were re-erected in the park and now head the wisteria walk. (BMCC HR SP 9).

Charles Moore, after whom Moore Park in Sydney is named, was a Mayor of Sydney. He also served as a member of both the Legislative Assembly and the Legislative Council. He built his country residence in 1876 on the corner of Sylvania Avenue and the main road. His crest is carved into the gate-posts.

For a time Springwood Ladies College functioned there. The house was demolished in 1958, leaving the gateposts and nearby Moorecourt Avenue as reminders.

Christ Church of England (BMCC HR SP 8)

The nave and temporary chancel were built in 1889 on land given by Charles Moore. Plans and specifications were provided free by the architect Sir John Sulman. The church remained uncompleted until 1962.

Southall (BMCC HR SP 6)

This handsome stone residence was originally built by Charles Moore in 1886 for the use of the Church of England rector and was called *The Vicarage*.

It has been variously used as a grammar school and a girls' school and a maternity hospital. An army nursing sister, Matron Sophie, O.B.E., later named the house *Southall* after an English hospital in which she served in World War I.

5 Hawkesbury Road

After passing by the turn-off to the Springwood Shopping Centre, take the left turn from the Great Western Highway towards Richmond along **Silva Road** into Hawkesbury Road. **Lawson Road** is on the opposite side of Hawkesbury Road.

Turn left away from Springwood along Hawkesbury Road, passing **Buckland Hospital** on the right and also **Ellison Road. St Columba's College** (private property) is on the left.

Turn right into Singles Ridge Road, 3½ km from Springwood. After 3 km of sealed road and 2 km of rough gravel road, you reach *Yellow Rock Lookout*. The view to the north along the Hawkesbury River is impressive, as is the craggy gully of Fraser's Creek. There is no safety fence; it is not an area for young children.

Return to Hawkesbury Road and turn right. One and a half km along turn left into White Cross Road. At the end of the road, the track to *Blue Gum Swamp* begins. This is a circular track about 8 km in length, with beautiful vegetation. At the northern end of the track, another leading north-west goes up onto the ridge and continues for several km to *Grose Head South Lookout*. This gives views of the Grose River and through Grose Gap towards Richmond. It is

certainly worth a rather long walk. Return can be by the track to White Cross Road or, keeping to the ridge, to come out at St Columba's College. Turn left into Hawkesbury Road and continue along it. **Hartfields** (private property) is on the left.

About 8 km from Springwood, *Hawkesbury Panorama Lookout* overlooks the Hawkesbury River and the Sydney plain, to the south-east.

Return to Sydney either via Hawkesbury Road and Richmond or via Springwood and the Great Western Highway.

Silva Road — Silva Plana

Springwood's level area covered with a magnificent forest is recalled by 'Silva Plana', the mansion built by the Hon. John Frazer, M.L.C., benefactor of the Frazer Memorial Presbyterian Church. The mansion was surrounded by carriage ways, and walks extended down into the bush. A stream was dammed to supply water to the house; the dam wall may still be seen in Else Mitchell Park, Prince Street.

The mansion was demolished in the 1940s, leaving the street name as a token of its existence.

Lawson Road

The first grant of land in the Springwood district was made in 1834 to Lt William Lawson, explorer and commandant of Bathurst. Part of his land is now the industrial area of Springwood and served by Lawson Road.

Buckland Hospital (BMCC HR SP 15)

The hospital stands on land originally owned by the Hon. James Norton, M.L.C., Postmaster-General of New South Wales in the Stuart Government of 1884. There he built 'Euchora'. The property was bought by Sir Thomas Buckland, a president of the Bank of New South Wales. After a town water supply was provided, largely due to his representations to the council of the day, he built the Buckland Convalescent Hospital for Women. The hospital was officially opened by the Premier, Sir Bertram Stevens, in 1936.

Ellison Road

This road is a reminder of Thomas Ellison, whose orchard of citrus, stone and pome fruit trees covered the area now occupied by the Springwood Golf Course. Planted in the 1880s, much of the orchard was still bearing in 1919.

Part of the orchard became a 9-hole golf course in 1903 and was extended to 18-holes in 1949.

St Columba's College (BMCC HR SP 17)

Part of the property on which the college is built belonged in 1839 to William Lawson. This and other land, including 'Elmhurst' built by W. Ipkendanz in 1884, was purchased by Cardinal Moran. The first section of the training college for student priests was constructed of stone quarried on the property. Twenty-six students were admitted in 1910.

A chapel, dormitory and classrooms were added in 1923, and other extensions were made in later years. 'Elmhurst' became a presbytery and is now a private home.

Hartlands/Hartfields (BMCC HR SP 3)

This elegant two-storey stone building was constructed in 1889 for Miss Janet Hooper who conducted a 'School for Young Ladies' there until 1897. She named it 'Hartlands' after her home in England.

For some years the house was rented, then vandals destroyed the fittings and it became known locally as 'the haunted house'.

Since 1962 it has been restored and is a private home, now called 'Hartfields'.

4 The Hollows — Linden and Woodford

1 Faulconbridge to Linden

Along this section of the road a number of properties were developed in the late nineteenth century. The first was **Metchley** now demolished and the site built over.

In about half a km, you pass the *Faulconbridge Lily Pond* on the left. The waterlilies were brought from Tasmania in 1945 by Charles H. Dilloway.

As you drive along this section of the highway, you will observe the narrowness of the ridge. The road and the railway occupy the whole of it.

Looking to the left, your passengers may get a glimpse of the ruined remains of **Weemala – Eurama** (private property). Nearer the highway is **Numantia – Weemala**, to be distinguished by its high encircling wall (private property). **Alphington (Danville)** now removed, was between them.

Round the next bend, turn left into Martin Place and cross the railway by the overbridge. On your right is **Banool** (private property) built on the site of 'Martin's Folly'.

A short walk from the further end of Numantia Avenue, below the water tower, will take you to LADY MARTIN'S POOL.

Return to the highway and turn left. The ridge is very narrow here. Somewhere in this vicinity may be the **Site of the Explorers' Camp, 17 and 18 May**.

At the top of a hill, you will pass, on your left, LINDEN LODGE (private property) for which the area is named and on your right **Linden Railway Station**.

Continue along this very narrow and hilly section of the ridge and take the next turn left. (Somewhere along this section of the highway is the **Site of Cox's Bluff Bridge**, perhaps near the watertower or possibly further west.)

Metchley and Western House

Professor Badham bought 14 acres (5.66 hectares) from Sir James Martin adjacent to Sir Alfred Stephen's block. he first built a wooden cottage called *Metchley* and later a brick house on a better site to the east and named it *Western House.* His family spent considerable periods of time there working in the garden and were often seen to stop work and line up to wave to the trains. Both these houses have been demolished.

Professor Charles Badham D.D. (1813-1884)

Born in Shropshire, England, son of a professor of Glasgow University, graduate of Oxford University, Charles Badham was ordained in the

FAULCONBRIDGE TO LINDEN

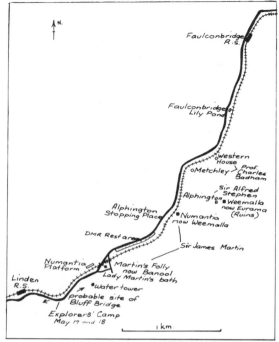

'Eurama' (formerly 'Weemala'). Ruin, viewed from the highway west of Faulconbridge, in 1982.

Church of England but his unorthodox ideas were not acceptable to the church. He became Professor of Classics and Logic at the University of Sydney.

Ruins of Weemala — Eurama (BMCC HR FB 1)

This stone house was built by stonemason Paddy Ryan for a Mr McCullock in 1881, when it was named *Weemala*. Later owners re-named it *Eurama*. For many years it was neglected, then a new owner spent time and trouble to restore it, only for it to be burnt in the 1968 bushfire.

Numantia — Weemala (BMCC HR FB 2)

Sir James Martin's *Numantia* estate, about 1½ km west of Faulconbridge and extending some 2 km along the ridge towards Linden, consisted of 954 acres (386 hectares). He so named it in honour of a town in Spain besieged by Roman Legions in 134 B.C. because he thought the scenery appeared similar.

In 1877 Martin built a wooden cottage beside the railway line and protected it by a high wall. Here he developed his country estate.

The *Alphington* Rail Stopping Place was near this cottage.

Later owners re-named it *Weemala*. It was destroyed in a bushfire but has since been rebuilt.

Alphington (Danville)

Sir Alfred Stephen built a wooden house on his block of 12 acres (4.85 ha.) which he had bought from Sir James Martin. He called it *Alphington* after his father's home in Exeter in Devon. The *Alphington* Stopping Place on the railway line served this group of properties between 1877 and 1881.

The house was later moved to Faulconbridge, where, under the name of *Danville*, it may be seen opposite Grose Road.

Sir Alfred Stephen G.C.M.G. (1802-1894)

Born in the West Indies and educated in England, he served as a lieutenant in a militia corps of Fusiliers for two years, after which he studied law.

Arriving in Tasmania in 1825, he was appointed Solicitor-General and Crown Solicitor, and later became Attorney-General of Tasmania. He was made a Judge of the Supreme Court of New South Wales in 1839, was Chief Justice from 1845 to his retirement in 1873. He became a member and was President of the Legislative Council, was Lieutenant-Governor in 1875 and President of the Trustees of the National Gallery in 1880.

He was highly thought of by his contemporaries; he was 'a clever pains-taking judge, with depth of learning and acute intellect', 'very active in political and community life', 'showed impartiality and incapability of the slightest feeling of resentment', his 'decisions were models of lucidity'.

Banool — Martin's Folly — Lady Martin's Bath (BMCC HR LD 1)

Sir James Martin planned to build a large stone mansion on the western edge of his land, a kilometre from the *Numantia* cottage. He laid the foundations and put in tanks to supply the garden and house with water. *Lady Martin's Bath* is one of these tanks. It was, however, never completed and became known as *Martin's Folly*. Lady Martin took a dislike to the place and refused to spend her inheritance on the elaborate project.

A private railway platform, *Numantia*, was opened nearby for Martin's use; it was closed in 1897.

In 1908 a cottage named *The Bungalow* was built on the foundations of Martin's Folly. A later owner changed its name to *Banool*.

Sir James Martin, K.C.M.G. (1820-1886)

Born in the County of Cork, Ireland, James was brought to Australia as a baby when his father was employed by Governor Brisbane as his private groom and horse trainer. Educated at Parramatta and Sydney, James began writing for *The Australian* newspaper, edited it for a while, and then studied law. He went into politics first as a member of the Legislative Council and then was elected to the Legislative Assembly when it was formed in 1856. In his long parliamentary career he was Premier of New South Wales for three terms, and friend and colleague of Sir Henry Parkes. He retired from Parliament to become Chief Justice of New South Wales in 1873.

Martin Place, Sydney, is named in his honour.

Site of Explorers' Camp, 17 and 18 May

Blaxland, Lawson and Wentworth camped, it is thought, in the vicinity of the present Linden railway station on the sixth and seventh nights of their journey, and Blaxland commented on the difficulty of ascending the mountains here — a difficulty encountered also by Cox and by later road and rail builders, as well as travellers on Cox's road.

From Blaxland's journal:

'Monday May 17th, 1815 ... in the afternoon they encamped between two very deep gullies on a narrow ridge of the Mountain where they were forced to fetch water up the Precipice they suppose six hundred feet or more of which they could get scarcely enough for the men — the Horses went without this Night ...'

'May 18th ... The day was spent in cutting a passage through the brushwood for a mile and a half further. ... The ridge which was not more than fifteen or twenty yards over with deep precipices on each side was rendered almost impassible by a perpendicular mass of rock nearly 30 feet high extending across the whole breadth with the exception of a small broken track in the centre. By removing a few large stones they were enabled to pass.'

The ridge has been changed by road and railway works and the spot is difficult to identify. The ridge is hilly as well as narrow.

Linden Railway Station

The Linden area was first distinguished from others by the number of miles it was from the ford on the Nepean River — as Seventeen Mile Hollow.

The railway to Weatherboard (Wentworth Falls) was opened in 1867 but a platform at 17 Mile Hollow was not opened until 1874 when a request was made by Mr D. Fletcher of Linden Lodge nearby. Seventeen Mile Hollow, Linden Tank, Henderson's Platform and then Linden were the names given to it in succession.

In 1882 two crossing loops, to enable more trains to run on the single line, were put in as well as other improvements. In 1885 a watertank was established and supplied from a dam and pumping station on Woodford Creek. Other re-organisation of the line took place over the years as well as up-dating the water supply. Then improvements to locomotives made the watering of trains at Linden unnecessary and use of the station decreased until it was closed in 1974.

Cox's Road — The Bluff Bridge

William Cox tells of his problems with the ridge near Linden. 'August 27 Measured to the 16th mile, immediately after which the ground got very rocky, and in half-a-mile we came to a high mountain, which will cost much labour to make a road over ...

August 29 ... Had to remove an immense quantity of rock, both in going up the mountain and to the pass leading to the bluff on the west of it. Examined the high rocks well and fixed on making a road off it from the bluff instead of winding around it.

September 12 ... The bridge we have completed is 80 ft. long; 15 ft. wide at one end and 12 ft. at the other; 35 ft. of it is planked, the remainder filled up with stones ... At the left there is a side wall cut from the solid rock. At the right, where the ground is lower, we have put up a rough stone wall about 100 ft. long, which makes the pass to the bridge quite a lane. It is steep from the top of the mountains quite to the lower end of the bridge, a distance of about 400 ft. The bridge and pass have cost me the labour of 12 men for three weeks...'

Governor Macquarie and his party crossed the bridge on the afternoon of April 27, 1815. Major Antill wrote that, after passing Caley's Repulse, 'About half a mile on we prepared a bridge extending from one rock to another across a chasm, which we named Bluff Bridge, ...'

All traces of this bridge have disappeared under earthworks for road and railway.

2 Linden

Drive along the highway from Faulconbridge, past Linden Railway Station, and turn left at the signpost: 'To Glossop Road, King's Cave and

King's Cave, Linden

Caley's Repulse, Linden

Donohoe's Headstone, Burke Rd, Linden

Remnant of Cox's Road, Linden

Caley's Repulse'. This road takes you by an overpass to the other side of the railway line. Turn right at Glossop Road and on your left, almost immediately, is a sign pointing to **Caley's Repulse.** Park and walk up the few steps. Straight up the hill, beside a house, you will find the heap of stones, surrounded by a low fence. If you walk on up the hill through the bush, in a very short time you will come to a vehicular track. Turn left and you will find some **Remnants of Cox's Road.**

Follow this track for about 500 metres until it comes out on a hill above the highway. Look across to the hill on the opposite side, to Woodford Trig Station. More remnants of Cox's Road are to be found there. Some historians think that the **true site of 'Caley's Repulse'** may have been on the top of the hill near the Trig.

Return to your car and drive along Glossop Road a short distance and turn right into Burke Road. About 200 metres along, down the hill, the road widens near **Donohoe's Headstone.** There is room to park nearby. Beside a (broken?) signpost is a track leading downhill to **King's Cave.** The walk is quite short and the result interesting.

The railway embankment opposite Donohoe's Headstone covers his grave, and also the **Site of the Toll Bar House** and the **Site of the Toll Bar Inn.**

Return to Glossop Road and turn right. This road takes you along Linden Ridge in a north-westerly direction at first. This is thought to be the area of the **Explorers' Camp, 19 May.**

Follow Glossop Road, noticing on your right *Linden Observatory*, said to contain the largest privately-owned telescope in the Southen Hemisphere. **Lake Woodford,** on your left, can be seen below the reservoir at the end of Glossop Road.

From the end of Glossop Road, a track takes you along Dawes Ridge. Keep to the left — the right fork follows Linden Ridge to the east. In about 3 km the track reaches **Mount Twiss,** the end of the attempt to reach Mount Hay made by **Lt William Dawes** and party in 1789. The track to Mount Twiss is very rough for a car but good for walking. Return along Glossop Road and retrace your route across the overbridge. Turn left at the highway for Woodford.

Caley's Repulse

This pile of stones was put together by members of the Australian Historical Society (later the Royal) in 1912, to celebrate the approaching centenary of the crossing of the Blue Mountains. They had been searching for the heap which had apparently disappeared over the years. The fence was placed around it by the Blue Mountains City Council in 1972.

There are two questions which will probably never be satisfactorily answered. Is the present site of Caley's Repulse the original one? Who heaped up the stones in the first place?

Early explorers and travellers always mention the pile of stones in conjunction with the view to be seen from the very high hill they (and the stones) were on. The view from the present site is not extensive, and rather closed in on the eastern side. It has been suggested that the first site could have been on the hill presently surmounted by Woodford Trig.

Blaxland, Lawson and Wentworth assumed that the pile had been heaped up by George Bass on his mountain

LINDEN

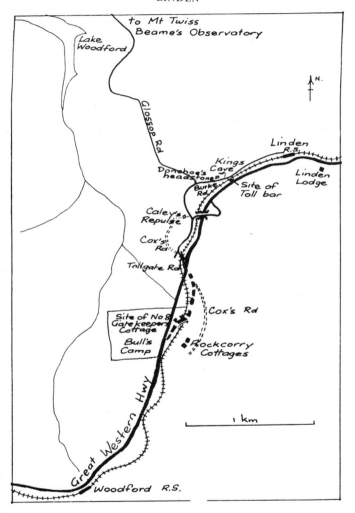

journey. At one time it was thought that Bass struggled up the Grose River as far as Mount Tomah, but later researchers have come to the conclusion that his attempt on the mountains was made south of the Warragamba River. On the other hand, Bass was known to be energetic and impatient and, while waiting for a

Blossoming street trees, Leura (p.89).

View from Govetts Leap Lookout, Blackheath (p.112).

Leura Cascades (p.91).

ship, he *could* have journeyed up into this part of the mountains. There is no record of such an excursion, however.

George Caley certainly made expeditions into the foothills near The Oaks in 1802 and to Mount Banks in 1804. He wrote voluminously to Sir Joseph Banks giving reports on his collecting efforts and his explorations. There is no record of his having been on the ridge at Linden, although in his account of his journey to Mount Banks, he writes of having seen Grose Head North from 'the other side'.

Other early explorers were Captain William Paterson, who stayed in the bed of the Grose; Ensign Francis Barrallier, who made his assault along the Nattai River and got as far as Christy's Creek, not far south of Kanangra Walls; the ex-convict John Wilson, who journeyed south of Barrallier's track; and Henry Hacking, former Quarter-master of the *Sirius*, who claimed he had penetrated the mountains for 20 miles but left no record or map of his track.

Some historians consider it more likely that the heap of stones was put up by Aborigines. Other heaps of stones were found at Mount Pleasant, near Bathurst, and were attributed to Aborigines. Why not the pile of stones originally found on Linden ridge? It will probably remain a mystery.

The pile of stones is interesting mainly as a landmark mentioned by journal writers. The earliest references to it follow:

> 'May 19, 1813 ... From this ridge they first began to have an extensive view over the settlements below at a little distance from the spot they ascended they found a heap of stones piled up in the Shape of a Pyramid ... they

conjectured it to have been the end of Mr Bass's track.'

Blaxland

'21st Nov. (1813) ... passed the Pile of Stones alluded to by a former party; soon after we were on a very high hill, which was clear of mist, but to my great disappointment the country to the Eastward being covered with a Vapour I could not be satisfied with the Prospect, which must have presented itself had the weather been clear ...'

Evans

'September 3 (1814) ... The road finished to Caley's heap of stones, 17½ miles ... From the bridge it continues rocky to Caley's Pile, from thence at least two miles further, the mountain is nearly a solid rock ... impossible to make a level good road...'

Cox

'... a pile of stones attracted attention; it is close to the road, on the top of a rugged and abrupt ascent, and is supposed to have been placed there by Mr Caley, as the extreme limit of his tour — hence the Governor gave that part of the mountain the name of Caley's Repulse.'

Macquarie

Remnants of Cox's Road

The old road is clearly visible here, with edges chipped out of the solid sandstone and a 'pavement' of rocky steps. This apparently did not make for a smooth cart or coach ride. Travellers remarked on the discomfort hereabouts. In the early 1800s a journey over the mountains was something to write about in your diary, as Mrs Elizabeth Hawkins did in 1822:

> '... We ascended. Our cart had now three bullocks, as we had so much trouble to get on with two, but we were

worse off than ever. As the ascent became worse, they refused to draw, and every few minutes first one and then another would lie down ... At length we came to a hill so steep it seemed we could never get up it. We alighted ... We were on the side of it; in front it was almost perpendicular; behind was a valley so deep the eye could hardly distinguish the trees at the bottom ... The first dray with the horses got up. They were then brought back to assist the rest with the bullocks, but they could not succeed in raising them from one rock to another. With great noise a sudden effort was made, and one shaft was broken...'

The difficulties of crossing the mountains were not ended by finding a route or building a road.

Cox described the mountain as being of solid rock here, impossible to make a good level road over. He added, 'The more the road is used the better it will be.'

Mrs Hawkins experience hardly bore out Cox's hope!

True Site of Caley's Repulse (?)

The hill surmounted by Woodford Trig Station and crossed by the line of the first road to Bathurst gives very good views back over the Sydney plain. Such views are described by the early diarists when they reached the hill near the pile of stones. For this reason some historians think the pile must have been originally situated nearer to this hill rather than on its present site further east.

John Donohoe's Headstone

The headstone bears the inscription: 'Erected to the memory of John Donohue who departed this life June 25 A.D. 1837 aged 58 years.'

The original engraving is still to be seen on the back of the headstone, barely legible in places, although it can be discerned that the name was spelt 'Donohoe'.

Donohoe was in fact buried in a spot now covered by the railway embankment. The headstone was removed each time the railway line was up-graded. In 1970 the Linden Citizens' Association had it placed in its present position near the path leading to King's Cave.

Legend has it that Donohoe was a constable who was shot by a bushranger, named King. No documentary evidence for this story has been uncovered to date. Although we do not know who he was, he did at least have one friend who bothered to record his death on a headstone erected over his grave.

King's Cave

Only a few steps below the road you find yourself under a wide overhang — a perfect mountain shelter for the aborigines, for the soldiers who levelled the floor, and obviously for others since. What more does one need — a dry floor, shelter from wind and rain, a hearth, morning sun, a stream nearby, *and* close to transport (or trade route).

King's Cave was probably used as a camping place by the King's Own Regiment — guarding convict road-builders, but tales of a bushranger named 'King' and his foul murder of Donohoe, whose grave is nearby, have grown around it. Allan E. Searle, in his book, *Historic Woodford and Linden*, presents some interesting and convincing facts about both these relics.

Toll Bar House

The western end of the railway embankment now covers the site of the Government Toll Bar constructed in 1848. A policy of paying for road construction and maintenance by the levying of tolls on travellers had been in operation since the days of Governor Macquarie. The site of the old 17 Mile Hollow Stockade was chosen, as the very narrow ridge there made it suitable. At the same time a Toll Bar and house was to be erected at Broughton's Waterhole (Mount Victoria); this house still exists and we can assume that the house at Linden was built to the same plan. Thomas Ellison was the toll bar keeper.

When the railway line was built at Linden in the 1860s the road was moved to allow the railway to have the best location, and the toll house and gates were demolished.

Toll Bar Inn

Thomas Ellison, toll bar keeper, acquired land to the east of the toll bar and in 1857 built an inn there of locally quarried stone with a shingle roof. It had two storeys, a stone flagged verandah, and a staircase which could be drawn up. With the coming of the railway a few years later, Ellison received compensation for the destruction of his inn, its site being under the railway embankment. He built the Alexander Hotel nearby. Of timber construction, it burnt down in 1869 and was not rebuilt.

Explorers' Camp, 19 May

Blaxland's journal for this day reads:
'.. proceeded about a Mile and a half in the track they had cut and marked the day before along a very narrow ridge not more than fifteen or twenty yards over with a very deep rocky precipice on each side when they ascended the second ridge of the mountains ... they first began to have an extensive view of the settlements below...'

The last bearing of their compass course given for this day is 'North West a quarter of a Mile.'

The heap of stones is mentioned. '...at a little distance from the spot they ascended they found a heap of Stones piled up in the Shape of a Pyramid by some European...' but this was probably passed while they were cutting the track for the next day after they had made camp.

Their bearings given for the next day are in a southerly direction.

From this evidence it seems likely that their camp for 19 May was a little way out along Linden Ridge, which they did not pursue as the watercourses on each side flow northerly and the ridge would not take them to the west, as desired.

Lake Woodford

This water storage system supplies Linden and a number of towns on the Lower Blue Mountains. The first small dam across Bull's Creek was built in 1885 to service the railway tank at Linden. The failure of the Wentworth Falls storage to provide adequately for trains in the 1920s led to a larger scheme being implemented downstream of the dam at Linden, and so Woodford Creek was dammed.

Requests from ratepayers on the lower mountains for a water supply and the lessening of watering requirements for trains over the years led to the Blue Mountains Shire Council acquiring the dam in the 1930s. The dam wall has been raised several times to increase the supply as required by the demand. The water requires considerable treatment before it is fit for household use.

Mount Twiss

A longish walk along the 4WD track on Linden and Dawes Ridges takes you to Mount Twiss. Dawes named this furthest point west reached on his expedition after a brother officer, Captain Twiss, R. E., to whom he also dedicated his map.

Lt William Dawes was the first to come so far into the mountains. He came in summer, in December 1789, with Lt George Johnstone and Mr Lowes, surgeon's mate, sent by Governor Phillip to reach a high point on the range of hills and to see the lie of the land. They were aiming for Round Hill, now Mount Hay, one of the knobs clearly visible from Sydney, which would promise a good view. The party is believed to have come by way of Sassafras Gully, past the south side of present Springwood, up to Faulconbridge and across Linden Creek, to Mount Twiss, in a direct line, climbing up and down precipitous ridges and gullies. Dawes' map of the journey and the profile he drew of Mounts Hay, Banks and Tomah from his Mount Twiss suggest that this may be the area he reached. He felt that he had penetrated about

twelve miles (19 km) into the mountains.

It was a hard and discouraging way to attempt the mountains, and a hot time of year for walking there. The party was out for five days in reaching Mount Twiss, carrying all their necessary food and equipment in back packs, through a steep, untracked, rocky scrubby wilderness.

Mount Twiss is fairly easy to locate as the track makes a U-shaped detour round its western side before returning to the main line of the ridge. The skyline view which Dawes recorded is visible to the north-north-west from the track (or from the rocks above) once you round the western curve of the U.

Lieutenant William Dawes (1762-1836)

A lieutenant in the Marines, Dawes volunteered for service with the First Fleet. He was a competent astronomer and was asked to observe a comet expected in 1788. An observatory was set up for him on Dawes Point (Sydney) but it did not long survive his return to England in December 1791.

Dawes accompanied Governor Phillip and Watkin Tench on several expeditions as well as leading his own party to Mount Twiss. His abilities in navigation and surveying were put to use in keeping the tally of distance travelled and the daily records of compass directions. His map of the colony, published later in Captain Hunter's *An Historical Journal of the Transactions at Port Jackson and Norfolk Island* is the most accurate which has come down to us. Tench remarks that Dawes was the only one who could keep count of the paces while travelling along, regardless of interruptions.

Dawes was also interested in botany and in the study of Aboriginal languages and customs. He wished to remain in the colony, but no suitable appointment was found for him, one difficulty being that he had disagreed with Governor Phillip over treatment of the Aborigines.

After leaving New South Wales, Dawes spent some years as Governor of the Sierra Leone Company in Africa and worked in Antigua in the West Indies for the anti-slavery movement. He was never able to return to Australia.

3 Linden to Woodford

Follow the highway from Linden towards Woodford. Cross the railway by the overbridge and turn right into **Bull's Camp,** a pleasant and historically interesting reserve, with facilities. (If you miss the turn, stop on your way back from Woodford.) Beneath the embankment at the overbridge just crossed is the SITE OF NO 8 GATEKEEPER'S COTTAGE, now to be found at Frederica Street, Lawson.

Points of interest to look out for are: THE WATERHOLE in the site of an old quarry, THE POWDER STORE OR CONVICT CELL and THE GROOVED ROCK. The last two are on the west of the picnic area, quite close by. Their actual use is uncertain.

Look up at the hill on the other side of the road and railway. **The Rockcorry Cottages** (private property) can be seen on the western side of Woodford Trig. **The site of Captain Bull's House** is said to be just west of the Rockcorry Cottages.

Turn right onto the highway and drive towards Woodford.

The Rockcorry Cottages (BMCC HR LD 8)

These cottages were once thought to pre-date the railway, but as they are not shown on the Railway Survey Plan, it is now realised that they are of a later time.

The land on which they are built was first granted to John Taylor in 1879 as a reward for his services in the Volunteer Defence Forces prior to that date. He sold it in the same year and after a time these two blocks came into the hands of David Moore, a Presbyterian minister who retired and built the cottages.

Captain Bull's House

This house was also known as the 'Twenty Mile Hollow Government House'. The hollows were indicated somewhat loosely, as Bull's Camp was at 18 Mile Hollow.

This stone house of five rooms and offices was built in 1842 and sold in 1844 when Captain Bull moved to Blackheath. Built fairly close to the Bathurst Road, it overlooked the camp.

Uncertainty surrounds the disposal of the house — it is thought that Michael Hogan used the materials to build extensions to the King's Arms Hotel at 20 Mile Hollow (Woodford). No building is shown at this particular spot on the Railway Survey plan of 1862, which shows that the old Government House had been removed before that date.

Bull's Camp

This large open space, now a pleasant picnic area, has had a variety of uses over the years.

It was set aside as a stock reserve in 1829 by Lieutenant G. M. C. Bowen, during his brief period with the Survey Department. Bowen settled at Bowen Mount, in the 1840s.

Later the area was used as a camp for convicts employed in repairing the Bathurst Road, the length through Linden and Woodford always needing particular attention. It was then referred to as the 18 Mile Hollow Stockade and was a military police post established to keep the road in order, to protect travellers, and in the 1850s, gold shipments.

Between 1842 and 1844 Captain Bull was in charge of the road camp. He sent the 'flogger' back to Sydney, as he believed in more humane methods. He gave convicts who died proper burial. Records show that his authority was respected by the convicts and, although he was there for such a short time, his name has been perpetuated.

After the convict road gangs were broken up in 1849, civilian workers camped in the area on several occasions. In 1866 railway workers were there for the construction of the first single track line; they moved on as soon as that section was complete. In 1896 they were back again to construct a deviation to the line.

The area is now under the control of the Blue Mountains City Council.

Captain Bull (1806-1901)

John Bull was born in Ireland, the son of Colonel Bull, Companion of the Bath and a Knight of Hanover, who served in the Royal Horse Artillery in the wars against Napoleon.

John Bull joined the army, served in Ceylon and England, joined the 99th Regiment and arrived in Sydney in 1842. Almost immediately he was appointed a magistrate and Assistant-Engineer in charge of work on the Western Road and with his wife and three children, set up his headquarters at the 18 Mile Hollow Stockade. In 1844 Bull was transferred to Blackheath, where he stayed until the convict road gangs were broken up in 1849.

Captain Bull then retired from the army and after a short period at Newcastle went to Victoria as Commissioner of Crown Lands, Magistrate and Warden at Bendigo and later at Castlemaine. He died at Goulburn at the home of his daughter and is buried in Goulburn cemetery.

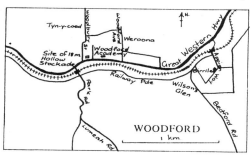

4 Woodford

Drive along the highway about 2 km from Bull's Camp. Turn left into the Appian Way, where a sign directs you to Bedford Road which leads to **Murphy's Glen**, 6 km from the highway, where the trees and bird life are particularly interesting. There are several easy walks from the picnic area.

Return to Railway Parade and stop opposite the **Woodford Railway Station**. Above and just past the station is a monument dedicating *Wilson Glen* to the Blue Mountains Shire. Thomas M. Wilson did this in memory of his wife on 24th May, 1932. A steep walking track leads down into the glen.

Follow Railway Parade; it is steep and hugs the bottom of a very high rock which carries the railway embankment. Turn right to cross the railway line and right again onto the highway. After a short distance you come to **Woodford Academy.** This is a National Trust Property yet to be restored. Pause to look at the outside of the building. (There is space to park in Woodford Academy Park on the opposite side of the road.)

A few metres up the hill, between Arthur Street and Woodbury Road, is the **Site of 18 Mile Hollow Lockup**. Woodbury Avenue is the site of property owned by **Sir T. W. Edgeworth David, Tyn-Y-Coed** now subdivided.

Downhill from the Academy, beyond Woodford Avenue, is **St Paul's Church of England.** Continue down the hill to return to Sydney.

Woodford Railway Station

The present station was built in 1902 when the line was duplicated. Earlier stations had been situated further west. The first opened in 1869 near Woodford Academy. This was named Buss's Platform, after William Buss, licensee of the King's Arms Hotel. The name was changed to Woodford to follow the change of name of the hotel in 1871. Other sites were further west in 1877 and then to the east in 1880.

A crossing loop was built at Woodford in 1896.

Woodford Academy

This Colonial Georgian group of sandstone and brick buildings now belongs to the National Trust of Australia (N.S.W.), being transferred as a gift from Miss Gertrude MacManamey in 1978.

The site was first occupied by a weatherboard building called The Woodman's Inn, probably built about 1833 by Thomas Pembroke, recipient of the original grant of land. An early diarist noted that he kept a good inn, in contrast to another which had a reputation for rowdiness, next to it. This building existed until at least 1842.

Michael Hogan acquired the inn in 1836 and, although he owned the property for 19 years, his name does not appear on the list of licensees. In 1843 as the King's Arms Hotel at 20 Mile Hollow, it was licensed to James Nairn. Probably at about this time, the weatherboard structure was replaced by the single storey stone building which has remained relatively unchanged, and the ground floor of the kitchen wing. Next a two storey stone wing was added, and a second storey in brick was built above the kitchen block. A ground plan shown in the 1862 survey plan for the railway shows Woodford House as the building is today.

William Buss was licensee from 1856 to 1867, when it was known as Buss's Inn and the nearby railway platform took its name from the inn. After Buss's death in 1867 when the railway took away much of the road traffic and custom from the inn, Albert Fairfax bought it as a private residence and re-named it Woodford House. The railway platform was also changed to Woodford.

The Woodford Academy, Great Western Highway

From 1884 to 1907 the property was in the hands of several boarding-house keepers. Then John Frazer MacManamey, B.A., opened Woodford Academy as a school for boys. Over the years the land belonging to the estate was subdivided and sold, only the small block on which the house stands remaining.

Site of 18 Mile Hollow Lock-up

'The Hollows' were often used somewhat loosely, as Woodford was usually known as 20 Mile Hollow.

When the watch house at Weatherboard (now Wentworth Falls) needed to be replaced in 1854, it was decided to choose a site nearer to Penrith, and land to the west of The King's Arms was chosen. The building was completed by Thomas Boland, of Springwood, in 1855, between present day Arthur and Woodbury Streets. Ten acres (4 hectares) was surveyed for police purposes and it became the mounted patrol station.

In 1874 a temporary observatory was set up in the police paddock to observe the transit of Venus between the earth and the sun.

Mr P. F. Adams, Surveyor-General of New South Wales, assisted by Messrs Vessey, Bischoff and Du Faur, set up and operated the required instruments, sent from Sydney and elsewhere.

Tyn-Y-Coed

This Welsh word meaning 'hut in the bush' was an appropriate name for the weatherboard cottage built by Sir T. W. Edgeworth David in 1898. Later considerably extended and with a large garden and orchard, it became the permanent home of his family.

Professor Edgeworth David (1858-1934)

Born at St Fagan's Rectory, near Cardiff in South Wales, and educated at Magdalen College School and New College, Oxford, he attended the Royal School of Mines and became an assistant geological surveyor with the New South Wales Department of Mines.

David became professor of Geology and Physical Geography at the University of Sydney in 1891. He worked in many parts of Australia and in the Ellice Islands, and went to the Antarctic with Shackleton's and Mawson's expeditions. His book, *The Geology of Australia*, became a classic in its field.

St Paul's Church of England, Woodford (BMCC HR WD 1)

Services for the congregation of Linden and Woodford were held in a variety of venues from the mid 1880s onwards, but the church was not erected until a decision about the site was made and funds raised.

The old booking-office from Linden Railway Station was moved to Woodford and used as a hall for a while.

St. Paul's Mission Hall was dedicated and opened 1919. A new Sunday School room was added in 1979.

5 Hazelbrook to Wentworth Falls (The Weatherboard)

1 Hazelbrook — Lawson — Bullaburra

Drive up the Great Western Highway to HAZELBROOK RAILWAY STATION. You may like to turn left to cross the railway line by the over-bridge, to visit some galleries and antique shops. A rough track leads to the OLD BATHS AND SWAMPY LAND. This was the kind of area chosen for the **Explorers' Camp 20 May**.

About 1 km along the highway, on the left, is the great mass of SYDNEY ROCK (BMCC HR LN 9), a well-known landmark. From the top of the rock, Sydney is visible.

After following the highway over the railway line, notice on the corner of Kitchener Street, the STONE HOUSE, THE CONVENT (BMCC HR LN 5) (private property), built in the 1890s. Follow the highway to **Lawson Railway Station**.

Turn left through DOUGLAS SQUARE, formerly known as 'Grand Square'. Turn left into Honour Avenue and pause at the HONOUR GARDENS. Walk through the gardens and notice the memorial plaques to individual servicemen beside the shrubs and trees.

On the left at the head of the avenue, is an old **Horse Trough**. A few buildings further along is the MASONIC LODGE, once the first primary school, opened in 1888. **Emmanuel Anglican Church** is on the opposite side of Honour Avenue.

Continue along Honour Avenue and Broad Street to a signpost indicating the start of the track to *Adelina Falls*, named for Henry Wilson's daughter. The old track to the falls led down the gully to *Junction* and *Federal Falls* but it is now overgrown and hard to find.

A short distance along Broad Street is a vehicular track leading to a turn-around and a picnic area. A further half km along is another track, with turn-around and picnic area, leading to *Cataract Falls*. The old track went on to Federal Falls.

Return via Broad Street to Honour Avenue and turn left into the

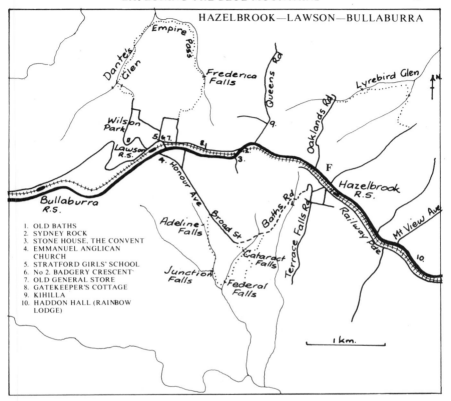

HAZELBROOK—LAWSON—BULLABURRA

1. OLD BATHS
2. SYDNEY ROCK
3. STONE HOUSE, THE CONVENT
4. EMMANUEL ANGLICAN CHURCH
5. STRATFORD GIRLS' SCHOOL
6. No 2. BADGERY CRESCENT
7. OLD GENERAL STORE
8. GATEKEEPER'S COTTAGE
9. KIHILLA
10. HADDON HALL (RAINBOW LODGE)

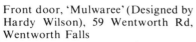

Front door, 'Mulwaree' (Designed by Hardy Wilson), 59 Wentworth Rd, Wentworth Falls

Old baths and swampy land, Hazelbrook

highway. A short distance along you will pass the Lawson Primary School. The site of **Blue Mountains Inn** is in the playground.

Drive on along the highway to **Bullaburra**. In this vicinity is thought to be the **Site of the Explorers' Camps,** 21 May and 3 June, on their return journey. Drive on towards Wentworth Falls.

Explorers' Camp, Hazelbrook, 20 May 1813

'They got ready at Nine O'Clock and proceeded about four Miles and three quarters encamped at 12 O'Clock at the Head of a Swamp of about three acres covered with rushy coarse grass with water running through the Middle of it. The Horses by necessity lived on the Coarse swamp grass or rushes nothing else could be got for them.'

BLAXLAND

He also describes 'a small swamp clear of trees at the heads of the different streams of Water which run down the side of the Mountain...'

The swamp with the stream running through it, and which was dammed to make the old baths, is one of the few swamps left and accessible to the tourist. This was the kind of place the explorers chose for their camps, some flattish ground for camping on, water and the only kind of grass available for their horses.

The camp of 20 May is thought to be a little way beyond the present Hazelbrook Railway Station, not necessarily this swamp.

Lawson Railway Station

This area was first known as 24 Mile Hollow, that being its distance from Emu Plains.

The railway platform was one of the four original stopping places on the line built in 1867, when it had a passing loop and was named Blue Mountains, from the inn close by. This name was often misleading to strangers to the area and was changed to Lawson in 1879. When the *Railway Guide* of 1886 was published, it took the traveller 3½ hours from Sydney to Lawson. Many boarding houses were established then and were patronised by invalids for whom mountain air was recommended.

Horse Trough

The trough was first placed near the shopping centre and later moved to Honour Avenue. It is inscribed:

'TO THE DUMB FRIENDS OF MAN presented to the Blue Mountains Shire Council by Mr R. D. Meagher. Lawson. 1921'

Emmanuel Anglican Church, Honour Avenue, Lawson (BMCC HR LN 7)

In the 1870s and early 1880s services were held in homes, in the railway waiting room and in the hotel.

In 1884 the original Emmanuel Church was built on land purchased and donated by the Hon. Charles Moore, of Springwood. It is now the church hall. It was of weatherboard and has recently been bricked over. The present church was built in 1910.

The Pre-Kindergarten School is the latest addition, opened in 1977.

Blue Mountains Inn

Thomas Pembroke, who later built The Woodman's Inn where Woodford Academy now stands, was granted this land. He erected a hut there about 1830 but soon lost interest in it.

Henry Charles Wilson was granted 100 acres (about 40 hectares) and in 1848 built an inn on what is now the school playground. A garden and large orchard surrounded it. The inn was popular with all classes of travellers, being the only one between the Weatherboard Inn at Wentworth Falls and Buss's at Woodford. One story concerning the origin of the inn's name was that Wilson's daughter Adelina was quite a chatter-box and was described as a noisy 'blue mountain parrot'.

In 1870 the license of the inn was transferred to the new Blue Mountains Hotel built nearer the railway station where it operated till 1923, when it was demolished to make way for shops.

The Blue Mountains Inn became known as 'The Old Farm'. It was then described as a stone building of eleven rooms, with an iron roof. In 1917 it was unoccupied and derelict and the council ordered it to be demolished.

Bullaburra

Land in this area was first owned by Sir Henry Parkes, who called it the *Village of Colridge*. It was later acquired by Arthur Rickard & Co., who developed the village of Bullaburra, an Aboriginal word meaning 'blue sky' or 'fine weather'.

Explorers' Camp 21 May and 3 June, on the return journey

'...they proceeded by the track they cut and marked the day before three miles and three quarters they encamped at the Head of a well watered Swamp of about 5 acres...'

Blaxland

During that night the dogs were disturbed and the explorers thought that one of the horses had got loose. In the morning they discovered that the horses were all there and so they thought it must have been a native, who was going to attack them but was driven off by the dogs.

According to the distances given in Blaxland's and Lawson's diaries, it is thought that they camped near Bullaburra on 21 May on the outward journey and at the same camp on 3 June on the return journey.

2 The King's Tableland, Wentworth Falls

From Bullaburra, drive to the top of **Bodington Hill.** Turn left into Tableland Road at the *Brown Horse Inn Restaurant*, which is licensed, and open for lunch: Wednesdays, Saturdays, Sundays and public holidays, 12 noon to 3 p.m.; and for dinner: Wednesdays, Thursdays and Fridays, from 6.30 p.m.

Turn right into Yester Road. At the end of the road, only 100 metres or so, is **Yester Grange** a gallery and tea-room open Wednesday, Thursday, Friday and school holidays, 10 a.m.

to 4 p.m. and on Saturday, Sunday and public holidays, for an hour longer. Admission is charged. A walking track leads to *Weeping Rock* and *Wentworth Falls*.

Somewhere in this vicinity is **The site of the Explorers' Camp, 22 May.**

Macquarie's Names. While Macquarie and his party were camping at The Weatherboard at Wentworth Falls in 1815, the Governor named some of the geographical features.

Continue south along Tableland Road. A short access road on the left leads to **Bodington Red Cross Hospital.**

A km further along Tableland Road on the left is Queen Elizabeth Drive. At the end of the short tarred section, the left-hand track leads to *Ingar Picnic Ground*, 12 km away in the Blue Mountains National Park. The right-hand track goes to a parking area with directions for a short walk to the **Kings Table Aboriginal Site.**

Return to Tableland Road and turn left. On the right Hordern Road leads to Little Switzerland Drive and the **Blue Mountains Deer Park and Zoo,** open daily from 9 a.m. to 5 p.m. Admission is charged. There is a barbecue and picnic area and a kiosk. Little Switzerland Drive runs along the cliff top, so that a short walk of about 10 metres gives splendid views of the full sweep of Jamison Valley.

Return to Tableland Road via *Hordern Road*, named for J. L. and C. S. Hordern, at one time owners of the nearby property 'Cherrywood'. (BMCC HR WF 10)

4 km from the highway, Tableland Road passes through the grounds of **Queen Victoria Convalescent Hospital** set in a very beautiful garden.

24 km from the highway, over an unsealed road for much of the way, you will find *McMahon's Lookout* with extensive views over *Lake Burragorang*. These are the waters of the Cox's and Kowmung Rivers held back by Warragamba Dam. The sight is well worth the drive. Several short walks along the cliff face reveal the scene from different angles.

Return via Tableland Road to the highway.

Bodington Hill (BMCC HR WF 1)

Cox reached this hill on 24 September 1814.

'...Removed on Saturday to the 26 mile, being just at the foot of a steep mountain. Examined it well, and found it too steep to ascend in a straight direction.

Sept. 25 (Sunday) Went up the mountain; examined it, and fixed on a way to make a winding road up. This is the highest mountain on the whole of the range we cross.' (One can only suppose Cox meant steepness not altitude.)

'Sept. 27 Finished the road up the mountain this evening. Made a very good job of it (cost 10 men two days.)'

Yester Grange (BMCC HR WF, 15 Nat. Tr.)

Yester is a Victorian country house, set in park-like gardens, a short distance above Wentworth Falls. The name of the property comes from Yester House, Gifford, near Edinburgh in Scotland. It was built in the early 1870s by Captain Smith, of the Granville timber firm Goodlet & Smith, of New Zealand kauri

WENTWORTH FALLS
(THE WEATHERBOARD)

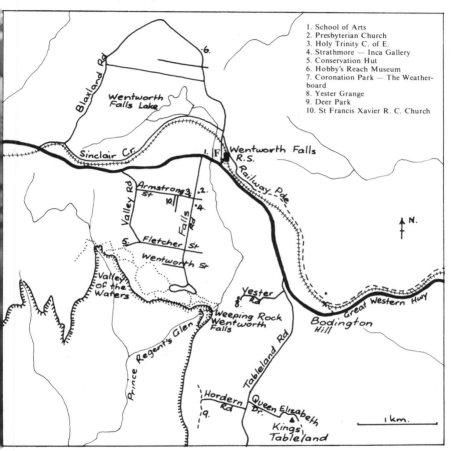

1. School of Arts
2. Presbyterian Church
3. Holy Trinity C. of E.
4. Strathmore — Inca Gallery
5. Conservation Hut
6. Hobby's Reach Museum
7. Coronation Park — The Weatherboard
8. Yester Grange
9. Deer Park
10. St Francis Xavier R. C. Church

Yester Grange, Yester Rd, Wentworth Falls

The intertwined initials, J and S, in the blue doors in the hall, commemorate the builder and his wife Susan. Soon after its completion the house was bought by John See (Premier N.S.W. 1901–5) and his wife Charlotte. In 1889 they added a large kauri-lined ballroom and the two rear wings. The house became their summer residence and was so used by their descendants until 1938.

Yester Grange is now an art gallery in a house furnished with museum pieces of the Victorian era. The cellar-gallery is used for changing exhibitions of paintings, ceramics, furniture and other crafts. Lunches and afternoon teas are available and may be taken by a log fire in winter or on the verandah overlooking the Jamison Valley when the weather is clement. Alternatively, you can bring your own picnic to have in the garden.

The walk to the falls is only 400 metres, and a further 200 metre walk below the cliff line is fascinating. The water drops 300 metres, making Wentworth Falls one of the highest falls in the mountains. 'Weeping Rock', about halfway to the falls, is a picturesque spot to stop for a rest on the way back.

Explorers' Camp, King's Tableland, 22 May

Blaxland describes this camp as being
'...on the top of the third and highest ridge ... by the side of the fine stream of water ... having a fine view of all the settlements and country eastwards ... but to the westward ... an impassable Clift of Rocks which appeared to divide the interior from the Coast as with a Stone Wall rising immediately perpendicular, out of the side of the Mountains...'

Instead of cutting their path for the next day, as had become customary, they spent the afternoon in trying to climb down the cliff or to follow the streams, hoping to get to the bottom and find some specimens of rocks which might explain the 'dreadful Convulsion of Nature', of the Jamison Valley.

It was a night of disappointment for the three men, as their path seemed to have become even more difficult.

To give their position a modern name, they had camped a mile and a half (say 2 km) south-west of the top of Bodington Hill.

Macquarie's Names

King's Tableland

The view of the Jamison Valley from the King's Tableland is breathtaking; no less interesting is the coastal plain stretching away to the east. In the account of the *Tour over the Western or Blue Mountains, 1815,* it is recorded:

> 'The majestic gradeur of the situation, combined with the various objects to be seen from this place, induced the Governor to give it the appellation of *The King's Table land.*'

Prince Regent's Glen

To the south-west '...the Mountain terminates in abrupt precipices of immense depth, at the bottom of which is seen a glen, as romantically beautiful as can be imagined, bounded on the other side by Mountains of great magnitude, terminating equally abruptly as the others; and the whole thickly covered with timber. The length of this picturesque and remarkable tract of country is about 24 miles, to which the Governor gave the name of *The Prince Regent's Glen...*'

Thus Macquarie honoured the Prince of Wales, eldest son of King George III, who had become Regent in 1811 as a result of his father's illness; he succeeded to the throne as George IV in 1820.

Pitt's Amphitheatre

As Macquarie's party journeyed on, the western side of the valley came into their sight, and the long vista to the south of

'...Mountains rising beyond mountains, with stupendous masses of rock in the foreground, here strikes the eye with admiration and astonishment. The circular form in which the whole is so wonderfully disposed, induced the Governor to give it the name of *Pitt's Amphitheatre* (in honour of the late Right Honourable William Pitt)...'

William Pitt the Younger served two terms as Prime Minister of England, from 1783 to 1801, and from 1804 to 1808, during the founding of the colony of New South Wales and its early years.

Campbell's Cataract

Macquarie and party camped at Cox's Weatherboard Hut at the second depot on 28 April 1815 and again on the return journey on 15 May. On this second occasion the party spent some time exploring the cliffs of Prince Regent's Glen and discovered a waterfall estimated at 1000 feet high. Macquarie named this *Campbell's Cataract* for his secretary, J. T.

Campbell. We now know it as Wentworth Falls.

Jamison Valley

Macquarie also changed the name of the area of the Weatherboard Hut to Jamison Valley and gave the name of Jamison Creek to the stream which runs beside it, for his friend Sir John Jamison of Regentville on the banks of the Nepean River. (More details of Sir John Jamison in chapter on Lapstone Hill.)

Bodington Sanitorium

Bodington Sanitorium was founded about 1908 by Dr Sinclair, who had been resident medical officer at the Queen Victoria Sanitorium, further along Tableland Road. Bodington is now a Red Cross Hospital.

Aboriginal Site

King's Table is a prominent hill capped by a broad flat rock, on which are to be found grooves for tool sharpening near rock pools. If you wish to photograph them, morning or afternoon shadows give excellent results.

A rock shelter, giving protection from rain and wind, has been excavated by archaeologists. Carbon dating from charcoal found in the cave shows occupation from 22 000 years before the present.

All Aboriginal artifacts, rock grooves and so on, are under the protection of the National Parks and Wildlife Service.

Wentworth Falls Deer Park and Zoo

The heath type vegetation of this valley gives rise to the name of Little Switzerland, from its resemblance to the Swiss Mountains and the Scottish Highlands. Here is situated the 14 hectare Deer Park and Zoo. There are many native Australian animals and exotic birds as well as deer of all species. It is a very pleasant and interesting place to have a barbecue and picnic.

Little Switzerland road runs close to the edge of the King's Tableland escarpment and the view of the Jamison Valley is unobstructed and magnificent.

Queen Victoria Sanatorium (BMCC HR WF 11)

The Queen Victoria Sanatorium was opened in 1903 for the treatment of tuberculosis. A hospital to treat this disease had already been set up at Leura three years earlier and was reputedly successful. The resident medical officer was Dr Sinclair. He resigned to go into private practice in 1908 and later founded the Bodington Sanatorium.

Now called Queen Victoria Memorial Hospital, it is set in beautiful gardens. The expanse of lawn and picturesque trees are a pleasure to see.

3   Falls Road, Wentworth Falls

From Tableland Road, turn left into the highway and drive about 1½ km to Wentworth Falls village, where you pass on the left GRAND VIEW HOTEL. The present building replaces the original weatherboard structure. There are photographs of the old building in the bar.

Keep to the highway for about 400 metres to Falls Road. Opposite is the old SCHOOL OF ARTS — COMMUNITY HALL (BMCC HR WF 19). Turn left into Falls Road. On the left is *Wilson Park*; the *Charles Darwin Walk* starts from behind the tennis courts. A plaque nearby gives interesting information.

Towards the end of the first block is the **Presbyterian Church.**

On the corner of Armstrong Street, on the right, is HOLY TRINITY CHURCH OF ENGLAND (BMCC HR WF 4). Turn right into Armstrong Street. The second on the left is Day Street, for **St Francis Xavier Roman Catholic Church.**

Return to Falls Road and turn right. In the next block, on the left is STRATHMORE, 74 Falls Road (BMCC HR WF 21: Nat. Tr.).

Continue along Falls Road, past Fletcher Street. On the left is an OLD HORSE TROUGH. Turn right into the one-way circular drive to the parking area. There are views of the *King's Tableland Escarpment* (BMCC HR WF 18). Walking tracks lead to a lookout closer to the falls and down into the *Prince Regent's Glen* below, and to the *National Pass* going round to the *Valley of the Waters* where you can climb out at the Information Centre at the end of Fletcher Street. It is as well to allow at least 3 hours for the round walk. A number of other walks along the cliff top give good views of the *Valley of the Waters*.

From the Scenic Drive return to Falls Road and then turn left into Wentworth Street. MULWAREE, 59 Wentworth Street, was designed by architect Hardy Wilson. (BMCC HR WF 20; Nat. Tr., private property).

Turn left at Langford Street or Falls Road and left again into Fletcher Street. At the end you will find a TEAROOM AND INFORMATION CENTRE (Conservation Hut), open weekends. Walks along the cliff top, down into the valley and to the **National Pass** begin here.

Turn left into Valley Road, follow it to the Highway, and turn left. Drive along about 1 km and, keeping right, pass under the railway. Turn right immediately into Sinclair Crescent, to explore the north side of Wentworth Falls.

Presbyterian Church (BMCC HR WF 3, Nat. Tr.)

St Andrew's Presbyterian church is unusual in having a cross over the belfrey. Albert Smidmore, the benefactor, was a Roman Catholic. He had married twice, each of his wives being a Presbyterian. A condition of the gift was that a cross should be erected over this memorial to his wives.

St Andrew's Presbyterian Church, Falls Rd, Wentworth Falls

St Francis Xavier's Roman Catholic Church (BMCC HR WF 9)

Recent additions have been made to the original small wooden building which was hauled by a bullock team from the old Gladstone Colliery, which was below Leura Golflinks on the other side of the Valley of the Waters.

National Pass

The feat of cutting steps into the rock to make a track down to the bottom of the Valley of the Waters was begun in 1890. The difficulty of completing the path to the top of the Wentworth Falls was overcome by Captain Murray; he was lowered over the cliff on a rope to find a path up which steps could be cut. Five men completed this heroic task.

4 Wentworth Falls — Northern Side of Railway Line

Follow the highway beneath the railway line and turn right immediately into Sinclair Crescent and then immediately turn left into BLAXLAND ROAD. This road follows the first line of the Old Bathurst Road, built by William Cox in 1814.

Continue along Blaxland Road for c. 2½ km to No. 99, **Hobby's Reach Museum**, open only on Saturday and Sunday 2 to 4 p.m. There are interesting historical exhibits and a commanding view from the rear of the grounds. The new museum is on the property of TARELLA, oldest building on the north side of the railway line.

Somewhere in this area between Hobby's Reach and the railway line is the **Site of the Explorers' Camp 23 May**. Turn left into Blaxland Road and right into Sinclair Crescent before the railway line. In about 1 km you reach **Wentworth Falls Lake**. There is a picnic and barbecue area here. Return to Blaxland Road. On the left is Railway Parade; about 3 km along a very bad road is RHONDA VALLEY (private property; BMCC HR WF 8).

Cross the railway line by the overbridge and stop beside **Coronation Park. Wentworth Falls Railway Station** is nearby. The Blue Mountains Historical Society Marker stands in the park.

On the opposite side of the road in front of the post office is the Wentworth Falls 'Footsteps in Time' marker, commemorating George William Evans' crossing of the Great Dividing Range. He camped in this vicinity on 4 January 1814.

The **Site of the Weatherboard Inn**, about 200 metres west of the railway overbridge in Pitt Park, is markd by an evergreen oak (*Quercus ilex*). Access is from the end of Adela Avenue, beside the old SCHOOL OF ARTS on the highway.

Continue along Station Street and turn left onto the highway. Drive back towards Bullaburra.

Hobby's Reach

William Cox writes: 'Oct 3 ... at the 29th mile is a very handsome long reach, quite straight, which I call, for the Layer of it out, "Hobby's Reach".' This was Lieutenant Thomas Hobby, who was Cox's assistant on the project. (Cox always refers to him as Mr.)

Hobby was rewarded with 500 acres (about 200 hectares) of land and 6 cows at the conclusion of the work on the western road.

Explorers' Camp, 23 May — Wentworth Falls

The explorers found that day's journey difficult as they had not marked out and cleared the track the day before. They camped three and a half miles to the north '... on the side of a Swamp with a beautiful Stream of Water running through the Middle of it...'

This camp would be north of the present Wentworth Falls Railway Station and perhaps beside Jamison Creek, but probably further along the ridge north of the spot where Cox built his Weatherboard Hut.

They spent the afternoon in clearing a track ahead.

Wentworth Falls Lake

The lake began its life as a reservoir for the railway, when a concrete dam was built across Jamison Creek in 1878. In 1908 a new dam was constructed to increase the storage, making Wentworth Falls the main supply source until electrification in 1957.

Now the lake is used for the recreations of fishing, swimming and sailing at the weekends.

Coronation Park — The Weatherboard

'...Went forward to fix on a site for a second depot. Chose one ... close to a stream of excellent water...' Cox's Journal, 25 September 1814.

This spot is now in Pitt Park and the stream was named Jamison Creek by Governor Macquarie in 1815.

Cox wrote on completion of the building:

> 'Oct. 1. Began on Friday to put up the building for the second depot. The situation is very pleasant, being on a ridge high enough in the front (which is due east) to overlook the standing timber altogether, and at the back there is a considerable quantity of ground without a tree,· and a rivulet of fine spring water running through it. ... The building for the store is 17 x 12, with 3 ft sides, gable-ended, all weatherboards, and a door on the east end. Finished on the 8th inst. Cost me eight

men, six days. It is 28 miles from Emu Ford.'

The building was used as a store while Cox was building the road and in later years it was a depot for the military, who had to supervise convicts working on the upkeep of the road, and to protect travellers from bushrangers.

Governor Macquarie gave the name of *Jamison Valley* to the whole area, but *Weatherboard* remained in local usage till the end of the century.

Site of the Weatherboard Inn (BMCC HR WF 7)

'January 17, 1836. In the middle of the day we baited our horses at a little inn, called the *Weatherboard...*' So wrote Charles Darwin in his Journal.

In 1833 William Boyles had 100 acres (about 40 hectares) granted to him and on it built the Weatherboard Inn on the site of Cox's store hut, which had burnt down.

The Quaker James Backhouse described it in 1835:

> 'After travelling eighteen miles, we arrived at the Weather-board hut where we had intended to lodge; but the only good room was occupied. One in which we had an excellent meal of beef and bread, with tea, was without glass in the windows, and could not have the door shut, for the smoking of the wood fire. This, as is common in this land of trees, was a very large one, and it was acted upon by a fierce and piercing wind; we therefore determined on making another stage.'

Boyles willed the land to his daughter in 1842.

With the coming of the railway in

the late 1860s, the role of the Inn changed from being a coaching house and lodging for travellers to providing accommodation for visitors to the mountains.

In 1894 the property was bought by Robert Jones, and two years later by Mrs G. M. Pitt.

The Naturalists' Society of New South Wales has planted an oak tree there to commemorate the visit of Charles Darwin.

Wentworth Falls Railway Station

The railway line over the Blue Mountains opened as far as *Weatherboard* on 3 July 1867, and for the next ten months, until the line was extended to Mount Victoria, it was the terminus. Coaches to carry passengers to the west met the trains and waggons and teams delivered and collected goods.

The name was later changed to Wentworth Falls.

5   Bullaburra — Lawson — Hazelbrook — North Side of the Railway Line

From Wentworth Falls, drive east along the highway through Bullaburra to Lawson and, turning left, cross the railway line at the overbridge. Park beside the Bowling Club or in San Jose Avenue on the right, as there are several interesting buildings in the area. They are BOWLING CLUB HOUSE, Loftus Street, which was originally a reservoir for the railways, in use until electrification in 1957. **Stratford Girls' School,** San Jose Avenue, (Private property). No 2 BADGERY CRESCENT (BMCC HR LN 6) and the OLD GENERAL STORE next door to it (BMCC HR LN 4).

From San Jose Avenue turn left into Park Road and right into Evans Street. Walks from *Wilson Park, Lawson,* to *Dante's Glen* and the *Empire Pass* start here. A short path brings you to *St Michael's Falls. Frederica Falls* is at the further end of the track which comes out at Hughes Street. Allow about 3 hours for the complete circuit.

Drive back along Evans Street to **Lawson Baths.** Follow Bernard Drive out of the park and turn left into Badgery Crescent. Pass The Old General Store and turn left into Hughes Street. A walking track from the end leads to *Frederica Falls* and via the *Empire Pass* to Wilson Park. Turn left into Badgery Crescent and rejoin the highway opposite *Sydney Rock.* Keep left and soon turn left into Queen's Road.

Not far along, turn left into Kangaroo Street and park beside the ABORIGINAL ROCK ART SITE. Stand well back from the National Parks and Wildlife Service Marker to get a good view of the kangaroo outline. Best photographed in the early morning or late afternoon.

Opposite Kangaroo Street in Queen's Road is *Kihilla* (BMCC HR LN 2, private property).

Return to the highway and keep left. About 500 metres along pull off beyond the safety fence. A short walk back brings you to ABORIGINAL TOOL SHARPENING GROOVES on a rock below the embankment of the highway.

A little further down the highway, turn left into Oaklands Road and follow it to *Horseshoe Falls Reserve* (right). A walk of about 500 metres beside a cascading stream brings you to *Lyrebird Falls*. A further 2 km along the track reaches *Horseshoe Falls*. There are interesting outcrops of ironstone in the walls along the track. A round walk via The *Amphitheatre* and *Burgess Falls* would take two or three hours.

Return via Oaklands Road to the highway and turn left. A short block along is Village Place; outside the chemist's shop is the Hazelbrook 'Footsteps in Time' marker. About 2 km along turn left into Mount View Street, which leads to walking tracks to *Edith* and *Fairy Falls*. A short distance further down the highway, shielded by a tall hedge, on the left is HADDON HALL, now *Rainbow Lodge* (BMCC HR H 1, private property).

Stratford Girls' School (BMCC HR LN 3; Nat. Tr.)

This area was part of Joseph Hay's San Jose Estate. He was an official of the Lands Department. In 1878 he built a substantial house, used as a Sanatorium in 1882. In the 1890s it became *The Palace*, a guest house. In 1919 Stratford Girls' School, under the direction of Miss E. Wiles, was transferred to the building from Honour Avenue; later it was controlled by the Stratford School Council. Stratford closed in 1960 and the house was later used by the Blue Mountains Community School. In 1980 a fire reduced it to a shell.

Lawson Baths

At this station, originally Blue Mountains, water was supplied to the engines from a creek dammed in a gully to the north of the station and pumped to tanks from which the water gravitated to stand pipes at the railway line. This supply was unreliable in droughty periods and after 1908 water was piped from Wentworth Falls to obviate the necessity of water trains.

The pool at Lawson, in its beautiful surroundings at Wilson Park, has been elevated from its status as a railway dam to an Olympic heated pool.

Kihilla (BMCC HR LN 2)

The first landowner was W. H. Pinney. The property was taken over by R. Fitzstubbs in the 1880s. He built *Kihilla,* a substantial stone house. The next owner, A. Mitchell, added the west wing, stables and a coach house in the 1890s. The gardener's cottage still near the highway dates from this time.

In 1913 Sir John and Annie Sulman purchased it. Sir John Sulman was an eminent architect and town planner, and member of the Federal Capital Planning Committee. On his death Kihilla became a guesthouse. It is now a Christian Convention Centre.

6 Leura to Katoomba (The Crushers)

1 Sublime Point and Gordon Falls, Leura

From the Great Western Highway take the Alternative Route to Katoomba, turning left into Scott Avenue. Near this spot was a level crossing and a **Gatekeeper's Cottage**, before duplication of the line.

Turn left into Gladstone Road, and following the Sublime Point signs, turn left at Fitzroy Street, right into Watkins Road and again right into Sublime Point Road. Near the golf course is the site of the **Gladstone Colliery**, which operated in the 1880s. At the end of the road is the Lookout at *Sublime Point*. A path leads to the picnic area and a flight of steps to the lookout, revealing the broad sweep of Jamison Valley from the King's Tableland escarpment to the walls of Narrow Neck Plateau.

Return to Fitzroy Street, follow it to the T-junction with Denison Street, and turn left. On the right is **Everglades**. This is a National Trust Property open to the public, daily from 9.00 am. Admission is charged. Return via Fitzroy Street to Gladstone Road, take the third turn on the left into Megalong Street. On the left, on the corner of Grose and Megalong Streets, is MEGALONG MANOR. Built at the turn of the century, this gracious home now provides holiday accommodation. Turn right into Grose Street and left into Railway Parade.

Leura Railway Station is on the western side of the overbridge. **The Site of the Explorers' Camp 24 May**, is thought to have been near the station, but possibly on the other side of the line. Park and walk down The Mall, an 'old world' shopping centre. Look for A COTTAGE WITH ATTIC (BMCC HR LA 6) and A SHOP WITH RESIDENCE (BMCC HR LA 7).

On the corner of The Mall and Megalong Street is THE RITZ, (BMCC HR LA 9) once a fashionable hotel, during World War II a servicemen's convalescent home, now a nursing home.

Drive down Leura Mall to the T-intersection with **Olympian Parade** and turn left. On the left is LEURALLA, Toy and Railway Museum of N.S.W., and the Dr H. V. Evatt Memorial. Open 10 a.m. to 5 p.m. Wednesday to Sunday as well as public and school holidays; closed Monday and Tuesday. There is a refreshment room. Admission is charged.

At the end of the Parade is *Gordon Falls Reserve*. A short walk to the Falls Lookout starts here. Allow an hour for the walk to the *Pool of Siloam* and **Lyrebird Dell**. *Prince Henry Cliff Walk* goes all the way to Katoomba Falls. The walk to *Leura Cascades* takes about an hour. Return to Olympian Parade.

LEURA

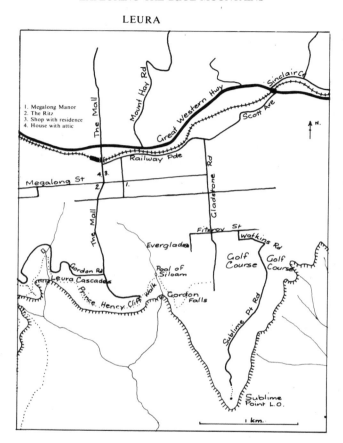

1. Megalong Manor
2. The Ritz
3. Shop with residence
4. House with attic

Site of Gatekeeper's Cottage, Leura

This cottage, No. 9, was sited west of the bridge at the start of the Alternative Route to Katoomba. The level crossing gate was kept by Mr and Mrs Claridge, an old English couple. Legend says that Mrs Claridge, always wearing a snow-white apron, chatted to travellers waiting for the gates to be opened.

The gatehouse was demolished when the line was duplicated in 1902, and some of the stone was used to build 'Bou Saada', 250 The Mall, Leura.

Site of Gladstone Colliery, near Leura Golf Links (BMCC HR LA 4)

In the days when Katoomba was a mining town, Leura too had its mine. Gladstone Colliery flourished for a while and Gladstone Railway Siding was made west of the 65 Mile Peg to serve its needs between 1885 and 1887.

Everglades Denison Street, Leura

This is a National Trust Property and work is being done to preserve the beautiful home and garden.

In 1932 Sydney businessman, Henri Van de Velde, bought a former fruit orchard, 5 hectares in extent, and built there his weekend retreat. With the help of Danish landscape designer Paul Sorensen, and a work force of up to 60 men at times, terraces were carved from the mountainside, reinforced with drypack stone walls, and planted with trees and shrubs from all parts of the world against the background of native bush. The spring displays of bluebells and daffodils are outstanding, and the rhododendrons and azaleas in both spring and autumn are glorious.

Leura Railway Station (BMCC HR LA 3)

The Leura Railway Station and its overbridge were built and opened in 1891. The district was to have been called 'Lurline' after the daughter of William Eyre, the man who subdivided the area, but the station was given the name 'Leura' and that was extended to the whole suburb. Leura is thought to be an Aboriginal word meaning 'lava', appropriate because of the large number of stones of volcanic origin found in the locality.

Site of the Explorers' Camp, 24 May, Leura

The explorers followed the top of the ridge which circles north from Wentworth Falls and then south-east; Cox made the Bathurst Road along this ridge, and today it is Blaxland Road. Their day's journey of four and a half miles brought them to '...the Head of a Swamp...' This spot was probably in the vicinity of Leura Railway Station, but below the ridge, on one side or the other.

While they were marking their road for the next day, they heard a 'native' chopping. The dogs chased him and they did not see him.

Olympian Parade

This street right on the edge of Jamison Valley was the scene, in the early years of the twentieth century, of advanced treatment of tuberculosis. Matron Robison set up the hospital after she had returned from the Black

Forest in Germany, where she had taken her young doctor husband for treatment. His disease was too far advanced for his life to be saved but his wife, a trained nurse, returned to try the effects of Blue Mountain air on Australian patients. Many years afterwards Matron Robison said she felt that the success of the treatment had influenced the establishment of the Queen Victoria Sanatorium at Wentworth Falls.

Lyrebird Dell Leura

Archaeologists Stockton and Holland have excavated the caves in this area. It is thought that at the time the Aborigines occupied the cave near the picnic shelter, it was probably drier than it is now.

2 Cliff Drive, Leura to Katoomba

From Gordon Falls Reserve, Olympian Parade leads to Gordon Road and the Cliff Drive which extends right round the edge of the Jamison Valley to the highway at the west of Katoomba. There are many lookout points, each with its own reward.

We have visited *Bridal Veil Falls Lookout, Flying Fox Lookout* where some of the old machinery is still to be seen, and *Leura Cascades Picnic Area.* This is a very pretty place with tree ferns and other rainforest plants. Beginning here are walks to *Bridal Veil Falls,* to *Gordon Falls* along the *Prince Henry Cliff Walk* and to *Katoomba Falls. Kiah Lookout* is another good place to begin walks along the cliff top.

Then you come to the most famous of them all, *Echo Point* and *Queen Elizabeth Lookout.* From Left to Right scenic features are **The Three Sisters** and the *Giant Staircase* (A slot machine tells their story). *King's Tableland Escarpment, Mount Solitary and The Ruined Castle, Narrow Neck Plateau and Escarpment* and **Pitt's Amphitheatre.** Walks lead along the cliff top via *Prince Henry Cliff Walk* to *Gordon Falls* and to *Katoomba Falls* in the other direction, via *The Giant Staircase,* going down beside *The Three Sisters* 996 steps to the *Federal Pass,* the path at the foot of the cliffs to *Leura Cascades* in the east, and to the west to the foot of the *Scenic Railway* (last car up leaves at 4.55 p.m.) and to the *Golden Stairs* at *Narrow Neck.*

The Information Centre at *Echo Point* is well worth a visit for the displays it provides, the information about walks, drives, etc., not covered in this book, and also about restaurants, accommodation, caravan parks, camping, the dates of special fixtures, as well as the delightful view from the window down into the gully below.

Return to Echo Point Road. Kedumba Emporium, on the left, provides restaurants and souvenirs. Lilianfels Picnic Park is next on the uphill side.

From Echo Point Road, turn left into Lilianfels Avenue, passing LILIANFELS (BMCC HR K 1, private property). Follow Cliff Drive to *Katoomba Falls Reserve.* From the reserve walks lead to *Katoomba Cascades, Katoomba Falls* with a drop of 240 metres, *Prince Henry Cliff Walk, Orphan Rock.* Many of these scenic features are floodlit at night.

A short distance along Cliff Drive, on the corner of Violet Street, is the *Skyway Revolving Restaurant,* from which *Katoomba Falls* and the *Jamison Valley* may be seen. The 15 metre diameter floor can seat 200 people. Open 10 a.m. to 4 p.m. Nearby is *The Three Sisters Fountain* and the *Scenic Skyway.* The aerial cable car travels slowly 275 metres above the valley floor and 350 metres across the gorge, but returns before reaching the other side. It was constructed in 1958, then being the first horizontal passenger-carrying ropeway in the Southern Hemisphere. It provides magnificent views of *Katoomba Falls,* the *Orphan Rock* and the *Jamison Valley.* Operates: 9 a.m. to 5 p.m.

Starting from the same place is the **Scenic Railway.** The 56 passengers who travel in the duralium car descend 230 metres into the Jamison Valley at an average incline of about 45 degrees. As they pass through the tree-clad gorge, approximately 445 metres in length, they get the heart-stopping thrill of a lifetime. It is not for the faint-hearted. Those who venture have spread before them one of the best views of the Jamison Valley, as well as passing close to the rock face. It is the easiest way to get down to the *Federal Pass,* and walks to the *Landslide,* the *Coal Mine* (the railway began life to serve this mine) and the *Ruined Castle.* Last car up leaves the bottom station at 4.55 p.m. daily.

Continue left along Cliff Drive to *Cyclorama Point,* the highest spot at Katoomba, with a view across *Narrow Neck,* and **Landslide Lookout.** Half a km further along Cliff Drive, a gravel road on the left (Glenraphael Drive on the map) goes out along *Narrow Neck.* A short way down the hill the rock walls of **'O'Sullivan's Folly'** are on the right above the Drive. (BMCC HR K 24). The road along *Narrow Neck Plateau* is fairly rough and at its further end is suitable only for 4WD vehicles. A permit is required to enter the Water Board area. Splendid and different views of the Jamison Valley to the east, and to the west of the Megalong Valley, with the Great Dividing Range in the background, are to be had from the road. From Narrow Neck, the *Golden Stairs* lead down to the *Federal Pass* going round as far as *Leura Cascades;* to the *Ruined Castle,* a full day's walk, quite strenuous. Take water with you. This track goes on to Mount Solitary. From the top of the stairs, you get a good view of *The Landslide.*

Back on Cliff Drive *Narrow Neck Lookout* gives a good view of the peninsula. Keep to the left on Cliff Drive and you will come to

CAHILL'S LOOKOUT named for Hon. J. J. Cahill, Premier N.S.W. 1952-9. This is a good picnic spot from which to see down into the *Megalong Valley*. Continue along Cliff Drive, turn left into Narrow Neck Road which takes you back to the highway west of Katoomba.

The Three Sisters

This is the most famous of the many strange rock formations on this eroded plateau of Triassic sandstone. An Aboriginal legend tells the story of its origin.

The three sisters, Meenhi, Wimlah and Gunedoo, ran away to make an illegal meeting with three tribesmen. A tribal witch doctor chased them and they took refuge on top of a rock. Their father, who was far off in the valley below, had some magic powers and changed his daughters into stone to protect them. In his excitement he dropped the stick or stone which produced the magic and he could not protect himself when the witch-doctor turned him into a lyrebird. The lyrebird heard calling in the valley below is the girls' father scratching about in the earth looking for his magic stick or stone, to turn himself and his daughters back into human form.

Pitt's Amphitheatre

Major Henry Antill, accompanying Governor Macquarie across the mountains in 1815, wrote glowingly of his first view of this scene.

'April 28 ... one of the grandest views that can be imagined was opened to our sight. In the foreground was a deep glen, part of which we had seen yesterday, and around it an immense amphitheatre of lofty hills crowned with rocks, upon which the sun was shining affording a variety of tints. In the distance were lofty mountains as far as the eye could reach, forming a grand circumference and background — the whole *coup d'oeil* grand beyond the power of my pen to describe; and until now most likely unseen by the eye of civilised man. Called it Pitt's Amphitheatre.'

The Scenic Railway (BMCC HR K 17)

The railway was built in the first place to haul coal to the top of the cliff. In 1872 John B. North, sometimes called the *Father of Katoomba,* began to work a coal mine at the foot of the cliff. A year later he discovered and began to work kerosene shale deposits at the Ruined Castle. He built a flying fox cableway to haul skips to the Orphan Rock, but when only 500 tons of the shale had been carried, the flying fox collapsed, and the equipment is still lying on the valley floor.

That company failed, but in 1879 another was formed by North and Thomas Sutcliffe Mort, of shipping (Mort's Dock) and wool brokering interests, and together they developed many mines, bringing vast quantities of shale and coal via a horse tramway from the Ruined Castle and other mines in the Megalong Valley by a 'daylight tunnel' through Narrow Neck to the foot of a haulage railway. Part of this tramway is now covered by the landslide. At the top, the skips were hauled along another tramway to the railway at 'Shell Corner', near the junction of Valley Road and the highway and near the spot where the first school was conducted.

Some of the miners who worked these mines lived in the valleys to minimise travelling and small villages existed at the Ruined Castle and in Nellie's Glen. Some houses were also clustered round the siding near 'Shell Corner'.

This shale could not be refined in Australia at that time, and was taken to Italy by sailing ship and shipped back as kerosene. It burned very well and was in great demand for use in the lamps of the day.

The shale gave out about 1895 and the haulage of coal alone from the valleys was not economic. The tramway at the bottom was torn up in 1897, but the railway siding remained until 1918.

In the late 1920s Katoomba Colliery went into business once more. About 1930 they began using their coal skips to give tourists the thrill of their lives. This venture was so successful that a more comfortable conveyance was designed. And so we have the Scenic Railway!

J. B. North purchased much of the land on which Katoomba is now built. He had always encouraged his friends to visit his mines and spoke highly of the scenic beauties and healthful qualities of the mountains and by the time his mines ceased to operate, the district was well on the way to becoming a major tourist centre. It seems fitting that part of his original venture should have developed into one of the most popular tourist attractions of the area.

Landslide Lookout

This geological feature reminds us of the way that the Blue Mountains gorges have been formed. Softer shale and coal beds underlie harder sandstones. The coal measures are weathered away by forces of water and temperature and wind. The sandstone is undermined and the upper rock breaks off at the cracks and joints characteristic of it. Then there is a rock fall and the cliff line has moved back a little further.

The landslide occurred recently, in geological terms, in 1932.

O'Sullivan's Folly (BMCC HR K 24)

This is the beginning of the road which was to be blasted out of the side of Narrow Neck and down into the Megalong Valley. This work was never completed — as the year was 1899 one can understand the technical difficulties — and it was named for the Minister of Public Works of the Day, E. W. O'Sullivan.

3 Katoomba

At the corner of Valley Road and the highway, at *Shell Corner*, in a fenced area is an Historic Marker recording the site of the **First School at Katoomba**. (You may not see it unless you stop and it is difficult to find a

KATOOMBA

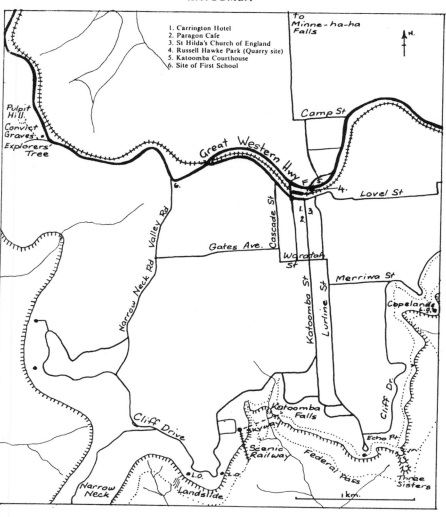

1. Carrington Hotel
2. Paragon Cafe
3. St Hilda's Church of England
4. Russell Hawke Park (Quarry site)
5. Katoomba Courthouse
6. Site of First School

parking space nearby.)
Turn left into the highway and drive west about 1 km to **The Explorers'**

Tree and **The Site of the Explorers' Camp, Pulpit Hill, 25 May**. Park opposite the signpost to the **Six Foot**

Convict graves, Pulpit Hill, near Katoomba

Track, re-opened in 1984 (see article Chapter 7, page 107). The track goes through **Nellie's Glen** in the valley below. Walk up Pulpit Hill Road about half a km to the **Convict Graves**.

Return to the highway and turn right for Katoomba. Do not cross the railway line but turn right into Bathurst Street (the Old Great Western Highway), on the southern side of the line.

On your right watch for BALMORAL HOUSE (BMCC HR K 7, private property), which was one of the first boarding houses in Katoomba, built in 1876.

Turn right into Parke Street where you pass the site of the first permanent school building in Katoomba. Turn left into Waratah Street. Park your car and walk up the hill to see the **Paragon Cafe** and the **Carrington Hotel** both on the left side of the street. Opposite is **St Hilda's Church of England** (BMCC HR K 14).

Return to your car, drive up Katoomba Street and turn left into Bathurst Street. Turn right at the roundabout to cross the railway at the overbridge and right at the highway. Turn left at the lights to park near the Blue Mountains City Council Chambers.

Site of First Katoomba Public School

Historic Marker No. 15, erected by the Blue Mountains Historical Society, reads:

> 'A public school was opened in this area of Katoomba on 6th February, 1882. It was a tent which accommodated about 40 children. A motel is now built on the site where the tent was erected.'

Near North's siding, where coal and shale was loaded into railway trucks, a few houses had been built and a store set up to serve the miners. In 1880 the Rev. Thomas Harrison and Mr J. B. North requested a school to serve this population, North donating the land to the Education Department.

John Douglass was teacher for 15 years, and during this time a permanent building was erected in Parke Street, Katoomba, the main population having moved to the developing tourist centre. An old photograph of the building shows that it was in the regulation style of that time. This school served not only the children of Katoomba but those from as far away as Lawson.

The Explorers' Tree, Pulpit Hill, Katoomba (BMCC HR K 18, Nat. Tr.)

Explorers' Camp 25 May

The plaque beside the tree reads:

> 'This wall and fence were erected by the Minister for Lands (the Hon. J. S. Farnell) in the year 1884 to preserve this tree which was marked by the explorers Gregory Blaxland, William Lawson and William Charles

Everton House Restaurant, Faulconbridge (p.52).

Imperial Hotel, Mount Victoria (p.121).

Wattle in bloom near the top of Neates Glen (p.109).

Wentworth who discovered a way over these mountains in the month of May, A.D. 1813.'

The unfortunate effect of the wall was to kill the tree it was intended to preserve. The dead trunk became dangerous and the top was sawn off and taken to the grounds of the Hydro Majestic at Medlow Bath were it remained for many years until burned in a bushfire. The initials have rotted away, no trace of them remaining. A roof has recently been provided to minimise the effect of the weather.

A letter in the *Sydney Morning Herald* of, 26 August 1867 (the year before the railway was extended from *Weatherboard* to Mount Victoria), under the initials of W.W., probably those of the Rev. William Woolls, Ph.D., F.L.S., a botanist, records that

'...the blackbutt on which the late Mr W. Lawson cut his initials with a tomahawk in 1813, still presents the letters as legible as ever. This interesting tree, so intimately connected with the first expedition over the Mountains, is standing on the side of the Bathurst Road at the summit of Pulpit Hill.'

In 1884 another writer reported that only part of the 'W.L.' remained.

In the journals of the three explorers, there is no mention of the marking of the tree. On the day in question, 25 May, they travelled three and a half miles from their previous camp site in the vicinity of Leura and made their camp beside a swamp. There is water about 45 metres to the north of Pulpit Hill, making it a possible camping spot. They followed their usual procedure of leaving the horses and gear in the charge of some member or members of the party and others going forward to cut a track for

the next day.

The tree is the only reputed relic of that historic journey.

Convict Graves, Pulpit Hill, Katoomba (BMCC HR K 19)

In F. F. Bailliere's *Gazetteer of New South Wales* of 1866, Pulpit Hill was the only place named between Weatherboard and Blackheath. It was listed as

'...a lofty peak of the Blue Mountains on the Great Western Road lying about 70 miles west of Sydney... It derives its name from the fact of the Rev. S. Marsden having performed Divine Service from a peculiarly shaped rock upon it, to the stockade party located there.'

As Marsden died in 1838, the tradition goes back a long way.

We counted 21 heaps of stones, some of them having a larger flat stone upright at one end.

The Blue Mountains Tourist Association notice gives this information:

'These graves are purported to contain the remains of convicts who died during the maintenance of the Bathurst Road circa 1815-1870. Church services were held here most Sundays. The Lock-up was nearby. Please help us preserve this link with our past by leaving the graves unmolested.'

The names of the convicts buried here were not recorded.

Nellie's Glen, near Pulpit Hill, Katoomba

The glen was named after a daughter

of J. B. North, whose mining company worked the kerosene shale and coal mines there. Tracks led down to the mines and these were followed by the formation of Nellie's Glen Road and the walking track at the end of it to the bottom of the Bonnie Doon Falls. In recent years the road has been blocked off.

When the mines were working some of the miners used to live in a small settlement at Pulpit Hill. An inn called the 'Shepherd and Flock' was built at the foot of Pulpit Hill as early as 1835 and was still serving the miners in the 1880s.

The *Six Foot Bridle Track* to Jenolan began at Nellie's Glen and was opened for use in 1884.

In the 1890s, after the mines had closed, an Aboriginal tribe was living in the Glen. They decided to open a 'tucker shop' to cater for tourists, and the head man, named Billy Lynch, a well known identity in Katoomba, worked at the ham-and-beef shop in Main Street, Katoomba, to learn the trade.

Paragon Cafe, 65 Katoomba Street, Katoomba (BMCC HR K 4, Nat. Tr.)

Established in 1916 by the Simos family, *The Paragon* has been famous since the 1920s for its hand-made chocolates and candies and its morning and afternoon tea fare. If you have not been to *The Paragon,* you have not tasted the flavour of Katoomba.

This cafe/tearoom is in a conventional row of two-storey shops in Katoomba Street. The original section was fitted out in 1925 by H.

and E. Sidegreaves. Two dining rooms were added, the Banquet Hall in 1934 and the Blue Room in 1936, both designed by architect Henry White. The following comment on the interior, for which it is justly famous, is made in *The Heritage of Australia:*

'Of the many such buildings erected in Australia between the wars, none were as sumptuously finished as the Paragon and it has survived relatively unaltered.'

The Carrington Hotel (BMCC HR K 2, Nat. Tr.)

The Carrington is hard to see from Katoomba Street these days because the growth of trees and shrubs, as well as the bus shelter, screens it almost entirely. When you do get a glimpse, it is reminiscent of an old English Manor, but with a difference. There is a large flat observation roof from which long distance views may be seen of the Sydney skyline and across the Jamison Valley to the Gib at Bowral, when the atmosphere is right. Walk up the drive and look at the graceful colonnaded verandah and leadlight glass.

Mr H. G. Rowell began to build his new hotel, to be named the *Western Star,* in 1880. The architect employed was C. Kirkpatrick, of Kirkpatrick and Bosser; the builder was F. Drewett of Lithgow. Stone blocks for the original part of the building came from the local stone quarry just across the railway line. It was the first tourist hotel built in Katoomba and it was to accommodate up to seventy people. Soon after its opening, it was re-named the *Great Western Hotel.*

The corridors were made unusually wide, and in wet weather served for

Narrow Neck from Cliff Drive, Katoomba

Front entrance, Carrington Hotel, Katoomba St, Katoomba

the guests to walk in, as on the deck of a ship. The large sandstone verandah facing east was another unusual feature. The unique artistry of the stained glass windows has been accorded a special classification by the National Trust.

In 1886 the hotel was acquired by Mr F. C. Goyder, who made consider-able additions. In that year the Governor of New South Wales, Lord Carrington and Lady Carrington visited the mountains and stayed at the hotel, and from that date made it their mountain retreat. With the Governor's permission, Goyder changed the name of the hotel to *The Carrington.*

Other names associated with the development of *The Carrington* have been Mr A. L. Peacock, manager under Goyder's ownership, owner Sir James Joynton Smith, M.L.C., and Mr Theo Morris.

A water supply for the hotel was an urgent necessity. A Blake's Hydraulic Ram was installed to pump water from Katoomba Creek. In working to provide a water supply for the hotel, Mr A. L. Peacock provided the whole town with reticulated water, and in the process became Mayor of Katoomba. The electricity plant, with its tall smoke stack, still a town landmark, supplied light and power for the town as well as for the hotel. The growth and development of the town of Katoomba has paced along beside that of *The Carrington Hotel*.

1980 saw the celebration of the centenary of *The Carrington*, one of the lasting achievements of that event being the book on the subject by Geoff Gates, entitled *Centenary of the Carrington Hotel 1880-1980*. Access to a copy will make your stay at the hotel more pleasurable.

In 1981, *The Carrington* was used as a set for a film *The Burning Man* starring James Mason.

4 Katoomba and Leura — North Side of Railway Line

Cross the railway line at the overbridge, turn right onto the highway and left at the next lights to park at the Blue Mountains City Council Chambers. Between it and the highway is the Katoomba 'Footsteps in Time' marker commemorating the survey of the proposed line of road by G.W. Evans. He camped in this vicinity on 2 January 1814.

There are a number of interesting buildings in this area. On the south side of the highway are the **Katoomba Railway Station**, once called **The Crushers**, THE SITE OF A GATEKEEPER'S COTTAGE, HOTEL GEARINS, formerly *Biles*, built in 1883 (BMCC HR K 22).

The highway at the lights has replaced the Russell Hawke Park, once the site of the STONE QUARRY, connected with the crushing plant. Opposite the Council Chambers, across the old highway, is the **Katoomba Courthouse**.

Across Station Street are THE MASONIC TEMPLE (BMCC HR K 12) and the *Renaissance Centre* in the former MOUNT ST MARY'S CONVENT (BMCC HR K 5).

Signposts for *Minne-ha-ha Falls* direct you along Station Street, turn left into Camp Street, right into Victoria Street, right into Verdun Street, left into Burke Street and diagonally right into Minne-ha-ha Road. From the picnic area a dirt track leads across a ford to a walking track which follows Yosemite Creek. As the water tumbles over a series of cascades beside the path, the name meaning *Laughing Waters* and taken from the Hiawatha story, seems appropriate. The water finally plunges off a ledge into a pool, which, according to Aboriginal legend, is bottomless. It takes about 10 minutes to walk to the top of this fall and another 10 minutes to climb down to the bottom of the falls.

Return to the highway and turn left towards Leura, drive east along the highway for about 2 km, passing the Alexandra Hotel, on the right, which has provided accommodation for many years. As you travel this stretch of the ridge, recall that the explorers, Blaxland, Lawson and Wentworth, camped somewhere in the vicinity of Leura Railway Station and the overbridge to Leura Shopping Centre.

Turn left into Mount Hay Road. About 9 km along, you will come to *The Pinnacles. Lockley Track* leads to *Lockley Pylon* and a track into the Blue Gum Forest.

Five km further on at the end of the road is a picnic area and a walking track to **Mount Hay.** There are wonderful views of the *Grose Gorge* from the shoulder of the mountain.

Return via Mount Hay Road to the highway and turn left for Sydney.

Katoomba Railway Station — The Crushers (BMCC HR K 20)

Katoomba was first known as **'Stone Quarry'** the quarry being in what is now Russell Hawke Park, a pond occupying the depression left by excavation. The stone was used for building purposes (e.g. The Carrington) and a large quantity of it was crushed for use as ballast on the railway line being extended from Weatherboard to Mount Victoria. When the wooden platform was built in 1874, it was known as **'The Crushers',** and passengers had to instruct the guard to stop the train there.

After the development of coal and shale mines in the Jamison Valley and the encouragement given to tourists by J. B. North, the mine owner, a new platform was built and the name changed to *Katoomba,* possibly as a corruption of *Kedumba,* meaning 'Falling Waters'. It should be noted, however, that Assistant-Surveyor Govett reported to Surveyor-General Sir Thomas Mitchell as far back as 1833:

> '...That part of the country where the Cascade Creek from the Weatherboard Inn joins the Cox's River, is called (by the natives) GO DOOM BA.'

On the north side of the railway gates was a huge turntable, used to turn the pilot engines which had to help the trains up the steep grades from Valley Heights, to ready them for their downward run. The turntable was removed in 1958 when the line was electrified.

Katoomba Courthouse (BMCC HR K 11, Nat. Tr.)

The foundation stone was laid on May 4, 1895 by His Excellency Sir Frederick M. Darley, Lieutenant Governor, whose summer residence was *Lilianfels* near Echo Point.

Mount Hay

This is the Round Hill of the early colonial writings, a suitable name for identification. Lt William Dawes was making for this mountain in 1789; the view of the wild ridges to the east to be obtained from the track is adequate explanation of some of his reasons for his being unable to reach Round Hill.

Assistant-surveyors Govett and Dixon mapped much of this area in the 1830s.

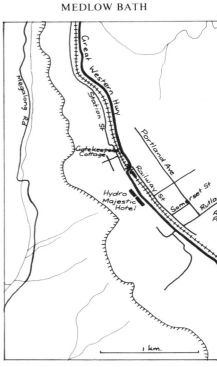

MEDLOW BATH

No 11 Gatekeeper's Cottage, Station
St, Medlow Bath

Hydro Majestic Hotel from Hargreaves Lookout, Shipley

7 Medlow Bath and Blackheath

1 Medlow Bath

Take the Great Western Highway from Katoomba to Medlow Bath. Stop on the left at the **Hydro Majestic Hotel**. The building is interesting. A short walk at the rear of it will take you to splendid views of the *Megalong Valley* and *Shipley Plateau.*

Opposite is the **Medlow Bath Railway Station.**

Without crossing the railway line, continue along the highway into Station Street. About 400 metres along is the **No. 11 Gatekeeper's Cottage** (private property).

Return to the highway and turn left across the railway and immediately right into Railway Street. About 1 km along, turn left into Somerset Street and then right into Portland Avenue. At this junction is THE CHALET, Restaurant and Guest House at 40 Portland Avenue. It is a house of old world charm, built in 1892.

Turn left out of Portland Avenue into Rutland Road. About 2 km along, a road on the left leads, in about 1½ km, to *Lake Medlow* (BMCC HR MB 5). A further 1½ km along Rutland Road is the *Katoomba Airfield.* Scenic flights over the mountains are available every weekend. About 2½ km beyond the airfield is *Point Pilcher.* This is indeed a beauty spot. The view is to the north into Govett Gorge. There is a picnic area with facilities.

Retrace your route to the highway and turn right to travel towards Blackheath. This section of the ridge is very narrow. The headwaters of one of the creeks on the right could have provided water for the **Explorers' Camp of 26 May** and **2 June** on their return. Continue towards Blackheath.

The Hydro Majestic, Medlow Bath (BMCC HR MB 9, Nat. Tr.)

Historical Marker No 8, erected by the Blue Mountains Historical Society, reads: 'Hydro Majestic. Built upon the site of Hargraves' old home. Hargraves received the reward for the discovery of gold in Australia'.

Edward Hargraves discovered gold near Bathurst in 1851 and as a reward was appointed Commissioner for Lands and given £10 000. This enabled him to acquire land at Medlow Bath, which he had noticed as a particularly beautiful spot. He built a home there and lived to enjoy the view until 1891.

The Belgravia Hotel was constructed on land next to Hargraves' house in 1891, with machinery installed for generating electricity which could pump water from the valley below.

At the turn of the century Mark Foy, Sydney business man, bought the Belgravia and Hargraves' old home as well as another, the Tuckers'

House, and combined them into a 'Hydropathic Establishment'. He engaged Dr Bauer of Germany to conduct the latest therapeutic methods from Europe. Very rigid rules were observed.

To keep up the supply of fresh vegetables Foy bought Valley Farm in the Megalong Valley and hauled the produce, including milk and poultry, to the hotel by flying fox worked on a balance system. Traces of the flying fox may still be found in the valley.

The health resort aspect of the venture was not very popular, and so Mark Foy operated the Hydro Majestic as an ordinary hotel, but retained the name.

Foy built a special art gallery and filled it with paintings and other exhibits, but unfortunately it was destroyed by fire in 1922.

During World War II the building was used by the American Army as a base hospital for servicemen wounded in Pacific Islands battlefields.

Medlow Bath Railway Station (BMCC HR MB 4)

The siding opened in this vicinity in 1880 was known as Brown's Siding. There was another Brown's Siding in the Lithgow Valley, which made for some confusion and so eventually the name was changed to Medlow. After the opening of the Hydro Majestic by Mr Mark Foy in 1903, the station was called Medlow Bath, indicative of the 'spa' nature of the hotel.

No. 11 Gatekeeper's Cottage, Medlow Bath (BMCCHR MB 2, & Nat. Tr.)

This gatekeeper had charge of a level crossing to the west of the present overbridge, about 300 metres from the railway station, and the portion of Station Street that leads to it would then have been the Bathurst Road.

Until recently the cottage was *The Cottage Shop* for antiques and craft goods, with the *Gatehouse Inn,* named for it, next door.

The cottage, built in 1867, has been preserved in memory of Robert William Hazelgrove, Per-Way Ganger, N.S.W. Dept of Railways. This was made possible by his daughter Elena.

Explorers' Camp, 6 May & 2 June

They progressed only two miles and three quarters, as '...the bush continued still thorny...' Blaxland, 26 May.

They thought that the land below them to the westward was sandy and barren, a disappointing conclusion.

Further on in the same entry Blaxland wrote: '...this day they saw the fires of the natives below ... by the number they computed they amounted to in all ... about thirty Men Women and children...' They also saw the track of a wombat.

This camp is estimated to be somewhere on the western side of Medlow Bath. They used this camp site on their return journey on the night of 2 June.

2 Blackheath — Shipley — Megalong

Approaching Blackheath from Medlow Bath, Neate's Park is on the left. Here is **The Statue of Govett the Bushranger (legendary)**.

Turn left across the railway at the level crossing opposite Govett's Leap Road, into Bundarra Street which leads to the start of the *Centennial Glen-Porter's Pass* walking track. The glen was named on the One Hundredth Anniversary of the founding of New South Wales in 1888. The track emerges at Burton Street. The return to your car along Station Street beside the railway is a reasonably level walk.

Return to the railway line and turn right into Station Street. Somewhere near the Shipley Road turn-off was the shed to which sheep were brought up from the western sheep stations to be shorn, during the time when Cox's descent of Mount York was in use.

Keeping to the left and following Station Street for about 1 km, you come to *Paul Harris Lookout,* with interesting views into the *Megalong Valley*. Return along Station Street and turn left into Shipley Road. Half a km along is *Centennial Glen Road* (BMCC HR BH 12) on the right, leading to walking tracks, one through the Glen to Porter's Pass and another, 'Wall's Ledge', along the cliff top.

Return to Shipley Road and follow it out to the **Shipley Plateau,** famed for its apple orchards. *The Shipley Tea Room* is a pleasant place for refreshments. Keep left along Hargraves Lookout Road to *Hargraves Lookout* and magnificent views down the Megalong Valley and south to Kanangra Walls.

Return to the fork and take Mount Blackheath Road on the left to *Mount Blackheath Lookout* with extensive views of the *Kanimbla Valley* and the Great Dividing Range to the west.

Return along Shipley Road and turn right into Megalong Road, for a drive through **Megalong Valley**. About 2 km down through the rainforest is a walking track to *Mermaid's Cave* and the *Coachwood Glen Nature Trail*. The village of Megalong stretches along several km of sealed road, from THE TEA ROOMS to THE CHURCH (BMCC HR MG 2). Megalong Road (part gravel) next passes a *Picnic Ground on Megalong Creek*. Just beyond it, the **Six Foot Bridle Track** crosses the road. At the end of the road, you will find *The Packsaddlers,* Green Gully, Megalong Valley, where horse riding trips into the mountains are organised. Camping and motel style accommodation is available.

Before the advent of the white man, the Megalong Valley supported a population of **Aboriginal People**. As you drive up Megalong Road, you may catch a glimpse of the Hydro Majestic on the cliff top. Turn right into Shipley Road, and left along Station Street, and return to the highway.

Legend of Govett the Bushranger

The story goes that a bushranger named Govett, when chased by police and called upon to surrender, did not do so, but instead spurred his horse over the cliff edge, where the water falls 450 metres into the valley below. The story has persisted, become elaborated and entered into the folklore of the place, being used to advertise the beauty and excitement of a holiday at Blackheath.

When given publicity in 1873, a descendant of William Romaine Govett, who discovered the waterfall in 1831, protested. Mr John Dunmore Lang replied with·an explanation of the possible origin of the legend. He tells of a bushranger who always eluded the police at a cliff regarded as impossible for any man or beast to scale. The bushranger, however, had a wonderful horse which he had trained to leap this gorge. Eventually he was caught, but the suggestion is that the stories have become confused.

The statue in Neate Park, created by Arthur Murch, was erected by the Blackheath Rhododendron Festival Committee in 1974.

The Shipley Plateau

The Shipley Road originally began at the horse paddock belonging to the Blackheath Stockade which was on the site of the present public school on the corner of Leichhardt Street. This of course was long before the railway was built.

The plateau was named after the town of Shipley near Bradford in Yorkshire, England, by Mr R. S. Longton who took up land there in 1892. His property was *Chellowdene*. At that time the road was a difficult winding track, and required many changes to make it what it is today. In 1929 the Tourist Road was opened to Mount Blackheath Lookout.

The Shipley Tea Rooms were built about 1935 by Eric Longton, son of the founder of the district.

Megalong Valley

Megalong is an Aboriginal word thought to mean 'valley under the rock'. The first record of a European coming to the valley was of Thomas Jones, a natural history specimen collector, who followed the course of Cox's River from Burragorang to Hartley in 1818.

The first land was taken up in 1838, those settlers travelling from Burragorang and Camden. Later there was a track down from Nellie's Glen, giving access to Katoomba.

When J. B. North's mines in the Jamison and Megalong Valleys were operating in the 1880s and 1890s, a flourishing settlement grew up in the Megalong. A thirteen room hotel was built there, but when the mines closed, it was demolished and the materials used to build homes at Katoomba. The Great Bushfire of 1904 wiped out the remains of the settlement.

After the track from Blackheath was improved, more durable housing materials were imported into the district. Pise (earth walls) were also used and some are still in use today.

The Six Foot Bridle Track (BMCC HR MG 3)

In 1884, a bridle track from Katoomba via Nellie's Glen was made through to Jenolan Caves. £2 500 was spent on this *Six Foot Track*, as it was called and is still so marked on maps today. It crossed Cox's River at the junction with Gibraltar and Murdering Creeks, following them for a distance to Black Range and joining the Jenolan Caves Road at the top of the Great Divide.

When Lord Carrington was staying at Katoomba in 1886, he visited Jenolan Caves, travelling on horseback along this track.

Aboriginal People of Megalong Valley

A number of Aboriginal people lived in the valley along with the white settlers on a very friendly basis. At one time the valley could field two cricket teams, one being the 'All Blacks', and being mostly Aboriginal. One chief of the Gun-dun-gorra tribe, Werriberri or Billy Russell, dictated to a resident a record of his life, *My Recollections*. The two Billy Lynches, father and son, were well known about the turn of the century in Megalong and Katoomba.

In the ages before the advent of white settlers, the tribe spent the winter in the warmer Burragorang and the summer in the higher and cooler mountain area of Wallerawang, moving through the Megalong Valley in spring and autumn.

This old Aboriginal route was used by stockmen as an alternative to the difficulties of the mountain crossing.

3 Blackheath

Drive along the highway towards Mount Victoria for a short distance past the bridge over the railway, and turn right into Ridgewell Road. This road becomes a bush track and eventually a walking track. It ends at *Baltzer Lookout* directly above the landslide on Burramoko Head. The view is over the Grose River Gorge. Return to the Highway, turning left; drive one block and turn left at Sturt Street, left at Inconstant Street, and right at Bacchante Street. On the left is the entrance to the *Blue Mountains Rhododendron Garden*, (*Bacchante Gardens*), established by the Blue Mountains Rhododendron Society, which has its headquarters here. This beautiful and interesting garden is especially worth a visit in the spring. open daily: 9 a.m. to 5 p.m. Membership subscriptions and visitor donations held towards upkeep and are appreciated. (BMCC HR BH 10).
Inconstant Street leads to Hat Hill Road. Turn left for views of and access to the Grose River and its Gorge. After passing the abandoned airfield a drive of 10 km brings you to the end of Anvil Ridge. Halfway

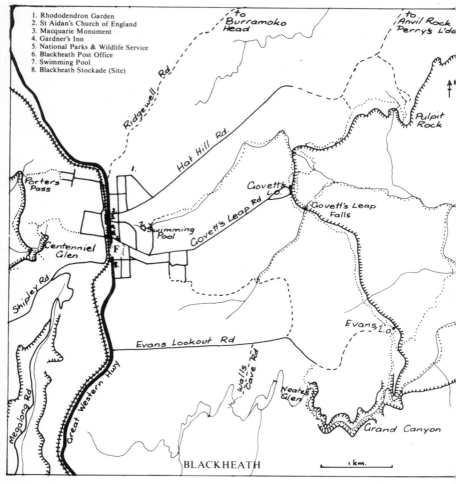

Map legend:

1. Rhododendron Garden
2. St Aidan's Church of England
3. Macquarie Monument
4. Gardner's Inn
5. National Parks & Wildlife Service
6. Blackheath Post Office
7. Swimming Pool
8. Blackheath Stockade (Site)

to Burramoko Head

to Anvil Rock Perry's L'do

Pulpit Rock

Ridgewell Rd

Hat Hill Rd.

Govett's L.O.

Porters Pass

Govett's Leap Rd

Govett's Leap Falls

Swimming Pool

Centenniel Glen

Shipley Rd

Evans L.O.

Evans Lookout Rd

Walls Cave Rd

Neates Glen

Megalong Rd

Great Western Hwy

Grand Canyon

BLACKHEATH

1 km.

along on the left is **Hat Hill**. At the end of the road is *Anvil Rock*, situated above *Blackheath Walls*, with a good view to Mount Banks Walls across the gorge. *Windswept Cave* is a short walk further on.

Return to Hat Hill Road and turn left into the road leading to **Perry's Lookdown** and, as the name suggests, the view below is just as startling as that across the valley. This is the start of the shortest but most precipitous track into the *Blue Gum Forest*.

Return to Hat Hill Road, turn left and drive 2 km to turn left to **Pulpit Rock Lookout**. From this point there is a 270 degree sweep of view. A cliff top walk starts here and continues for 7 km, with a lookout about every kilometre, to *Evans Lookout*. Look for the place from which both *Horseshoe Falls* and *Govett's Leap* can be seen at once. Most of the cliff top track is unfenced and so care needs to be taken. The walls below the track are here called the **Griffith Taylor Walls**. There is a branch track from the cliff top going up *Pope's Glen*, above *Horseshoe Falls* to emerge at Prince Edward Street or onto Hat Hill Road.

Return to Hat Hill Road and turning left, follow it back to the highway. **St Aidan's Church of England** is on the corner of Hat Hill Road and the highway. Turn left into the highway and stop where the road widens outside the Community Centre. Look at the **Macquarie Monument, Blackheath**. Opposite is **Blackheath Railway Station**. A short distance along the highway is **Gardner's Inn**.

A short distance along the highway, opposite the level crossing, turn left into Govett's Leap Road. On the right, outside the New Ivanhoe Hotel, is the Blackheath 'Footsteps in Time' marker, memorial to George William Evans who surveyed this area on 1 January 1814 on his return from crossing the Great Dividing Range.

A short distance along, on the left is the **Post Office, Blackheath**.

Turn left into Prince Edward Road for the *Memorial Park and Swimming Pool*. The rhododendrons, planted in the park many years ago, are worth seeing in the spring.

Return to Govett's Leap Road and turning left, continue to the roundabout just past Connaught Road. The BLUE MOUNTAINS HERITAGE CENTRE is on the left; it is the headquarters of the National Parks and Wildlife Service. It is open daily, including holidays except Xmas Day, from 9 a.m. to 4.15 p.m. There are leaflets, books and interesting displays inside. Don't miss the *Fairfax Heritage Walk* which begins from the car park and circles round via *George Phillips Lookout* and *Govett's Leap Lookout*.

Turn left into the loop road and drive slowly through an avenue of eucalypts which has been admired for a hundred years. Park at the *Govett's Leap Lookout* and admire the view of Grose Gorge and of **Govett's Leap**. Think of its discoverer, **William Romaine Govett**.

The Cliff top walk may be followed in either direction, to *Pope's Glen* and *Pulpit Rock* or to *Braeside Walk* along *Govett's Brook* and *Evan's Lookout*. A track also goes down to the bottom of *Govett's Leap* and to the *Bridal Veil Falls* and joins *Rodriguez Pass*, which climbs out at Evans Lookout, as well as going to the *Blue Gum Forest*.

Return via Govett's Leap Road to the highway and turn left for one block to Leichhardt Street. Pause here to look at **Historic Marker No 9 — Blackheath Stockade**, and notice **Blackheath Primary School**.

Return to the highway, turn left and drive along for about 2 km. Turn left into Evans Lookout Road. It is about 4 km to *Evans Lookout*. The track connecting this lookout with *Govett's Leap Lookout* via the valley is **Rodriguez Pass**. The track also leads on to the *Blue Gum Forest* and another goes to the *Grand Canyon* and *Neate's Glen*.

Return via Evans Lookout Road to turn left into Wall's Cave Road. There is a walking track to **Wall's Cave**.

Return to Evans Lookout Road, turn left and at the highway left again. As you approach Medlow Bath, you may get a good glimpse of the Gatekeeper's Cottage in the half km before you cross the railway. The Great Western Highway takes you to Sydney via Emu Plains.

Hat Hill

The extensive views to be seen from the top of this hill have been popular since the 1890s, when horse coaches brought tourists to its foot. First a walk up Hat Hill to see the view, and then out to Anvil Rock and Pulpit Rock — this was the routine of the day. There was a picnic shelter at the foot of the hill.

Perry's Lookdown

This track down into the Blue Gum Forest was in existence as far back as 1884 and possibly earlier, when the climber descended by Docker's Ladder. The Railway Guide of that date advised, however, that exploration of the gorge should only be done with the services of a guide.

Pulpit Rock

The cairn and obelisk were erected by the Blackheath Sights Trust and the Lookout officially opened by E. A. Buttenshaw, M. L. A., Minister for Lands, on 14 December 1933.

Griffith Taylor Walls

It seems fitting that these magnificent cliff faces should be named for a man who did so much to extend our knowledge of the geological background to the Blue Mountains. Professor Griffith Taylor, born in London in 1880, arrived in Australia in 1893. He was the Senior Geologist in Captain Scott's expedition to the Antarctic in 1910-13, and later was Professor of Geography at Sydney University and at universities in Canada and U.S.A. He was the author of forty books on a variety of subjects related to geography and geology. *Sydneyside Scenery* has the most relevance to the Blue Mountains.

St Aidan's Church of England (BMCC HR BH 2)

The original part of this church was consecrated in 1884. In time it was found that the church was too small to accommodate the increase each summer from the visitors Blackheath was then attracting, and a wing was built on each side, the extensions being dedicated in 1902.

St Aidan's Rectory is also an attractive building.

Macquarie Monument, Sutton Park, Blackheath

The monument bears this inscription:
'This locality named "Hounslow" by Governor Macquarie on his way to the newly discovered country to the westward of the Blue Mountains was renamed by him "Black-heath" on May 15, 1815, during his return journey to Sydney.'

Major Antill, who accompanied Macquarie, was of this opinion:

> 'May 15 . . . From the appearance of this Station, it being a kind of heath, but a very wild and dreary scenery, the Governor gave it the name of Blackheath, though to my eye, very unlike its namesake.'

Stones from the original building of nearby Gardner's Inn were used to build the monument.

Blackheath Railway Station (BMCC HR BH 7)

When the extension of the railway from the Weatherboard was planned, Blackheath was to be the terminus. However, floods on the Nepean River washed away the bridge there, and the line was not opened as planned, the work being continued on to Mount Victoria. The handsome two-storey stone building was constructed there instead of at Blackheath. Blackheath did not even have a station at all!

A platform was completed by December 1869 and called Govett's Leap, but the name was changed to Blackheath in 1871. It was then the only stopping place between the Weatherboard and Mount Victoria till the siding at The Crushers was opened in 1874.

The first station buildings were constructed in the 1870s. The present station and platform were built in 1883 and improvements added in the following years. In 1898, after duplication of the line, Blackheath Station was made into an island platform.

Gardner's Inn (BMCC HR BH 8)

In 1830 Governor Darling inspected the land at Blackheath, for which Andrew Gardner, an ex-soldier, had applied and, being impressed with the situation, gave permission for the grant for the purpose of the building of an inn. Gardner built his inn and it was licensed as the *Scotch Thistle* in 1833, although the land grant was not registered until 1844.

In 1835 James Backhouse, of the Society of Friends, travelling over the Blue Mountains, wrote:

> 'Sept 9 . . . and we reached the "Scotch Thistle", a solitary inn, at Black Heath, on the top of the mountains . . . 10th. The night was very cold, rendering the good fires, the soft, clean beds, and excellent provision of this homely-looking inn, very acceptable.'

An early visitor of note was Charles Darwin, who booked a room there in 1836, and was much impressed with the comfort and service supplied.

Over the years the inn was called the *Blackheath,* the *Thistle,* the *Govett's Leap, Hydora House* and the *Hotel Astoria.*

Extensions were added from time to time. In 1938 the original section was pulled down and rebuilt, care being taken to preserve the cedar staircase. It was then renamed *Gardner's Inn.*

The long and varied history of this inn has been recorded in the sesqui-centenary volume written in 1981 by Geoff Bates, *Gardner's Inn Blackheath Blue Mountains NSW.*

Blackheath Post Office (BMCC HR BH 1)

The present post office was built in 1910.

The first post office at Blackheath

was a receiving office, established in conjunction with a telegraph office on the railway station, in 1880. A full post office was opened in 1885.

Over the years several different buildings have housed the Post Office.

Memorial Park and Swimming Pool (BMCC HR BH 9)

The area covered by this park was originally a series of swamps at the head of Pope's Glen Creek and was used as a grazing and camping area by stockmen passing through the district, a use which probably started very early.

The railway engines required a water supply and a dam was built across the creek, the area being reserved as a Catchment in 1867. A pumping plant was installed to convey the water to tanks at the station. After 1924 the railway took its water from the Bridal Veil Scheme, and the area was set aside as a park, although no development took place for many years.

After the tragic drowning of two small boys in the abandoned water hole and after much opposition had been overcome, the Memorial Park and Swimming Pool was officially opened in November 1931. Over the years the area has been landscaped and gardens planted, so that the park is one of the beauties of Blackheath.

Govett's Leap (BMCC HR BH 11)

This waterfall has been described by

Professor Griffith Taylor as

'the finest of the innumerable falls whereby the little streams of the plateau dash over the amazing cliffs to reach the Grose or Cox Rivers some 2 000 feet (608 metres) below ... The ... Sandstone is about 600 feet (183 metres) thick hereabouts ... and the falls are rarely over 500 feet (150 metres). Govett's Leap is 527 feet (159 metres) in the first major fall . . . (It) is enhanced by the fact that it falls into the head of a stupendous gorge, about 10 miles (16 km) long and a couple of miles (3 km) wide, leading down in the main gorge of the Grose River.'

(from *Sydneyside Scenery*)

The Govett's Leap Lookout, from which one may safely look at the wonderful scenery and the 'leap', was opened in 1938 as an appreciation of the work of the Blackheath Group controlling the Blue Mountains Sights Reserves.

The falls were discovered by Assistant-Surveyor William Romaine Govett in 1831, when he was conducting the original survey of the district. Since that date they have been the most important tourist attraction in the area, their beauties extolled by tourist brochures and numerous visitors.

William Romaine Govett (1807-1848)

William Govett joined the surveying department in 1827 when he arrived in Sydney, then only twenty and inexperienced. He learned quickly and by 1830 was in charge of a surveying party. In February of that year, instructions were issued to him to survey the Blue Mountains Range which he proceeded to do. In July 1831 he was surveying the Blackheath

Govett's Leap, Blackheath

Swimming pool, Memorial Park, Blackheath

Govett's Leap Lookout, Blackheath

Avenue of eucalypts, Govett's Leap Rd, Blackheath

district and while there found the falls. Govett's equipment was somewhat primitive and to assess the depth of falls and cliffs he would throw down large rocks and time their fall, or dangle his chain with a piece of tin attached to the end over the cliff and get a man on the opposite side to judge the number of chains required to reach the bottom. He judged the perpendicular height of the cliffs near the falls to be 528 feet (160 metres).

After completing his work in the Blackheath area, Govett was instructed to continue the survey of the Clarence/Wolgan and the Mount Tomah areas. While doing this work he discovered Mount Wilson.

He returned to England in 1834.

Blackheath Convict Stockade

In the 1830s convict road gangs reconditioned the surface of the road and eased many of the bends. A stockade was established at Blackheath sometime towards 1840 and operated as a maintenance depot until 1849, when the convict gangs were disbanded. Captain Bull was in charge of the Blackheath depot from 1844, when he was transferred from Woodford, till closure in 1849. He had a stone house on this site.

For a time the Commandant's house was used as a Police Station but by 1862 it had fallen into ruin. Building stone was taken from the ruins for use in the first school house.

Blackheath Primary School (BMCC HR BH 3)

Application was made for a school for the village of Blackheath in 1884 and land was set aside for this purpose, divided into two blocks by Leichhardt Road. A school building was erected on the site of the former-stockade and commandant's house, stones from the ruin of which were incorporated in the building. A teacher's residence was erected on the other in 1889. In 1895 a new building was put up to house the increased school population, and the old school building was re-erected as a weather shed. Additions were made in 1912 and 1922.

Rodriguez Pass

This walking track was built to connect Evans Lookout with the bottom of Govett's Leap. It was opened to the public on 27th January, 1889.

The men who had organised its construction and overcome the difficulties of planning and finance were James Daly, J. P., and T. R. Rodriguez, Stationmaster of Blackheath. Mr T. Williams was the contractor (the second; the first had decided the task was too difficult) and with the aid of his son and much perseverance and great skill with explosives, the track was built. The steps had to be cut out of the rock and cemented.

T. R. Rodriguez was also responsible for tracks being made to the Grand Canyon and to Neate's Glen.

Wall's Cave (Permit needed)

Archaeological studies have been made of this cave by Dr Eugene Stockton and W. Holland, who found evidence suggesting that the cave had been first occupied 12 000 years ago. The earliest occupants left tools behind which had not been much worked over. Later occupants left tools of the Bondaian type, requiring greater skill in their making.

This cave is a very beautiful spot.
'Take nothing but photographs; leave nothing but footprints.'

To find it turn at the small heap of rocks on the right of the track.

In the canyon at Wall's Cave

8 Mount Victoria (One Tree Hill) and Mount York

1 Scenic Mount Victoria

Drive along the Great Western Highway from Blackheath. Pull off to the left at MOUNT BOYCE for views of *Shipley Plateau, Kanimbla Valley* and the *Great Dividing Range.* **Explorers' Camp, 27 May,** was somewhere between Blackheath and Mount Victoria.

Return to the highway and turn left, heading for **Mount Victoria**, with its reminders of past history and ever present natural beauties. After about 2 km, turn off on the left at Brownstown Oval and drive round the oval to park as near the railway line as possible. Here you will find the Mount Victoria 'Footsteps in Time' marker, recording George William Evans' camp in this area on 31 December 1813, on his return from crossing the Great Dividing Range.

At the highway turn left. Victoria Falls Road, half a km further along on the right, before the highway crosses the railway line, goes almost to *Victoria Falls.* A walking track to the Falls continues on to *Burra Korain Camping Ground, Pierce's Pass* and the *Blue Gum Forest*; it joins tracks leading to Blackheath and Leura. Return to the highway along Victoria Falls Road and turn right.

On the left of the highway notice the roof of No. 12 GATEKEEPER'S COTTAGE (MBCC HR MV 9, Nat. Tr., private property). Across the railway line, also on the left, is the **Toll Bar House.**

Take the next on the left, *Mount Piddington Road* and follow the signs for *Tourist Drive 7* to **Victoria Trig Station,** Apex Road and to *Mount Piddington Reserve.* You can drive right to the picnic area at the top. A walking track leads to *Fairy Bower.*

Return to Apex Road and turn left, and left again into Carlisle, Victoria and Innes Streets, the last named becoming Kanimbla Valley Road. Drive to the end of this street. Walk down the blocked off road. A few metres along a short track on the left takes you to *Pulpit Rock. Kanimbla Valley* is below, with an extensive view to the south. Return to the old road, which goes down to the *Little Zig Zag* (BMCC HR MV 18) part of an old road into the valley. Twenty minutes walking will bring you to a well defined track on your left, about two thirds of the way to the bottom. This side track leads to the *Bushranger's Cave.* You will need to allow about an hour for the walk there and back to the cave.

Return via Kanimbla Valley Road and Innes Street and turn left into Victoria Street. On the right hand side of Victoria Street is the **Mount Victoria Primary School.** Continue along Victoria Street for several blocks and turn left into Grandview Road and left again into Kenny Street. Park at the end of this street. Take the walking track on the right which leads to the edge of the escarpment. The track then turns left and goes down a short distance to the *Engineers Cascade.* This is a very cool and pleasant grotto. 'Cooee's' across the valley often give an interesting response.

Return via Kenny Street and Grandview Road to the highway.

Explorers' Camp, 27 May

This camp was between Blackheath and Mount Victoria. They '... encamped ... by the Side of a Swamp ...'

In cutting the next day's track they saw more 'native fires' and also some '... good timber for building ...' This day's track cutting would have taken the party through the Mount Victoria area, when they got onto the Mount York ridge.

Mount Victoria

The early name for this locality was *One Tree Hill*, the hill being marked by Sir Thomas Mitchell on the map drawn by him for the English Government in 1834. This name remained in use at the post office until 1876. When the railway was built, the name of Mount Victoria was officially given by the Governor of New South Wales, Lord Belmore.

Whichever line of road was in use, the traveller passed through Mount Victoria. For a short period, it was the terminus of the railway. School children came by train from the upper mountain villages to school here. Inns flourished before the advent of the railway and boarding houses and private summer residences proliferated in the later years of the

nineteenth century, as the age of tourism began.

A military post at *One Tree Hill* is referred to in early writings, but no trace of it remains.

There are a number of buildings over 100 years old remaining in the district.

Toll Bar House, Mount Victoria (BMCC HR MV 3, Nat. Tr.).

The turnpike system of collecting tolls for the maintenance of roads had been established in New South Wales in Governor Macquarie's time, and an Imperial Act in 1832 extended the powers of the Governor to appoint places where the tolls should be collected. In 1848 it was decided to place turnpike gates at the 17 Mile Hollow Stockade and at the 35 Mile Stone at Broughton's Waterhole (Mount Victoria). A stone cottage was to be erected for the toll keeper in each case.

The Mount Victoria Toll House is one of the few that has survived; it is now being restored. The bow windows enabled the toll keeper to watch the road in both directions, rather necessary during the busy period after gold was discovered at Bathurst and other places westwards.

Tolls were collected between 1849 and 1876. A coach with springs was charged 1/6 (about 15c) but goats, pigs and sheep only one farthing each. Heavy wagons with wide steel tyres were allowed through free, because it was thought they crushed the loose stones on the road. Isaac Shepherd, a toll keeper, built an inn adjoining the toll house to serve travellers.

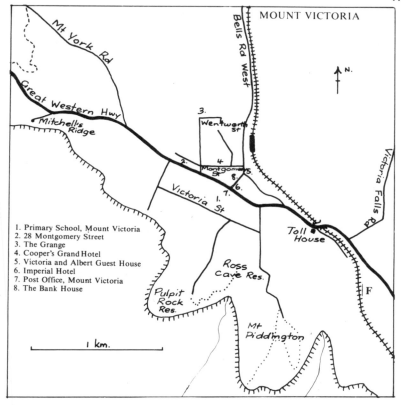

MOUNT VICTORIA

1. Primary School, Mount Victoria
2. 28 Montgomery Street
3. The Grange
4. Cooper's Grand Hotel
5. Victoria and Albert Guest House
6. Imperial Hotel
7. Post Office, Mount Victoria
8. The Bank House

Victoria Trig Station, Apex Road, Mount Victoria

The wooden sign was erected on 27 March 1982 as a reminder that the old name for Mount Victoria was *One Tree Hill.*

It is the highest point in the City of the Blue Mountains, being 1111 metres (or 3645 feet) above sea level.

The trig station was established on One Tree Hill in 1878.

Mount Victoria Primary School (BMCC HR MV 16, Nat. Tr.)

The school was established in 1868, the population having increased owing to the influx of families of workers connected with railway construction.

The sandstone building was used as both school and teacher's residence. It was the fourth structure provided for this purpose.

2 Mount Victoria Township

Cross the highway from Grandview Street and turn left immediately into Burwood Road and then right into Montgomery Street. On the right is a pair of cottages, **26-28 Montgomery Street** (private property).

Turn left up Selsdon Street (away from the highway), and drive up to its junction with Wentworth Street, to **The Grange,** now an outdoor education centre for Barker College, Sydney.

Return via Selsdon Street and turn left into Montgomery Street. On the left is the former **Coopers Grand Hotel,** now a guesthouse.

Cross Station Street and park near the **Mount Victoria Railway Station** and the **Museum** conducted by the Mount Victoria and District Historical Society. The Museum is open on Saturdays, Sundays and Public Holidays from 2 to 4 p.m. Admission is charged.

Walk up Station Street towards the highway. On the left is the **Victoria and Albert Guest House.** On the right hand side of Station Street are THE POLICE STATION No. 32 Station Street, dated 1875 (BMCC HR MV 24), No. 30 Station Street, dated 1875, No. 28 STATION STREET (BMCC HR MV 24) which is now a craft shop, THE BAY TREE TEA SHOP (BMCC HR MV 3, Nat. Tr.). The next three houses are THE BANK HOUSE, formerly the bank, 22 Station Street (BMCC HR MV 2, Nat. Tr.), LOUGH SWILLY 20 Station Street (interesting antiques here), THE FOYLE 18 Station Street (books and antiques here).

On the left, on the corner of the highway, is the **Imperial Hotel.** On the opposite side of the highway is the **Post Office and Old Stable.**

Collect your car and turn right into the highway from Station Street and head west towards Mount York. One block along to the west is ST PETER'S CHURCH OF ENGLAND (BMCC HR MV 7). The building is dated 187 I; the church was dedicated in 1875. Continue towards Mount York.

26-28 Montgomery Street (BMCC HR MV 11, Nat. Tr.)

These cottages were built about 1885-1886 as part of a boys' school. The main building *Glen Ogie* has been demolished. It is thought that Henry Lawson had some connection with the school. His father was employed in the construction of these and other

The former Coopers Grand Hotel, Mount Victoria

The Bank House, 22 Station St, Mount Victoria

Mount Victoria Railway Station

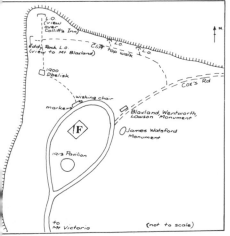

MOUNT YORK

Mount Blaxland from Eddy Rock Lookout, Mount York. The white dot indicates the marker on Mount Blaxland which has been outlined faintly.

buildings at Mount Victoria and perhaps the writer and poet-to-be visited his parent.

The Grange (MBCC HR MV 1, Nat. Tr.)

Tucked in under the hill, the row of five brick chimneys and the ornamental ridge capping first meet the eye. The house was built in 1876 by William Richman Piddington, a local landowner and a liberal Member of Parliament.

Mount Piddington, on the other side of the highway, beyond the toll bar house, is named for him.

Coopers Grand Hotel (BMCC HR MV 4, Nat. Tr.)

This imposing building was erected in 1876 for the Fairfax family of the *Sydney Morning Herald.*

Mount Victoria Railway Station and Museum (BMCC HR MV 6)

The museum is housed in the impressive railway refreshment rooms, built 1872. The smaller room was used as a dining room where a full meal could be served, when the train stopped long enough. Light refreshments were served from a long counter in the large hall during the 20 minute stops, all the time that was allowed on many train journeys. As you visit the museum and wander among the interesting exhibits collected there, imagine the scene as hungry and thirsty travellers struggled to be served in time to drink their tea before the guard blew his whistle. Mount Victoria was a renowned refreshment stop until well into this century.

Mount Victoria was the first headquarters of tourism, many places which could be visited in horse-drawn vehicles being listed in the guide books.

A fast passenger service from Mount Victoria was established early in the history of the line. One of the early drivers of the *singles* locomotives was Jock Heron, who had a reputation for fast and reliable running, and for being merciless with his engine and his firemen. When the blast of his engine whistle was heard, the station men would say, 'Here comes the big fish!' — confusing *heron* with *herring* perhaps? Thus *The Fish* became established. After the Second World War a second-division of the fast train was called *The Chips*, and later yet another was given the original driver's proper name, *The Heron.*

Victoria and Albert Guest House (BMCC HR MV 21, Nat. Tr.)

This very attractive building began life as the Royal Hotel. An early owner of the land was Mary Finn, of Hartley, who mortgaged it shortly afterwards to a Mr Peden. It was kept by various licensees, including P. Matthews. In the later half of the century it acquired its present name. J. T. Lees partly rebuilt and extended the hotel early this century.

There was a good trade while the railway was being built and when

Mount Victoria was the terminus for tourist coaches to Jenolan Caves and other attractions.

Imperial Hotel (BMCC HR MV 5)

The Imperial was built in 1878 and is unusual among mountain inns because it has always traded under its original name. There is an impressive sketch made about 1885 reproduced in *Excursions into History* published by the Blue Mountains Historical Society. Many changes have been made to the hotel in recent years.

Post Office and Old Stables (BMCC HR MV 15, Nat. Tr.)

The first post office was opened in 1866 and was known as *One Tree Hill*, retaining this name until 1876. The present building, designed by W. L. Vernon, was erected in 1895-7.

3 Mount York

Drive 1 km west along the Great Western Highway from Mount Victoria and turn right into Mount York Road. One km along, several Lands Department Walking Tracks begin. On the left is **Berghofer's Pass.** Estimated time for return walk: 1 hour. Easy grade. On the right, from a larger parking area, are **Lawson's Long Alley.** Estimated time: 4 hours to complete circuit, returning by **Lockyer's Road.** There are some steep grades in the 11 km.
Returning to Mount York Road, continue along it. After about 1½ km on the right are directions to a nature trail to Lockyer's Line of Road, 1829, a track to Lawson's Long Alley, and a walking track following *Cox's Road* along the *Mount York Ridge.*
Next on the left of Mount York Road are the historic wells, thought to have supplied the construction camp for the making of Cox's Descent. A short distance further along is *Barden's Lookout.* Mitchell's *Victoria Pass* and *Berghofer's Pass* below may be seen from this point.
At the end of the road is **Mount York.** There is parking space as well as picnic and barbecue areas. Here are many monuments erected over the years to the men whose combined efforts were needed to bring to fruition the great project of a road across the Blue Mountains to Bathurst. First, at the entrance is THE PAVILION erected in 1913 for the centenary of the crossing.
A short walk to the left through an archway brings you to *The Obelisk* erected in 1900 by a group of historically minded citizens headed by J. Berghofer. This white monument can be seen from many distant places across the valley. Inscriptions commemorate: **Blaxland, Lawson and Wentworth, Surveyor George William Evans, William Cox** and **Governor Lachlan Macquarie.**

From the *Eddy Rock Lookout* there is a wide view westward across the Vale of Clwydd to *Mount Blaxland,* the end of the explorers' journey, indicated by a shining marker. The Mount is some kilometres this side of the Great Divide and is below the skyline. A second lookout gives a view northward over Hartley Vale. Collits' Inn is in the valley below, marked by a group of large pine trees.

Another interesting monument is the block of stone bearing the HEADS OF BLAXLAND, LAWSON AND WENTWORTH, sculpted by Josef Nesteriuk; it was erected by the Blue Mountains City Council in 1969. Recording a different historical event is the monument memorialising **James Watsford**.

The walking tracks begin here, leading to *Cox's Descent of Mount York.* Circuit routes may be followed, returning via *Lawson's Long Alley* or *Lockyer's Line of Road.* Allow 4 or 5 hours.

At the far end of the central picnic area is the Mount York 'Footsteps in Time' marker, unveiled in 1988. This records the survey of the road made by George William Evans on 31 December 1813.

Return via Mount York Road to the highway and turn right. Drive down Victoria Pass about 500 metres and turn left at the *Mitchell's Ridge Lookout and picnic area.* Observe the *Pass of Victoria Monument* and the sign pointing to MOUNT BLAXLAND, the terminal point of the first crosing. If you stand on the pedestal of the monument and look along the top of the sign, you will see the triangular sign glinting on the top of **Mount Blaxland.** It is some kilometres this side of and below the top of the Great Dividing Range.

Return to the pass and turn left. Half way down the Pass on the left is a STONE MONUMENT with the words 'Mitchell's Pass 1832' carved into the rock. Where the Pass narrows, you are driving over the CONVICT BRIDGE OR RETAINING WALL (BMCC HR MV 12, Nat. Tr.). Near the bottom of the pass, a walking track starts up the hill along BERGHOFER'S PASS from which you can see the retaining wall.

On the side of Mount York ridge, opposite the convict bridge, the **Marcus Clark Cross** once stood.

Return to Sydney via the Great Western Highway.

Berghofer's Pass (BMCC HR MY 5)

Mitchell's Victoria Pass was too steep for the early motor cars and a new road around the side of Mitchell's Ridge was built at the instigation of John Berghofer, community leader and first president of Blaxland Shire Council. Building of the pass began in 1907 and after five years of drilling and blasting to cut away the tremendous cliffs and of building culverts across the many little watercourses which had to be crossed, the pass was opened in 1912. Although the grades were easy, the road had many sharp curves. Nevertheless, Berghofer's Pass was the main road until 1920, when Victoria Pass was up-graded and came into use again by the higher powered cars which had by then been developed.

Both roads were used for some years, but by 1934 further improvements had been made to Victoria Pass, and Berghofer's Pass was closed.

Recently opened as a walking track by the Department of Lands and appropriately sign-posted, Berghofer's Pass gives access to an excellent view of the buttressed walls of masonry built under Mitchell's direction to support the filling required to bring Victoria Pass to an even grade of 1 in 15.

As you walk down the gentle slope, step aside to look at the stone construction of the culverts. In one place there is a shallow water trough of the same design as the one on Watertrough Hill on Bell's Line of Road. At another, you will see the distance to Sydney and Bathurst carved into the rock. The name of the pass was apparently scraped out during World War I, when Berghofer's German ancestry was considered offensive. In spite of his work for the community and the fact that he was a naturalised British citizen, he was disqualified as a Councillor in 1916.

Lawson's Long Alley (BMCC HR MY 4).

This road was built through a long narrow gully and was nearly as steep as Cox's Road. In places the sides were supported with masonry walls, more time having been spent on it — Cox had been under pressure to make his road as quickly as possible.

Built by Lieutenant William Lawson, then Commandant at Bathurst, this road was not very satisfactory, either, as it was steep and also subject to flooding by the creek sharing the gully. Another line was drawn up and started on after Lawson's road had only been in service for a few years.

Lockyer's Line of Road (BMCC HR MY 7)

As neither of the roads down Mount York, that is Cox's Road and Lawson's Long Alley, were satisfactory, Governor Brisbane offered a reward for the finding of a better line. Already Archibald Bell Jnr. had in 1823 crossed the mountains to the north of the Grose River and found his way into the Vale of Clwydd, now Hartley Vale. When submitted to Major Mitchell as a possible route, it was rejected on the grounds that it was even steeper at Kurrajong Heights and at Mount Tomah.

Hamilton Hume set out in 1827 and discovered the extension of the Blue Mountains Range across the Darling Causeway saddle between the Grose and Cox's Rivers and which circles north towards Wallerawang. Mitchell disliked this suggestion on account of its length and its direction away from Bathurst. Instead he found a companion gully to Lawson's Long Alley and Major Lockyer set to work with gangs of convicts to build a broader and 'better' road.

Lockyer started at the bottom end near Collits' Inn and the part completed is broad and well made; its retaining walls are impressive. But barely had this work been started than Major Mitchell discovered what he considered a much superior route and whisked the workforce away to the Pass of Victoria.

Memorial to Blaxland, Wentworth and Lawson, Mount York

Memorial to James Watsford, Mount York

Remnant of Cox's Road, Mount York. Note where sandstone has been chipped away to form the road.

View over Hartley Vale from Cox's Road, Mount York. Collits' Inn is marked by the group of large pine trees near the centre of the picture.

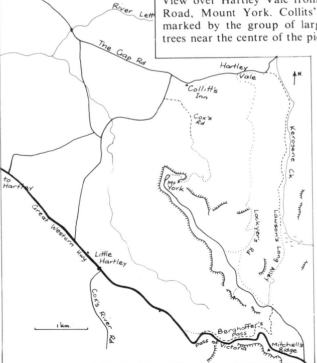

Mount York (Mount York & Environs — BMCC HR MY 6)

Mount York has an altitude of 3 490 feet (1063 metres). Governor Macquarie named it when he crossed the mountains in 1815, in honour of His Royal Highness the Duke of York, the second son of King George III.

Blaxland, Lawson and Wentworth

When the three explorers came to this point, they knew that they had crossed the mountains, and had only to get down to the easier looking country at the bottom. This was on 28 May 1813, and they had made a rather long day's journey, for them, of five and three quarters miles as '...not being able to find Water they did not encamp until five o'Clock when they encamped on the edge of the precipice...' Blaxland.

They were pleased to find that they had been mistaken about the land at the foot of the mountains and that there was good grass and forest. They took the horses down the mountain '...in a small trench made with a hoe, which kept them from slipping.' They found water at the River Lett two miles further west.

The following day they brought their camping gear down the mountain through a pass between the rocks found by Wentworth and later used by Cox for the Bathurst Road. Lawson discovered the stream which was afterwards 'named' by Evans the Surveyor, as a result of his mispelling of 'rivulet', the River Lett, and so confirmed by Macquarie.

Assistant-Surveyor George William Evans

In his journal Evans wrote:

'Wednesday, 24th (November, 1813) . . at 9 o'Clock came to the end of the Range from which the Prospect is extensive and gives me sanguine hopes, the descent is rugged and steep; I stowed away here a week's provisions in some hollow Cliffs in hopes of it being sufficient for our use back from this place; it was 12 o'Clock when we got into a Valley of good feed and appears a fine part of the Country; I have no doubt but the points of Ridges or Bluffs to the N.W. and S. . . . are the termination of what is called the *Blue Mountains* and that we are now over them; at 1 o'Clock I stopped on the bank of a Riverlett. . . .'

Governor Lachlan Macquarie

The Governor named the pass for its maker. In the report of his 'Tour', the ridge

'suddenly terminates in a nearly perpendicular precipice of 672 feet (205 metres) high . . . The road constructed by Mr Cox down this rugged and tremendous descent, through all its windings, is no less then 3/ fourths of a mile (about a km) in length, and has been executed with such skill and stability as reflects much credit on him.'

Major Antill, supervising the baggage, had this to say:

'April 29 . . . This pass had been made with great labour down a very steep mountain of upwards six hundred feet, and the way the road is made traversing the face of it makes it nearly a mile long; it was with much difficulty and exertion we got the carts down by fixing drag-ropes behind and holding on with the people; it was so perpendicular in places that the cattle could scarcely keep their footing...'

James Watsford

His monument is inscribed:

'NOT OF AN AGE BUT FOR ALL TIME
IN COMMEMORATION OF
AUSTRALIA'S FIRST ROYAL MAIL
COACHMAN
*JAMES WATSFORD
ON APRIL 6TH 1832 JAMES
WATSFORD PIONEERED THE
FIRST OFFICIAL MAIL SERVICE
PARRAMATTA, PENRITH,
COLLIT'S INN AND BATHURST.*

*THIS MARKED THE ESTAB-
LISHMENT OF A REGULAR
CARRIAGE CONVEYANCE OF
THE MAILS OVER THE BLUE
MOUNTAINS ROAD. JAMES
WATSFORD REACHED THE
SUMMIT OF MOUNT YORK AT
NIGHTFALL, PASSENGERS AND
HORSES WERE RESTED WHILE
HE ATTACHED DRAGS TO THE
COACH TO SLOW IT DOWN THE
STEEP SLOPES OF THE MOUN-
TAIN. HIS AMAZING DESCENT
TO THE VALE OF CLWYDD WAS
THEN ACCOMPLISHED IN
DARKNESS AND MIST. THE
NIGHT WAS SPENT AT COLLIT'S
INN AT THE FOOT OF MOUNT
YORK. ON THE FOLLOWING
DAY JAMES WATSFORD
CONTINUED HIS EPIC JOURNEY
VIA WILLIAM COX'S FIRST
ROAD THAT LED ACROSS THE
GREAT DIVIDING RANGE AND
O'CONNELL PLAINS TO BATH-
URST.*

*THIS COMMEMORATIVE
PLAQUE WAS UNVEILED ON
SEPT. 14TH 1974 BY HIS
WORSHIP, ALDERMAN K. D.
DASH, MAYOR, COUNCIL OF
THE CITY OF BLUE MOUNTAINS
IN THE PRESENCE OF ALBERT H.
WATSFORD ESQ.*

*THE DESCENDANTS OF
JAMES WATSFORD EXPRESS
THEIR EVERLASTING GRATI-
TUDE TO THE COUNCIL OF THE
CITY OF BLUE MOUNTAINS FOR*
*RESERVING THIS HISTORIC
SITE AS A COMMEMORATIVE
MEMORIAL TO THEIR FIRST
AUSTRALIAN ANCESTOR WHO
ARRIVED IN THE COLONY OF
NEW SOUTH WALES ON JAN-
UARY 14TH 1812.'*

Cox's Descent from Mount York (BMCC HR MY 3)

William Cox, with the experience of three months' road building in the Blue Mountains, was appalled at the difficulties he was faced with in getting down off Mount York. To do the job at all, he had to lower his standards. In his diary on 3 November he wrote:

'I have therefore made up my mind to make such a road as a cart can come down empty or with a very light load without a possibility of its being able to return with any sort of a load whatever, and such a road will also answer to drive stock down to the forest grounds. It is a very great drawback to the new country, as no produce can be brought from thence to headquarters except fat bullocks or sheep. The sheep will also be able to bring their fleeces up and be shorn on the mountains'.

In many places it is evident that the road was simply hacked through the rock. It is very steep; the grade is 1 in 4. Extra width had to be made in one place for Governor Macquarie's carriage to be got through the very first time the road was officially used. Ropes had to be used to help the horses to pull carts up the hill, often passed through rings set in the rocks. Bullocks would be yoked up to pull down hill. Standard practice was to tie on behind a whole tree, branches and all, to act as a brake. Convicts had to be sent from time to time to burn the dead trees scattered at the foot of Mount York. Its steepness made it a difficult road to keep in even a reasonable state of repair and complaints were frequent in the next few years about its bad condition.

The Pass of Victoria (MBCC HR MV 12)

This pass was constructed under the direction of Sir Thomas Livingstone Mitchell, Surveyor General, and completed and opened on 23 October 1832 by Governor Sir Richard Bourke, and, except for the eight years when it was supplanted by Berghofer's Pass, it has carried the traffic flowing to and from the west of the state. The continuous use of the road justifies Surveyor-General Mitchell's self-confident statement made in one of the letters he wrote to Governor Bourke during his fight for permission to construct the pass:

> '...I defy any man ever to point out any material improvement in the lines laid down by me for they have been marked only after a more careful survey of the ground than is made for such a purpose even in Europe.'

To build the Pass of Victoria, Mitchell had his convict gangs cut down parts of the cliff and use that material to fill the rift across his marked line, and then support the earthworks with massive masonry walls. This is the narrow part of the pass which cannot be widened without destroying a tremendous 150 year-old piece of engineering. The slowing of traffic at this point is a small price to pay for the preservation of our heritage. Elsewhere the pass has been widened and the surface improved.

The Marcus Clark Cross

This cross was a memorial to Byron Henry Clark, son of Henry Marcus Clark, who fell to his death when aged 6½ years on 1 April 1899. The little boy had followed his brother and sister, aged 9 and 12, who were climbing down the cliff to look at a cave.

The cross was placed near the site of the family mountain resort, *Drachenfels*, which was completely destroyed in a bushfire in 1902. The family never again stayed at the house after the boy's death. The cross was erected sometime after 1912.

Henry Marcus Clark had founded the retail store in Central Square, Sydney, in 1883 and the business operated there until the 1970s

Convict bridge or retaining wall, Victoria Pass

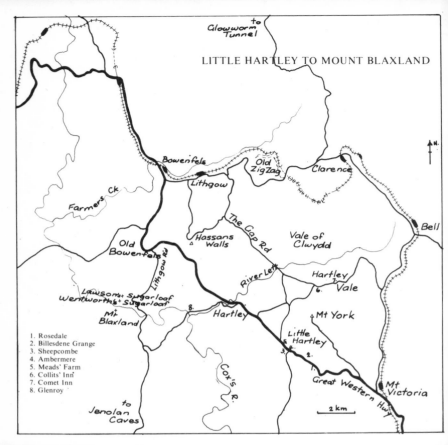

LITTLE HARTLEY TO MOUNT BLAXLAND

to Glowworm Tunnel

Bowenfels
Lithgow
Old ZigZag
Clarence
Bell

Farmers Ck

Old Bowenfels

Hassans Walls
The Gap Rd
Vale of Clwydd

Riverlett
Hartley Vale
6.

Lawson's Sugarloaf
Wentworth's Sugarloaf
Lithgow Rd
8.
Hartley
Mt York
Mt Blaxland

Little Hartley
5.
3.
2.

Cox's R.

1.
Great Western Hwy
Mt Victoria

to Jenolan Caves

2 km

1. Rosedale
2. Billesdene Grange
3. Sheepcombe
4. Ambermere
5. Meads' Farm
6. Collits' Inn
7. Comet Inn
8. Glenroy

N

Collits' Inn, Hartley Vale

'Rosedale', Little Hartley

'Sheepcombe', Little Hartley

Former school, Little Hartley (p.129).

Comet Inn, Little Hartley (p.130).

Balcony of the Visitor's Centre, Mount Tomah Botanic Garden (p.158).

9 Little Hartley (The Vale of Clwydd) to Mount Blaxland

1 The Western Foot of The Blue Mountains — Little Hartley — Hartley Vale

Remnants of these townships survive from their more thriving days. On the left is **Rosedale** (private property). About 1 km along on the right is BILLESDENE GRANGE — art gallery open week-ends.

Next on the left, after Cox's River Rd, is SHEEPCOMBE, formerly William's Store, built in the 1830s (Nat. Tr., private property). On the opposite side of the road is AMBERMERE, formerly the Rose Inn (Nat. Tr., private property). Further along on the right is **Meads' Farm** (private property).

Turn right down the road to Hartley Vale, and follow its curves. Keep right where the road forks to The Gap. After about 1 km, you will find on the right **Collits' Inn**. A short distance along on the left is the **Comet Inn** (private property).

Walking tracks start at a picnic area nearby; signs point the way to COX'S ROAD, LAWSON'S LONG ALLEY and LOCKYER'S LINE OF ROAD.

Opposite the Comet Inn some mullock heaps have been left by past **Shale Mining**. THE EXPLORER'S CAMP ON 1 JUNE on their return journey, was at the foot of Mount York.

Back track to the Gap Road which crosses the *River Lett*. The **Explorers' Camp of 29 May** was on the bank of this river.

Return to the highway and turn right towards historic Hartley Village.

Rosedale (Nat. Tr.)

First licensed as the *Coach and Horses,* and then as the *Victoria Inn,* the hostelry was built for William Cummings of Bathurst in 1839, the date being inscribed over the front entrance. Then travellers could drive directly up to the door; now there is an attractive garden. It is thought that Governor Fitzroy may have rested his horses there in 1847.

The large blocks of sandstone used in its construction were probably quarried nearby, perhaps by convict labour. The old bar has been removed from the eastern end.

In 1903 the old inn was renamed *Rosenthal* by its new owner, W. J. Berghofer.

Meads' Farm (Nat. Tr.)

The simple four roomed core of the house has been added to by later owners. It stands on part of the 100 acres (40 ha.) granted to Hugh Beattie in 1856. It is built of sandstock bricks and was originally roofed with shingles.

From 1867 to 1880 it operated as the *Kerosene Inn* and was patronised by the miners at the kerosene shale mine and works at Hartley Vale. Louis Meads was licensee in 1872.

Later owners were Captain George Stevens, who collected exotic bird and from 1887, Captain Thoma Stephenson Rowntree, Mayor of Balmain in earlier days, who used the farm as his country retreat. It was named *Culver* until recently.

Collits' Inn

Pierce Collits was transported to Australia in 1801 for receiving stolen goods, silk handkerchiefs, muslin and lace among them. His wife and two daughters came with him as free settlers. He built the inn early in 1823 and carried on a successful trade there until the traffic moved away to use the Pass of Victoria. The inn was first called the *Golden Fleece* and had a high reputation for good quality service. In 1831 a post office was established at Collits' Inn.

After the inn closed, Pierce Collits continued farming below Mount York and on other land granted as compensation in the Hartley Valley and at Canowindra. In its farming days it was known as *Mount York House* or *Farm*.

In 1877 John Kelly held the licence when kerosene shale was being mined in the area.

Comet Inn

When the Hartley Kerosene Oil and Paraffin Company began developing shale mines at Hartley Vale in the 1860s, the miners had to go as far as the *Kerosene Hotel (Meads' Farm)* at Little Hartley, for a drink. In 1877 John Kelly had a licence at *Collits' Inn*, but it was better for the miners when Thomas Thompson opened the *Comet* nearer the mines in 1879. Ann Curnow opened the *Vale Hotel*

nearby at the same time. Joseph Blenkinsopp took over the *Comet Inn* in 1880 and held the license till the turn of the century. The inn was named for the brand of kerosene made from the shale. The inn remained in business till 1913, when the shale works were closed.

The wide verandahs were added after the inn became a private home

Shale Mining, Hartley Vale

In 1824, when William Lawson's convict workmen were cutting the Long Alley, they came upon kerosene shale, but it was thought to be coal. Kerosene shale does look like coal but is lighter in weight and ignites more easily. Until 1850 when James Young in Scotland patented a method of getting coal oil or kerosene from coal and shale, nothing could be done with this *different* coal.

Hartley Vale was prospected in the 1850s and both coal and kerosene shale were found there. Coal was worked on the north side of the Hartley Vale Road just below the cliffs of Darling Causeway.

In 1866 the Hartley Kerosene Oil and Paraffin Co. erected a refining plant in the valley and the first oil was put on the market. Another company, Western Kerosene Oil, started a mine on the northern side of Hartley Vale and carted their shale to Mount Victoria and sent it to their refining plant in Botany Road near Waterloo. When the railway was extended to Bowenfels, a siding was put in 6 km north of Mount Victoria and a narrow gauge line from the bottom of the valley was constructed. The two companies merged to become New South Wales Oil and Shale Co. The high grade ore was sent to Sydney from Hartley Vale Siding, the Vale Refinery being closed. The product was marketed as *Comet Oil*; gasoline, benzine, spongaline and paraffin were also produced.

It was economic to send only the high grade shale to Sydney and in 1880 another refinery was erected at Hartley Vale to deal with the low grade shale which had accumulated.

The shale beds were worked out and the company closed down by 1913. There are mullock heaps left opposite the Comet Inn. Once the site of the tramway was visible down the cliff, but the bush has grown and obliterated it.

The Explorers' Camp, 29 May

The explorers' party made camp beside the River Lett and found that winter had set in on this western side of the mountains, and observed that what they had thought was sand was dead grass killed by the frost.

They decided to rest at this camp and stayed there a second night, 30 May, to take advantage of the grass and water for their horses.

Surveyor Evans also camped at the river. This was the end of the sixth day of his journey.

2 Historic Hartley Village

Drive along the Great Western Highway from Victoria Pass and turn left at the well-signposted **Historic Village of Hartley**. Park near the **Courthouse**. This historic building is well worth a visit.

Opposite the courthouse is the *Information Centre* in the old **Post Office**. Literature about the site may be obtained here. The National Parks and Wildlife Service is in charge of restoration work. A 15 minute film on the history of the district and on life in the gold mining days may be seen. This is free. Conducted tours, for which a charge is made, start at intervals during the day. A walk along the street takes the visitor back to times a hundred years ago. Next to the Information Centre is **St Bernard's Roman Catholic Church** and its **Presbytery**.

On the other side of the Information Centre is OLD TRAHLEE, probably built by John Finn, constable of the courthouse in the 1840s. On the hill a hundred metres along is BUNGA-RIBEE built in 1859 by John Finn's son, Patrick. This is private property and not part of the NP & WS Site.

On the left is the **Royal Hotel, Hartley** and at the top of the hill, on the right is **St John's Anglican Church**.

Return to your car and to the highway, where you turn left, and left

HARTLEY VILLAGE

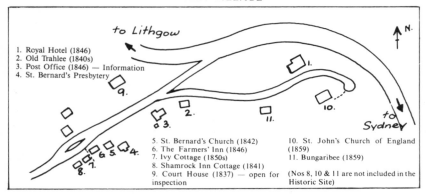

1. Royal Hotel (1846)
2. Old Trahlee (1840s)
3. Post Office (1846) — Information
4. St. Bernard's Presbytery

5. St. Bernard's Church (1842)
6. The Farmers' Inn (1846)
7. Ivy Cottage (1850s)
8. Shamrock Inn Cottage (1841)
9. Court House (1837) — open for inspection

10. St. John's Church of England (1859)
11. Bungaribee (1859)

(Nos 8, 10 & 11 are not included in the Historic Site)

Presbytery and St Bernard's Roman Catholic Church, Hartley

St John's Anglican Church, Hartley

Courthouse, Hartley

Farmer's Inn, Hartley

again into Jenolan Caves Road. This road goes to *Glenroy*, the next point of interest.

Hartley Village

Not far from the banks of the River Lett, on a slight hill out of danger of floods, a village began to grow at Hartley in the mid-1830s. Cox's Road had passed to the east and south of Hartley, to cross both the River Lett and Cox's River at Glenroy, then the focus for travellers along the road.

The Pass of Victoria was opened in 1832 and the road following Mitchell's new line, curved away from Glenroy. The new crossing of the River Lett was set up as the Town of Hartley and gazetted 1 January 1838. Only then did land become available from the previous Government Reserve along the River Lett.

A Police District was proclaimed for the Vale of Clwydd and a courthouse was completed in 1837. The number of travellers increased, as did the population of the surrounding district, and a store and several inns were established to serve their needs. Churches followed the increase of permanent population. Business throve there especially after gold discoveries to the west increased the traffic in the 1850s. The advent of kerosene shale mining in the 1860s brought added population to the valley. This was the heyday of Hartley.

Then the railway was completed to Bowenfels and to Bathurst in the 1870s and heavy goods no longer passed through Hartley; patronage by teamsters disappeared. Travellers used the train to connect with coaches at the railhead. Court business was more often conducted at Lithgow and no cases were heard at Hartley Courthouse after 1887. In 1927 the site of the historic village was transferred to the care of Blaxland Shire Council, and in 1972 Hartley Historic Site was declared and came under the management of the National Parks and Wildlife Service.

How the name of the Vale of Clwydd was changed to Hartley is unclear. Hartley is thought to be of Teutonic origin and to mean 'dweller by the lea of the stag'.

Hartley Courthouse

Built by convict labour of local sandstone, the courthouse was completed in 1837 and cases were heard there until 1887. Designed by Colonial Architect Mortimer Lewis in his favourite Greek Revival style, it was maintained by Blaxland Shire Council in excellent condition and is now recognised as one of the few examples of colonial architecture remaining in its original state.

The building consists of the Court Room, Magistrate's Room, Clerk's Room, Constable's Room and lock-ups. Sometime in the first few years and before the cross-bars were placed on the windows, a prisoner made his escape by soaping his body and squeezing out between the bars. Solitary cells were built in 1841 and the ruins are to be seen on the left of the building. Before any churches were built, services were held in the courthouse.

In the years following World War II, the courthouse was opened as a museum. Now the NP&WS has furnished it as it was in the 1840s and at the press of a button one can listen to court cases of the time being heard.

St Bernard's Church and Presbytery (Nat. Tr.)

The building of the church was begun in 1842 and completed in 1848. It was built to cater for a population then 90% Irish Catholic. It is still a sanctified church but is rarely used. The church was designed by a Mr Binning of Hassans Walls, cedar and locally quarried grey and black sandstone were used in the interior, which shows a strong French influence.

The presbytery built nearby is in its original state and is now used as the Information Centre by the National Parks and Wildlife Service.

Street Scape, Western end of Hartley Village

The Farmer's Inn, Ivy Cottage and *The Shamrock Inn.*
In the 1850s the gold miners' thirst for a drink demanded more than the Royal could supply, and in 1856 Robert Evans opened *The Farmer's Inn* by adding side wings to a cottage built by John Finn.

Next door is *Ivy Cottage,* also probably built by John Finn. Here the Magistrates lived.

At the western end is the *Shamrock Inn,* licensed to Patrick Phillips in 1861. Old shingles are still under the roofing iron. Bush timbers were used in its construction. This house is private property and not included in the historic site.

When these inns were patronised, charges were: 'ostler 1/-, supper 2/-, breakfast 2/-, bed 2/-, spirits 6d and horse 8/-'. (2/-=20c; 6d=5c).

The Post Office

This was the main residence of John and Mary Finn who came out from Trahlee in Ireland in 1839. John was constable at the courthouse. The slabs used in the garage came from the old store which was the Finns' first home. This more substantial house was then built and in 1846 became the post office. It may be the oldest post office building extant. The side wings were probably added when the Finns took over the post office; members of their family conducted it for some years.

The Finn family are thought to have built other houses in Hartley, including *The Farmer's Inn, Old Trahlee* and the magistrate's house, *Ivy Cottage.*

The Royal Hotel, Hartley

This graceful stone building, constructed about 1846, was first licensed by James Nairn in 1849. He catered for the coach trade to Bathurst; the central doorway served the refined travellers, the door at the eastern end led into the long bar-room and the western end was for the owner's family.

After many successful years as a hostelry, the *Royal* became the rectory of the Anglican Church and a school was conducted in the grounds. Today it is a private home, although part of the Historic Site.

St John the Evangelist, Church of England, Hartley (Nat. Tr.)

Although there were a considerable

number of members of the Anglican Church in the district, the building of St John's was not begun until 1853. Before that date services were held at irregular intervals in the courthouse. Designed by architect E. T. Blacket and completed in 1859, St John's is still in regular use.

3 Glenroy to Mount Blaxland

From the highway beyond Hartley Village, turn left onto Jenolan Caves Road, which follows the course of the River Lett for about 2 km. On the right before the bridge over Cox's River is **The Macquarie Monument, Glenroy**. *Glenroy Picnic Area* gives access to Cox's River and its junction with the River Lett. Admission is charged. **Cox's Road** passed through *Glenroy*.

Cross the bridge; almost immediately **Mount Blaxland**, with its shining marker, is visible on the right. Follow Jenolan Caves Road for several km to Lithgow Road. Turn right at this sharp intersection for a closer view of the end point of the first crossing of the Blue Mountains. LAWSON'S SUGARLOAF and WENT-WORTH'S SUGARLOAF are to the north.

The Explorers' Camp, 31 May was near Cox's River in this area. On private property at the foot of Mount Blaxland there is a CAIRN: MONUMENT TO BLAXLAND, WENTWORTH AND LAWSON, near the landowner's house. Mount Blaxland is Crown Land and climbers wishing to emulate the explorers should follow Cox's River from McKane's Bridge, as permission to approach the mountain over private land will not be given for insurance reasons.

Further along Lithgow Road there is a good view of Mount Blaxland looking back from the hill above *McKane's Bridge*, a beautiful old timber-truss bridge.

Return to the Great Western Highway via Lithgow Road or by retracing the route through Glenroy and Hartley. For Sydney, turn right onto the highway.

Macquarie Monument, Glenroy

The monument is inscribed:

> 'The first divine service west of the Blue Mountains was held hereabouts on April 30, 1815, in the presence of Governor Macquarie. Nearby he established a military station to guard the original western road which passed here, crossing the River Lett and Cox's River by the first bridges built west of the Blue Mountains.
>
> Blaxland Shire Council'

The account of Macquarie's tour in this area is as follows:

> 'The valley at the base of Mount York he called the *Vale of Clwydd*, in consequence of the strong resemblance it bore to the vale of that name in North Wales. . . . a rivulet of fine water runs along it from the eastward, which united itself at the western extremity of the vale with another rivulet containing still more water. — The junction of these two streams forms a very handsome river, now called by the Governor *Cox's River*; which takes its course, as has since been ascertained, through the *Prince Regent's Glen*, and empties itself into the River Nepean. ...'

It is interesting to note the wide application of the names just mentioned. Macquarie and his party spent two nights at this camp, 29 and 30 April, and again in 13 May 1815, on their return journey from Bathurst.

On his arrival back in Sydney, what the Governor had to say about the western country he had visited was this:

> 'The Governor deems it expedient here to notify the Public, that he does not mean to make any Grants of Land to the Westward of the Blue Mountains until he shall receive the Commands of His Majesty on that subject, and in reply to the report he is now about to make them upon it.
>
> In the meantime, such Gentlemen and other respectable free Persons as may wish to visit this new country, will be permitted to do so on making a written application to the Governor to that effect; who will order them to be furnished with written Passes . . .'

Cox's Road, Glenroy

Cox spent some time determining the line his road should take over the Vale of Clwydd and towards the Great Dividing Range.

> May 20 (Sunday) . . . Went with Mr Hobby, Lewis and Tye to examine the rivulet, river and ground as far as Blaxland's Mountain . . .
>
> Dec. 1 Mr Hobby and Lewis again examined the river to find a proper place for a bridge . . .
>
> Dec. 4 . . . there is a most beautiful ridge, near three miles long, that leads direct to the spot (decided on for the bridge).
>
> Dec. 6 . . . Examined the river and rivulet up and down, and fixed on a spot over each as being less trouble and more convenient than making one bridge over the river . . .
>
> Dec. 16 At 2 p.m. finished the bridge

over the west branch of the river, 45 feet (13 metres) long, 14 feet (4.27 metres) wide. It is a good strong job. There is also a causeway on each side to the high land, which is filled up with stone and covered with earth.'

Glenroy

Government cattle were sent over the mountains shortly after Macquarie's return, at first being kept at Mount Victoria. It was soon found to be too cold for them there and W. Hassall, the superintendent of Government Stock moved them to Glenroy, as that was a sunnier location. A stockyard was built in 1816, as well as the military stockade. John Maxwell, a Scotsman who had been Superintendant of Stock at Bathurst, was transferred to Glenroy in 1828. Here he obtained a grant of land on both sides of Cox's River. Later he had this grant transferred to the Wellington Valley area.

Other grants were made in the Vale of Clwydd from 1821 onwards and settlement began. In 1823 a reserve along the River Lett was declared. Then, after the completion of the Pass of Victoria and the construction of Major Mitchell's new road, which bypassed Glenroy and went through Hartley on the route taken by the highway today, Cox's Road fell into disuse. The village development which might have taken place at Glenroy occurred at Hartley instead.

Mount Blaxland

> 'Three miles to the westward of the Vale of Clwydd, Messrs Blaxland, Wentworth and Lawson had formerly terminated their excursion; and when

the various difficulties are considered ... their patient endurance of such fatigue cannot fail to excite much surprise and admiration. — In commemoration of their merits, three beautiful high hills joining each other at the end of their Tour at this place, have received their names in the following order; viz., — *Mount Blaxland, Wentworth's Sugarloaf* and *Lawson's Sugarloaf.*'

> *Macquarie's Tour of the Blue Mountains, 1815*

Today six large silver-coloured sheets placed in the pattern of a triangle have been affixed to the top of the mountain. The light glinting on the sheets makes Mount Blaxland visible against the background of the Great Dividing Range from Mount Victoria and Mount York.

Blaxland writes of the last day of their outward journey thus:

> 'May 31st ... They left their camp in the afternoon and ascended to its top which terminated their Journey —from which place they saw forest land all around them sufficient to feed the Stock of the colony, in their opinions for the next thirty Years...'

Explorers' Camp, 31 May

From the camp beside the River Lett, the explorers journeyed for about 6 miles (10 km), crossed the Lett and Cox's Rivers and camped beside a

'...very fine stream of water...'. Perhaps this was Cox's River or a tributary of it, such as Lowther Creek.

During that day

> '...they came on some Natives fires which they had left the day before they appeared to have been very busy sharpening their spears from the shavings and pieces of sharp stones they had left behind they appear on this side of the mountains to have no huts nor to bark or climb the trees like the natives on the other side the only remains of food they had left round their fireplaces — was the flower of the Honey suckle tree which grows like a bottle brush and are very full of Honey which they had sucked out.'

From this camp they made their climb of Mount Blaxland and their decision to return, mission accomplished.

Concerning their decision, Blaxland wrote the next day:

> 'June 1st ... their provisions being nearly expended, their clothes and shoes in particular worn out and all of them ill with Bowel Complaints which determined them to return home by the track they came at the same time having no doubt but that they had effactually accomplished the Object of their Journey and that all the difficulties were surmounted which had hitherto prevented the interior of the country from being explored and the Colony further extended...'

10 Jenolan Caves — Kanangra Walls

1 Jenolan Caves (map page 2)

Travel via the Great Western Highway to Hartley. Turn left onto Jenolan Caves Road, cross Cox's River at Glenroy. There are several places on the left where you can pull over to see extensive views of the Blue Mountains massif to the east.

The road rises to the top of the Great Dividing Range at **Halfway House, Hampton**. 'Million Acre' Rest Area is 5 km further along at the turn-off to Oberon. Jenolan Caves Road goes south for about 13 km through the Jenolan State Forest where there are several attractive rest areas.

At Binda Flats the *Six Foot Track* from Katoomba to Jenolan crosses the Caves Road. There are bush cabins for hire and a picnic area here. The road now leaves the Great Dividing Range and begins the steep, winding descent of 'Five Mile Hill'. Eight km brings you to **Jenolan Caves** and **Caves House**. Drive through the *Grand Arch* to spacious parking areas up the hill. A number of caves are open for inspection; there are tours daily at regular intervals, taking between 1½ and 2 hours. Obtain details from the Ticket and Information Office.

Walking tracks are: *Carlotta Track* (1.2 km), *McKeown's Track* (3 km), *River Track* (5 km), *Weir Track* (1 km). *Nature trails* are also laid out along points of geological, botanical and ecological interest. The head of the *Six Foot Track* is opposite the Caves House entrance.

Halfway House — Hampton

The Halfway House at Hampton was so named for being halfway between the railway at Mount Victoria and the Jenolan Caves. It was a welcome resting place when charabancs used to carry sightseers to the caves, and it is a pleasant stopping place today.

Jenolan Caves — Discovery and Development

The first white man known to have entered the caves was James McKeown, an escaped convict who was also a bushranger. He had built a hut in McKeown's Valley near to the caves, and used one of the caves, now known as McKeown's Hole as a retreat. About 1840 James Whalan, a property owner of the Fish River, near Oberon, had a horse stolen and tracked it to McKeown's Valley. He brought the mounted trooper from Hartley, and together they captured McKeown. When taking their captive back to Hartley, Whalan saw the immense opening of one of the arches in the limestone as they rode by. Charles Whalan, his brother, was interested in the report and explored the arches. He eventually discovered the caves and was delighted with their magnificent formations. He continued to search for new caves and enjoyed taking his friends to see their beauties. Their fame soon spread and visitors not only explored the caves but also took many pieces away with them. The caves were being destroyed.

At last the Government took action and in 1867 appointed a guide and caretaker, Jeremiah Wilson, with the title of 'Keeper of the Binda Caves'. The name was changed to Jenolan, Aboriginal for 'high mountain' in 1884. Another Aboriginal name for the caves area was Binoomea.

When visitors let Wilson know they were coming, he met them at Tarana Railway Station, four stops beyond Bowenfels on the line to Bathurst. He drove them in buggies through Oberon as far as the road would allow and they then had to walk the last steep descent to the caves. They were provided with candles, with holders to catch the drips, but otherwise little had been done to make viewing the caves an easy matter. It was a visit of high adventure, as well as an artistic feast. The night was spent camping in the Grand Arch in minimum comfort. In 1869 a dancing platform was built, by subscription, in the Grand Arch. It has long since disappeared.

Gradually over the period of 33 years while Jeremiah Wilson was caretaker, improvements were made in access to the caves, and in ease of viewing the formations. Rope ladders were replaced with steel ones, steps were cut and built up with concrete, handrails were added, formations were protected with wire netting, dangerous places were bridged over and sealed off. New entrances were cut into the Lucas and Imperial caves and strong doors set in to protect the caves. Electric light was installed in 1887, the installation being upgraded over the years, with lights extended to more of the caves.

In the late 1880s the road from Mount Victoria and Hartley was built and superceded the Tarana — Oberon route.

In 1884 the 'Six Foot Track' allowed horsemen to ride from Katoomba.

It took many years for all the caves now shown to the public to be discovered. The Arch Cave and the Elder Cave were discovered in the 1840s. The Lucas Cave was discovered in 1860 and was known as the New Cave until 1878, when it was renamed for John Lucas, M.L.A., who was instrumental in bringing the caves under government control. In 1879 Wilson found the Right Imperial Cave and in 1880 the Left Imperial Cave, and the Jubilee in 1893-4.

In 1903, James Wiburd, a guide since 1885 and now caretaker, with help from other guides, discovered the River Cave and then the Skeleton Cave, where the skeleton of an Aboriginal is fastened into the rock. These caves were opened for public inspection in 1905. The Temple of Baal and the Orient Cave were discovered soon afterwards.

In 1952 the Left Imperial Cave was renamed the Chifley Cave after Joseph Benedict Chifley, Prime Minister from 1945 to 1949. In 1954 a new tunnel entrance was made to the Temple of Baal and Orient Caves, and named the Binoomea Cut, at last acknowledging the Aboriginal name for the caves area.

Caves House (Nat. Tr.)

Early visitors to the Jenolan Caves camped in the Grand Arch, sleeping near the fire in their clothes, and in the morning washing in the icy stream flowing through the arch.

Jeremiah Wilson, the first official caretaker, saw the need for permanent accommodation and in 1880 built a single-storey wooden house to which additions were made from time to time. Some years later he put up a wooden two-storey guest house to accommodate 30 visitors. Fire destroyed it in 1895 and a new Caves House was built of limestone a few years later. This is the central portion of the present building, which took shape from a two-storey wing added in 1907 and a four-storey part built between 1914 and 1918. The dining room came into use in 1916, when electric lighting was installed, and a large reservoir to supply house and grounds was completed in 1920.

2 Kanangra Walls

The lookout at *Kanangra Walls* is about 32 km south of Jenolan Caves, the road following the Kanangra Range. The road is unsealed.

KANANGRA WALLS LOOK-OUT gives magnificent views of the walls and also of the extremely wild country to the north and east, with *Kanangra Grand Gorge*, edged by *Mount High and Mighty, Mount Stormbreaker* and *Mount Cloudmaker*.

KANANGRA TOPS WALKING TRACK starts from the car park at the end of Kanangra Walls Road. A short descent takes you to a large rock overhang, supposed to have once housed a dancing platform for drovers' parties. It is only a short climb onto the Tops, where the track leads off in an easterly direction, later turning south. It takes 1 to 2 hours to cross the Tops and return by the same track. This track continues on to the Kowmung River, and is for experienced bushwalkers only beyond the Tops. There are views to the north and east, from the Tops, towards the *Megalong and Jamison Valleys*, and of the western escarpment of the Blue Mountains Plateau. But the views to the south are more to our purpose here. On the skyline is *Byrnes Gap*, in the *Colong Maze*. Barrallier came up from the south-east through this gap, and crossed most of the country between it and the Tops, before he was halted by the falls that bear his name — on Middle Christys Creek, a few km south-west of where you are standing.

As you look at this wild scenery, think of the early explorers who attempted these wild paths to the south of the Blue Mountains Plateau as we have seen it:

George Bass, 1796, north-west from Camden,
John Wilson, 1798, south and south-west from Camden,
Francis Barrallier, 1802, west from Camden and Nattai.

George Bass (1771-c. 1803)

George Bass came to Australia as surgeon on the H.M.S. *Reliance* and accompanied Matthew Flinders on a number of explorations by sea. They are remembered as the discoverors of Bass Strait, and for their circumnavigation of Van Diemen's Land (Tasmania).

Between voyages, Bass turned his attention to land exploration. He accompanied Governor Hunter and

Kanangra Walls and Kanangra Deep

Barrallier's Falls on Middle Christys Creek, south-west of Kanangra Walls

others to the Cowpastures, near Camden, and in the following year, 1796, he attempted to cross the mountains. He had some idea of the problems he would have to face and in preparation he had special scaling irons and hooks made, for use with long rope ladders to help in climbing the sheer rocky cliffs he expected to meet. No map from Bass's hand has come to light, although Flinders, who certainly had a first hand account of

Bass's journey, has marked the route as starting from Mount Hunter, to the west of Camden, and proceeding slightly north of west for 28 miles (45 km) 'beyond which the mountains were impassable'. Steepness of the cliffs and lack of water made him turn back, his attempt lasting 15 days. As in all the early trips of exploration, the necessity of carrying all provisions was an extremely restrictive factor. It is thought that he probably crossed country now drowned by Lake Burragorang, and penetrated far enough to be able to see the Kanangra Range in the distance.

It has been suggested by some that Bass struggled up the Grose River valley to Mount Banks, but the route inland from Mount Hunter, just described, seems a better fit to the meagre evidence.

John Wilson (d. 1800)

Convicted in 1785 in Lancashire, England, for stealing cloth to the value of tenpence, John Wilson was sentenced to transportation for seven years and arrived in Port Jackson in the *Alexander* with the First Fleet in 1788. After serving his sentence, he took to the bush and lived with the Aborigines, thereby gaining an extensive knowledge of the country round Sydney.

In 1798 John Wilson led a number of Irish convicts in search of a mythical inland settlement. John Price, Governor Hunter's servant, was of the party; his diary records their experiences but lacks details of the course. Wilson and companions may have reached the Wingecarribee River, or possibly even one of the headwaters of the Lachlan, thereby crossing the Great Divide. Their route appears to have skirted the southern edge of the Blue Mountains National Park area. No notice was taken of their report, and the diary was lost for many years.

Francis Barrallier (1772-1853)

Barrallier was the son of a French naval surveyor employed by the British after the capture of Toulon in 1793. He came to New South Wales with Governor King and, failing to be appointed deputy-surveyor-general, was employed by King as an architect and engineer. In the course of his work he showed talent for exploring and, although Colonel Paterson of the New South Wales Corps, to which by this time he had been appointed Ensign, demanded his attention to military duties, King appointed him his aide-de-camp and sent him on an embassy to the 'King of the Mountains'.

From a base camp at Nattai, a place he had previously discovered, Barrallier set out on 5 November 1802 with four soldiers and five convicts. At the beginning they had Aboriginal guides, but before long, owing to a misunderstanding, they parted company. Although the explorers followed the directions given to them, or so they thought, it was not good enough. The route they took lay across country since drowned by Lake Burragorang, passed Yeranderie, then went through Byrne's Gap and over numerous ridges to the Kowmung River and its junction with Christys Creek. Snakes, shell fossils, waterfalls and pools of water with steep rock sides all help to identify this area as the end of Barrallier's attempt. When their boots were worn out, their stock of food low, and their energy and enthusiasm at a low ebb, there was nothing for it but to turn back. A waterfall 100 metres high with a mountain of rock towering up behind it concealed entirely the fact that just beyond it, within a day's march, was the top of the Great Divide.

The area Barrallier reached is not far south-west of Kanangra Walls.

11 To the Foothills — Belmont and Vale Lookout

1 Belmont on Richmond Hill

Travel from Sydney to Richmond via the Windsor Road or through Blacktown and cross the Hawkesbury River over the **North Richmond Bridge.** The river was deeper when Governor Arthur Phillip passed this point.

At North Richmond turn left along Grose Vale Road. After about 2 km, on the left, is **Richmond Hill** on which stands the magnificent building of ST JOHN OF GOD HOSPITAL. About 1 km along the driveway is the car park. As this is private property, anyone wishing to see more than an out-side view should make arrangements beforehand to be shown over it. This is well worth doing.

The first settler in this area was **Archibald Bell** who built the **First Belmont. Sir Phillip Charley** built the **Present Belmont**.

North Richmond Bridge

Governor Arthur Phillip, first Governor of the Colony, passed the site of the present bridge in June 1789, during his voyage of discovery through Broken Bay and up the Hawkesbury River. He went only a little further upstream to the branching of the Nepean and Grose Rivers.

The bridge is the second one built on this location. The stumps of the piers of the earlier one could, until recently, be seen downstream.

The old ferry used for the crossing could not handle the increasing traffic of the gold rush days and the first bridge was completed in 1860. Silting of the river caused frequent covering of the bridge by floodwaters and it was replaced in 1902. In 1926 the Richmond to Kurrajong Line was built and the bridge also carried the train, variously known as 'The Apricot Express' or 'Pansy', until the railway closed in 1952 after damage from wash-aways.

The Hawkesbury River, spanned by the bridge at North Richmond was so named by Governor Phillip in honour of Charles Jenkinson, Baron Hawkesbury, who was President of the Council of Trade and Plantations at that time.

The Aboriginal name for the river is thought to be Deerubin or Deerabubbin.

Richmond Hill

After naming the Carmarthen and Lansdowne Hills, Governor Phillip's report continues, 'A mountain between I called Richmond Hill and from the rising of these mountains I do not doubt but that a large river would be found ...' So wrote Phillip after his exploration of the north shore of Sydney Harbour in May 1788.

His boat journey up that river in June 1789 ended at Richmond Hill, where the party landed, walked to its top and later described the soil as good. The hill was named for the Duke of Richmond, a man of influence in the English government of the day.

Archibald Bell (1773-1837)

Lieutenant Archibald Bell and his family arrived in New South Wales in 1807 aboard the *Young William*. Bell bought the Richmond Hill property from John Bowman, to whom it had been granted in 1803. Bell was later granted a further 200 hectares adjoining his purchase. He named the property Belmont and established a flourishing farm with the aid of convict and 'ticket-of-leave' labour. A friend of Governor Macquarie and of the Reverend Samuel Marsden, Bell became a magistrate and earned a reputation for strict enforcement of the law.

Bell was sent to England as a witness at Major Johnson's trial and was thought by some to have been implicated in the rebellion against Governor Bligh, but it seems that Governor Macquarie did not think so as the Governor confirmed his grants, and visited Mrs Bell at 'Belmont' in 1810 at a time when his lands were officially confiscated. Bell's interest in politics continued after his return and in 1832 he was appointed to the Legislative Council, holding the seat until his death in 1837.

Bell's second son, also named Archibald, explored the countryside, and with the help of native guides, discovered the route across Mount Tomah. The young man did this in 1823, at the age of nineteen. Bell's Line of Road, the alternative main road to Lithgow, now runs along this route.

Mount Bell, which the road crosses, and the railway station and village of Bell on the Darling Causeway are also named after him.

Belmont

The first 'Belmont' homestead was of timber, and was replaced by a stone building in 1834, but only the foundation stone is left today. Following the bank failures of 1849 the Bell family was forced to sell the property, which was then divided into smaller holdings. Henry Newcomen bought the 'Belmont' home portion in 1860, demolished the house and rebuilt twice on the site. His second house was pulled down to make way for the present mansion in 1889.

Philip Charley (1863-1938) and the Present Belmont Park

Philip Charley was born at Ballarat, Victoria, and left home to work in Melbourne as an office boy in a law firm. Later he joined a syndicate to prospect on Broken Hill. Charley was not satisfied when the other men thought the lead ore too low a grade for mining, and had samples analysed. Traces of silver were discovered and the 'Syndicate of Seven' established the Broken Hill Company.

Now a wealthy man, Charley bought the Newcomen property at North Richmond, called it 'Belmont Park', and developed a horse and cattle stud there. He imported English Hackney and Coach horses, Red Polled and Hereford cattle and Lincoln and Shropshire sheep. He married, and in 1892 spent the then tremendous sum of £38 000 on building this most splendid mansion standing on the old Richmond Hill.

Steps of imported Italian marble lead up to the verandah and vestibule, where the fine mosiac floor is crossed by two broad passages. There are fifteen large main rooms, many featuring beautiful fireplaces, magnificent woodwork, and in the library elegant carved bookcases cover one wall. *Home Magazine,* in the issue of 26 February 1949 described a sun parlour where sheets of plate glass could be let down into the cellar. In the 1890s, it said, this was used for amateur theatricals and the audience gathered in the stone courtyard. There was also an Italian bathroom of dark marble and tiles, several large glass domed bedrooms, a billiard room and a grotto and fern house in the garden. Aspects of English, French and Italian architecture have been incorporated in the building, executed by artisans brought to Australia for the purpose. The resulting Victorian home is now part of the National Trust.

In the depression years Major Philip Charley lost his wealth and his beautiful home. After years of neglect, the Order of St John of God bought the property in 1951 and there established a hospital. The house is being restored.

2 Vale Lookout

Return to Grose Vale Road and turn left along it, and then right where it forks with Grose Wold Road. Pass through the village of Grose Vale and turn left into Cabbage Tree Road, the first km of which is sealed; the second is gravel. At the turn-around at the end, park and walk along a short track, through bushes, in their season, covered with yellow pea-flowers (*Pultenaea* and *Dillwynia*) and white rice flowers (*Pimelia*) scattered among the taller wattles, casuarinas and eucalypts. This is *Vale Lookout,* with a view up the Grose River Valley. In the deep gorge below are pools of blue water, the streams supplying them cutting great gashes in the mountains, the lower slopes greeny-blue with eucalypts, perpendicular sandstone cliffs towering above. There are several lookout points and it is worth while scrambling about the rocks to see the view from all angles. Vale Lookout is so called from the poem by Thomas Moore (1779-1852), *Vale of Avoca*, the name given to the Grose Valley downstream of the Lookout.

The first explorer of this narrow valley was **William Paterson** who thought it might be a gateway to the interior. Some sixty years later the **Engineers Track** was made to facilitate a survey of the valley as a possible route for a railway.

Return along Cabbage Tree Road, and at Grose Vale Road turn left for **Kurrajong.** In Kurrajong Park notice the mill stones from the 19th century flour mill in Little Wheeny Creek. The road on the right goes past **St Gregory's Roman Catholic Church.** The road on the left takes you to

View of Grose River and Grose Head
South from Vale Lookout

VALE LOOKOUT

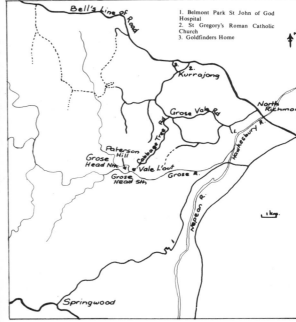

1. Belmont Park St John of God Hospital
2. St Gregory's Roman Catholic Church
3. Goldfinders Home

St John of God Hospital, Richmond
Hill. View from Grose Vale Road.

North Richmond Bridge. Piers of the earlier bridge.

Little Wheeny Creek and the former **Goldfinders Home,** a private residence now restored. Both these routes take you to Bell's Line of Road.

Turn left for Kurrajong Heights and right for Sydney.

William Paterson (1755-1810)

Paterson arrived in the colony in 1791, at that stage being a captain in the New South Wales Corps. He had previously been to South Africa and had published an account of his explorations there 'into the land of the Hottentot'. So it was natural for him to look for some unknown area to explore in this land new to Europeans.

Governor Phillip, on his Hawkesbury exploration, had been prevented by rapids from taking his boats upriver from Richmond Hill. Paterson got over this problem by taking with him light canoes which he used for the shallower waters of the Grose River. He and his party were able to manhandle these light craft over rapids and waterfalls, at least five being counted, for about sixteen kilometres up the river, possibly reaching the junction of Wentworth Creek with the Grose. They called the mountain they could see ahead of them, as they worked their way upstream, 'Harrington Peak', but this spot is hard to identify and does not appear on modern maps. When the level of water rose following a thunderstorm, their troubles were increased, especially by large rocks in the river bed and submerged branches of fallen trees. When their canoes were damaged, they most advisedly gave up, for we know today that heavy rain can make the Grose valley a dangerous place.

In his honour the peak on the right hand or northern side of the gap has been named Paterson Hill and the ridge running north to join Bell Range, Paterson Range.

From boyhood Paterson had been interested in botany and had collected specimens for Sir Joseph Banks while in Africa, from Norfolk Island and from Van Diemen's land during a subsequent tour of duty. As he found a number of new plants in the Grose valley, he was not entirely displeased with his excursion, in spite of failure to gain its objective.

He named the river after Lieutenant-Governor Francis Grose, who had supported and encouraged Paterson's attempt at the mountain crossing.

The Engineers Track

When an extension of the railway to the west of New South Wales was under consideration, it was suggested that the Grose valley would provide an easy grade with a tunnel through Darling's Causeway to Hartley. In 1857 the Royal Engineers were instructed to make a trial survey. After the preliminary survey, when it was discovered how very rough the terrain was, it was decided to make a track along the length of the valley so there would be easy access to obtain any information not recorded on the first survey. Mr Whitton, Engineer-in-Chief for Railways, supervised the work which was carried out by the Royal Engineers under Sergeant Quodling, with ten men doing the surveying and taking levels, and forty-nine labourers employed on the heavier work of making the track. In spite of more optimistic expectations, the track and survey were not completed till March 1860, almost three years being spent on it, as most of the track had to be cut out of the rocky sides of the gorge.

And after all, it was decided that the Grose valley route was impracticable! As we know, the railway followed the ridge south of the Grose to Mount Victoria, then diverging along the Darling Causeway to wind down into Lithgow via the famous 'Great Zigzag'.

The Engineers Track was neglected over the years, only being used by a few, such as botanist Louisa Atkinson, whose article 'The Ranges of the Grose' was one of her series 'A Voice From the Country', published in *The Sydney Morning Herald* in the early 1860s. Louisa found the track already damaged in many places by floods, and in some sections they were only able to negotiate it because the level of the water was low, it being a dry season. Her party attempted to climb out of the valley in the region of Springwood, but failed owing to the roughness of the ridges. Named for her are Louisa Hill and Atkinson Gully.

After a further hundred years or more of flood and fire, the track has disappeared for much of the length of the valley.

Kurrajong

An interesting book by Vivienne Webb, *Kurrajong, an Early History,* tells us that early spellings were Curryjong, Kurry Jung, Koryong and Corrygong.

Old Bell's Line of Road passes through the village, but through traffic is diverted along a modern highway.

St Gregory's Roman Catholic Church

Settlement spread out from Green Hills (now Windsor) and from Richmond across the river quite early in the eighteen hundreds and the population was sufficient by 1834 for the building of the first church in the district on this site. The building served as both school and church for many years. The church you see was erected in 1904, to replace the older structure.

Goldfinders Home

Built in 1851, the name reminds us that the inn was built to take advantage of the sudden increase in traffic to the gold diggings in the west, particularly the Turon diggins. The early Kurrajong racecourse was nearby. Later the inn was used by drovers bringing their cattle over Bell's Line of Road. There were resting paddocks for the cattle.

In 1860 the Wheeny Creek Post Office was opened in this building and there were three mail deliveries a week.

Now, under private ownership as a residence, the old inn is being renovated after years of neglect.

St Gregory's Roman Catholic Church, Kurrajong

Goldfinder's Home Kurrajong

12 The Carmarthen Hills — Bell's Line of Road

1 Kurrajong Heights

Bell's Line of Road, or Highway 184, begins at North Richmond Bridge and follows an easy grade to Kurrajong. From there it rises steeply. Up on the hill to the left, nestling among the trees, is NORTH KURRAJONG PRIMARY SCHOOL built in 1882. Climb *Bellbird Hill*, aptly named for its inhabitants, the Bell-miner (*Manorina melanophrys*), whose ting-ting-ting like a temple gong can be heard when the traffic is quiet. Clearing of scrub in this area threatened the habitat of this lovely bird, but fortunately there is still enough bush for the colony to shelter in and their numbers appear to be increasing rather than decreasing. In its season you will see wattle blossom and prolific yellow gorse (*Pultenaea flexilis*).

Where the passing lane begins, turn left into Bellbird Avenue and right into Stanley Avenue to *Powell Park*, named for early settlers. There are barbecue facilities here and the panorama of the Sydney plain spreads out before you. Look for the **Monument to Louisa Atkinson,** a sandstone boulder in a bushland setting, appropriate for a botanist.

Return to Bell's Line of Road. On the right is *Bellbird Hill Reserve* with another splendid view. On a clear day the city 'matchboxes' stand upright, and even the harbour bridge can be made out by the long-sighted. A Rotary Club reserve, with toilet facilities.

Continuing up the main road you reach Kurrajong Heights village. On the left are ST JAMES' CHURCH OF ENGLAND built in 1889. ST DAVID'S PRESBYTERIAN CHURCH, constructed by Charles Holdsworth in 1886. It has beautiful cedar fittings. KURRAJONG HEIGHTS POST OFFICE, pre-fabricated in England and shipped to Australia. **Lochiel House,** an art gallery and craft shop, open Thursday to Monday, 10 a.m. to 5 p.m. Turn left into **Wark's Hill Road** on the line of the early road route over the Heights. On the right is *Le Pressoir.* On the left is *The Opal Museum* with its large collection of Queensland boulder opal. Beyond it is **Belmore Lodge.** At the top of the hill, turn left along Burralow Road. On the left is *Cherry Park* (private property). At the top of the hill, not far from the house, is **Scott's Stone** marking the top of **Knight Hill**, thought to be the spot reached by Captain Tench and Lieutenant William Dawes in 1791. Tench named it for Sergeant Isaac Knight.

From the end of Burralow Road a fire trail leads down into Burralow Swamp. There the track to the right

KURRAJONG HEIGHTS

1. Kurrajong North Public School
2. Old Bell's Line of Road
3. Monument to Louisa Atkinson
4. St James Church of England
5. St David's Presbyterian Church
6. Site of 'Fernhurst', now demolished
7. Kurrajong Heights Post Office
8. Lochiel House
9. Opal Museum
10. Belmore Lodge
11. Scott's Stone

Lochiel House, Kurrajong Heights

Monument to Louisa Atkinson,
Powell Park, Kurrajong Heights

St David's, Uniting Church in
Australia, Kurrajong Heights

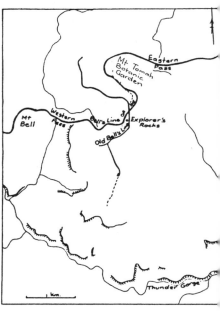

MOUNT TOMAH

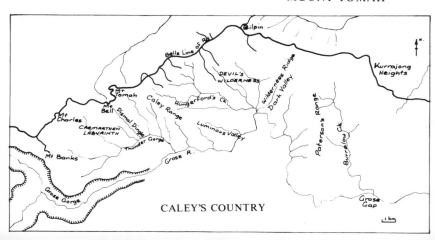

CALEY'S COUNTRY

leads to Bell's Line of Road near the *Fruit Bowl,* about 6½ km away. The left hand track leads up to Bowen Mount, named for an early settler, **G. M. C. Bowen.** The distance from Burralow Road to Bowen Mount is about 6 km. The condition of the fire trails varies, usually being open to 4 WD vehicles, but before venturing on them other than on foot, it would be wise to check with the police or the volunteer bushfire brigade captain. Return to Burralow Road.

Louisa Atkinson (1834-1872)

Caroline Louisa Waring Atkinson was the youngest daughter of James Atkinson, who wrote *An Account of the State of Agriculture and Grazing in New South Wales* in 1826, a publication which became an authority for intending migrants of the day and a mine of information for modern researchers into that period.

Although Louisa was born in the Berrima district and also died there, she spent most of her productive life at Kurrajong Heights, where she lived with her mother at 'Fernhurst', a residence now demolished. She became a botanist of note, and scientists such as Mr W. Macleay, for whom the Macleay Museum, University of Sydney, is named, Baron Von Mueller, Government botanist of Victoria, and the Reverend William Woolls, of Richmond, counted her among their friends. With Mrs Selkirk, of Richmond, she explored far and wide, both ladies wearing male attire, very practical but rather daring at that time. Her articles describing these botanical rambles were published in the *Sydney Morning Herald* in the 1860s under the title 'A Voice from the Country'. They have recently been collected and re-published by Mulini Press, of Canberra. She also wrote a number of novels, including *Gertrude, the Emigrant Child* and *Cowanda or the Veteran's Grant.*

The Kurrajong Heights Garden Club erected the monument in Powell Park to her in 1979, and also for the occasion produced a booklet about her life and work, entitled *Louisa Atkinson of the Kurrajong* by J. M. Smail.

Lochiel House

Lochiel House was built possibly as early as the 1820s. Its walls are of hand-hewn hardwood and the floor is sandstone. The original shingles are still there under the corrugated iron roof. It was built by Joseph Douglass who obtained the grant of land in 1825. It was for many years an accommodation house, being advertised in the *Sydney Morning Herald,* 4 July 1851, as 'Ivy Lodge — tea, a comfortable bed, breakfast, stabling and fodder for a horse all for 5/-'.

In those early times Kurrajong Heights was called after the settler, Douglass's Hill, or alternatively, the Big Hill, or Picture Hill, as you can easily understand after attaining the lookouts at the top.

Late owners of Ivy Lodge were Dr James Cameron, a doctor of divinity, and his brother, Dr Andrew Cameron, a doctor of medicine, who renamed it Lochiel House after the place in their native Scotland. For a short time Lochiel House was a post office, then a private residence for many years and now an art gallery.

Wark's Hill Road and the First Line of Road

The first road was built in the 1830s and 1840s when pick and shovel were the only tools used on minor roads and side cutting was difficult. The roads tended to go straight up the hills. Wark's Road was one of these places. Bell-bird Hill was another, the original line following an undeviating line on the other side of the Rotary Reserve from today's zigzag curves.

On the western side of Kurrajong Heights a zigzag was necessary to negotiate the steepness of the hill. A small section of an original convict-built retaining wall still remains and can be found by scrambling over the hillside. Side cutting was done there, and the name *The Cut Rock* was used as early as 1834, when Mrs Felton Mathew, wife of a surveyor, described the roughness of the road in her diary.

A local landholder, William Wark, gave his name to the eastern side of the hill. The road was often the scene of the finish of motor reliability trials in the 1930s.

A later line of road on the western escarpment curved to the south; it fell into disuse when the first cutting was made on the northern end of the Cut Rock Spur; it was used again as a deviation while improvements to today's road were in progress during World War II. Today the road winds through the gap in the Kurrajong Heights Range, hugging the man-made cliff which stands out to the observer standing on Mount Tomah as a great gash.

All these roads converged at the bottom of the hill to follow the same line along Bell's Range.

Belmore Lodge

This is an imposing sandstone house, and was built for Mr Wright of Hunter's Hill in 1866. It held a licence for a short while in 1900 and later was one of the many Kurrajong Heights boarding houses for holiday guests. It is now a restaurant and music centre.

Scott's Stone, Kurrajong Heights

In Cherry Park is a trig station, known as Scott's Stone, the original having been erected in 1860 by Canon William Scott, the first Government Astronomer, and warden of St Paul's College at Sydney University. Canon Scott built a cottage on 80 acres (about 32 hectares) at Kurrajong Heights and retired there in 1892.

A more modern trig stands next to the old one.

Knight Hill

Captain Watkin Tench and his party in 1891 could have reached Kurrajong Heights or Bowen Mount, the latter being more directly west of Richmond Hill. Of this journey, Tench writes,

'We set out on this expedition on May 24, 1791, and having reached the opposite side of the mouth of the Creek (South Creek) which had in our last journey prevented our progress, we proceeded from there up to Richmond Hill by the river side, mounted it, slept at its foot, and on the following day penetrated some miles westward, or inland of it, until we were stopped by a mountainous country, which our scarcity of provisions, joined to the terror of a river at our back, whose sudden rising is almost beyond computation, hindered us from exploring. To the elevation which bounded our research we gave the name of Knight Hill, in honour of the trusty serjeant who had been the faithful and indefatigable companion of all our travels.'

George Meares Countess Bowen (1803-1889)

Bowen Mount is named for an early settler, George Meares Countess Bowen. Lieutenant Bowen arrived in Port Jackson in the *Midas* in 1827 in command of a detachment of the 39th Regiment. After working in the Surveyor-General's office, he obtained, in 1828, a grant of 2 560 acres near Mount Tomah, Bowen said,

'I got 15 convicts assigned to me and plunged into the wilderness. It was a wilderness indeed. This wild tract was named by the Aboriginal natives "Bulgamatta", a compound of mountain and water and very descriptive since it included both high ridges and very deep ravines with never failing running streams. It was a solitary retreat with no near neighbours and about 25 miles from police protection. The choice was decidedly injudicious for though the soil was moderately fertile, so heavy was the timber and so expensive the carriage of heavy produce to a market that any experienced colonist would have predicted with certainty my ultimate failure.'

After five or six years, Bowen sold his Berambing estate and later bought land at Bowen Mount and in his twenty years there was more successful. It is even suggested that he may have planted what would have been the first rice crop in Australia in Burralow Swamp.

2 Caley's Country

The sketch map shows the ridge between the Grose and Colo Rivers, along which Bell's 'native guides' conducted him, and also the part of the Grose valley through which Caley struggled to Mount Banks. Before leaving Burralow Road, try to catch a glimpse through the trees of the tangled mass of ridges and gullies stretching away to the skyline of round basalt-capped mountains towards which Caley was attempting to make his way.

George Caley went down into the gullies. Take the easier route found by **Archibald Bell Junior.** Return via Wark's Hill Road to Bell's Line of Road and turn left to travel westwards.

Note as you descend from Kurrajong Heights, *The Cut Rock*. The road crosses the geological fault here. Today Bell's route through Bilpin is lined with orchards, apple in the main, with a few of peach and plum. Once oranges were grown here, but the climate proved too cold and the fruit could not compete with that grown at Kurrajong and elsewhere.

The fruit stall is part of the scene, and

at harvest time, January to May, almost every orchard opens its stall and fruit straight from the trees is available. Some more permanent stalls are the *Fruit Bowl* — also provides trout fishing and a picnic and barbecue area, and *The Pines,* both not far from the fire trail to Burralow Swamp.

Somewhere about here, within a km or two is the spot where Bell and his party pitched camp in 1823. Perhaps Allan Cunningham the botanist also had his base camp hereabouts.

At the village of Bilpin, branching off to the right, is the road to MOUNTAIN LAGOON. *The Ivy Inn* provides refreshments. About a km further on, also on the right, is the road to **Mount Tootie.**

The next turn-off, again on the right, will take you to *Mount Irvine* and *Mount Wilson* via Bowen's Creek Road, very winding and narrow. The scenery is spectacular, but the gravel road is often not trafficable.

On the western side of Bilpin other stalls are *Apple Trees Store* and *Miller's* (distinctive windmill sails).

The land from here to the foot of Mount Tomah was settled by **The Veterans** and G. M. C. Bowen, of Bowen Mount.

A km past Miller's, at the end of Valley Ridges Road on the left, is the **Waratah Native Garden** part of the Blue Mountains National Park. This is a pleasant picnic and barbecue area, with a walking track down to a little waterfall in a refreshing rainforest gully.

The road then crosses Caley Ridge, where the explorer struggled up out of the gorges. On the right is *Berambing Park* a picnic and barbecue area. Toilet facilities.

Then back to the main road and turn west towards Mount Tomah.

George Caley (1770-1829)

George Caley was born in Yorkshire, England, the son of a horsedealer. After four years at Manchester Free Grammar School, he was apprenticed to his father's farriery. In an age which saw the development of steam power and electricity and the publication of James Cook's journals of discovery, Caley was not satisfied with his life. He became interested in the study of botany as a hobby, and requested the help of Sir Joseph Banks to obtain employment in this field. Sir Joseph, well known for his assistance to many men of talent, arranged for Caley to work at Chelsea Gardens and later at Kew Gardens. When Mungo Park, explorer of the River Niger in Africa, declined Banks' offer to go to New South Wales to explore the country there and collect botanical and other specimens, the position was offered to Caley. After many delays, Caley arrived in the colony in 1799, on the *Speedy*, the ship which brought Governor King to replace Governor Hunter.

Caley wrote long letters to Banks about life in the new settlement and Banks expressed appreciation at learning about events from someone not attached to the government. Governor King and the Reverend Samuel Marsden both found Caley a difficult man to get on with, and Banks wrote to smooth things over and asked Governor King to let Caley go his own way, that he (Caley) was a wild man, but that Banks expected to get good service from him because he was hardworking. On another occasion Banks wrote of Caley, 'Had he been born a gentleman, he would have been shot long ago in a duel'. Robert Brown, also a protege of Banks, and the naturalist accompanying Matthew Flinders in the *Investigator*, said of Caley that he was an assiduous and accurate botanist.

Although Caley's duties were mainly to collect specimens, he was also to explore the country as opportunity arose. He made a number of journeys.

In November 1804 Caley set out to cross the Blue Mountains. He anticipated success where others had failed and completely underestimated the difficulties he would encounter.

Caley was accompanied by three ticket-of-leave convicts, described as 'three of the strongest men in the colony'. They carried three weeks' provisions and were to travel on foot, as Caley had decided that the terrain would be too difficult for horses. They crossed the Hawkesbury River at Richmond Terrace and, heading Little Wheeny Creek at Kurrajong, surmounted Kurrajong Heights to the south of the present road.

Their first camp was in the valley of Burralow Creek, which Caley called 'Swamp Creek'. There his men managed to set fire to the bush in their inexperience with Australian conditions. It needed quick action to save their camping gear and supplies.

Next day the party crossed Paterson Range and Brown's Ridge and camped in Dark Valley, so called by Caley, and retaining this name still. The following day they came to the almost perpendicular sides of the valley of Hungerford's Creek. After much searching, Caley and party found a way to climb down, lowering the baggage on a rope. Again much searching back and forth enabled them to cross the stream. Caley's name for this area, 'The Devil's Wilderness', expresses his feelings about it. It is thought that, though he did get down as far as the Grose River, he did not follow its course, but struggled across the rugged ranges to the north. The place they camped in that night he named Luminous Valley, because he had awakened in the night to see what he thought were stars, and then discovered they were luminous grubs on the rocky ledge above his head.

The following day, their fourth, they climbed out beside Pincushion Hill and followed the top of the watershed now called Caley's Ridge. This brought them near to the foot of 'Fern Tree Hill' (Mount Tomah).

On the fifth day, after some false starts, Caley found the saddle crossing the headwaters of Bowen's and Tomah Creeks and climbed onto his objective. Mount Banks, his next goal, seemed only a short distance away in a direct line. After camping on Tomah South at 'Station Rock', he set out to cross the country in between but found a 'dreadful chasm', with perpendicular sides, 'as if hewn by a chisel', across his path. Rocks thrown down took a long time to reach the bottom. We now know that Caley had stumbled across the top of part of the Carmarthen Labyrinth. Today the most intrepid bushwalkers* take ropes and climbing gear to get up and down into these canyons, and inflatable mattresses to help them through the icy waters of Carmarthen Brook. This is one part of the mountains to keep the name given to

*Three drowned in flash floods, January 1982.

it by Governor Phillip on 15 May 1788.

Fog kept Caley and his men on Tomah for another day. Then they worked their way round the mountain and down into 'Dismal Dingle', and at last up the side of square-topped 'Table Hill', (Mount Bell). Turning round the north of this mountain, they could then follow the ridge to Mount Banks, where they camped for a day.

Caley climbed to the top of Mount Banks with high hopes of seeing to the other side of the mountains, but here was another disappointment for him. All he could see was the impenetrable valley of the Grose. There was no way across and he could not see a way around it. It was left to Archibald Bell to be guided along the ridge to head the Grose and so find the track down through Hartley Vale to join Cox's Road.

Afterwards Caley described his journey as like travelling over the tops of houses in a town. One of his men, seeing a crow overhead, said that it must be lost or it would never stay in such a place! They arrived back at Parramatta after six days from Mount Banks with very few provisions left, which confirmed Caley's wisdom in turning back at that point. The monument on Mount Banks has been erected by the Blue Mountains National Park to record this furthest extent of his attempted crossing of the mountains.

Archibald Bell, Junior (1804-1883)

Mount Bell, Bell village, Bell Range, Bell's Line of Road and even Bilpin, which appeared as 'Belpin' in an early Post Office Directory, are all so called to commemorate the discoveries of Archibald Bell, Junior.

Bell's Line of Road, apart from several diversions to gradients better suited to today's traffic, follows the route taken by Bell and his native guides in 1823.

Second son of Lieutenant Archibald Bell, of Belmont at North Richmond, Archibald Junior, at the age of nineteen, set out with native guides to cross the mountains in August 1823. The crossing to the south of the Grose was already ten years old, but the steep descent at Mount York always created difficulty for travellers, and Bell was stimulated to find a new and possibly better track. On that first ocasion he got no further than Mount Tomah, where neither he nor his guides could find a way down the western side.

A month later he made a second attempt and found the western saddle connecting Tomah with Mount Bell. He followed the ridge over Mount Charles, beside Mount Banks, and around the head of the Grose, passing the spot where Bell Railway Station now stands. He found a route down into Hartley Vale to join the western road, then called Cox's, near where Collits' Inn had just been built, three or four miles, as he said, this side of Cox's River.

Bell's diary, recently presented to the Mitchell Library by his descendants and published in the Journal of the Royal Australian Historical Society, tells of trees of great size and very thick 'brush' through which they had to cut their way. He reported on the fertile soil of the Bilpin area and the lush growth of tree fern and rain forest on Mount Tomah. He also noted the comparative barrenness of the range from Tomah to the head of the Grose. Compared with Caley's journey, Bell's was an easy one. Only his horses suffered from pushing through the undergrowth.

Immediately after his return from showing the route to Assistant-Surveyor Hoddle, Bell set out for the Hunter Valley, following the recently discovered route of Howe and Singleton. He discovered Singleton dying of starvation at Patrick Plains. This expedition won him a grant of 1000 acres near Singleton. He built a two-storey stone house on his estate, 'Corinda', being one of the earliest settlers in that area. He spent the rest of his life there, dividing his time between farming, stock breeding, exploring and public affairs.

Mount Tootie

This mountain is another basalt cap, and its fertile soil has been farmed for many years. Lieutenant Frederick Bedwell, R. N., and Nicholas Garling were given the land there in 1830 by Governor Darling as a grant in trust as a dowry for Elizabeth Ward when she married Frederick Garling.

The Veterans

The land between Bilpin and the foot of Mount Tomah was surveyed and settled in the early 1830s by 10 or 12 veterans, old soldiers who had been persuaded to stay in Australia. They were supplied with rations from the general store for the first year, but when these were withdrawn, they all left the district, leaving only their names on the parish map.

Waratah Native Garden

This reserve is on the southern edge of Bowen's original grant, and backs on-to the Blue Mountains National Park. An extensive planting of native shrubs and trees was begun by Mr Frank H. Stone, whose chief interest was propagating waratahs from seed. The Society for the Propagation of Native Plants also took part in the project. In 1967 Mr Stone handed the property over to the Blue Mountains National Park. This authority has managed it since, and has made a walking track into the adjacent gully, where many water ferns adorn the banks of the stream and mosses cover the rocks. The path leads to a waterfall and rocky waterhole, a secluded and peaceful place. On our last visit one of the native mints, *Prostanthera cerulea*, was in bloom, a delicate blue mist.

3 Mount Tomah

A km past Berambing Park, the road crosses the narrow saddle of the eastern pass to **Mount Tomah**, George Caley's *Fern Tree Hill*.

At the top of the first steep rise, the road curves to the left leading to the entrance to the **Mount Tomah**

Botanic Garden, opened in 1988. This is the cold climate annex of the Royal Botanic Gardens, Sydney.

At the top of the mountain, pause on the left at the picnic area to look at THE EXPLORERS' ROCKS, a monument erected by the Mount

Tomah Society in 1973 to commemmorate the journeys of George Caley and Archibald Bell, and the work of **Robert Hoddle**, the surveyor, and **Allan Cunnningham**, the botanist (crossed Mt Tomah in 1823).

Follow Old Bell's Line up the hill from the picnic area and turn left down Charley's Road to look at the wild mountain scenery, to the east, with Caley in mind. From this southern end of the mountain he had attempted to cross straight over to Mount Banks, just visible through the trees. Then back to the main road and on westward, passing on the way over the narrow saddle on the western pass to Mount Bell. Then on to **Cave Hill** and further points west.

Robert Hoddle (1794-1881)

Robert Hoddle was the assistant-surveyor assigned to the task of surveying Archibald Bell's newly discovered route. In October 1823 he set out with Bell, two natives and five other men. In his report sent in a month later, he appeared impressed by the thickness of the 'brush' and the 'prodigious size' of the trees on Mount Tomah. He thought the line in general better than Cox's Road.

Some years later Hoddle was appointed Surveyor-General in Victoria, and designed the plan for the city of Melbourne.

Allan Cunningham (1791-1839)

Cunningham had been Assistant Manager of Kew Gardens. Sir Joseph Banks recommended him as a collector of botanical specimens and he arrived in New South Wales in 1816. When he heard of Bell's new route he decided to use it to reach Cox's River. He set out at the end of November 1823, following the line of marked trees left by Hoddle in his survey. His diary records his discovery of a wealth of new plants and he seemed satisfied with what he had achieved, even though he had to turn back at Mount Bell because there was not enough grass for his horses.

Later Cunningham explored much of northern N.S.W. and as far as the Darling Downs, Qld.

Mount Tomah

Both Caley and Allan Cunningham have left comprehensive records of the vegetation they found on the mountain and, in spite of much logging, there are still pockets of this rainforest left. Then it covered the entire mountain.

Still to be found there are the tree ferns which impressed them so much: *Dicksonia antarctica*, the soft or brown tree fern, and *Cyathea australis*, the black or rough tree fern.

Mount Tomah Botanic Garden

Part of the land grant made to Susannah Bowen in 1830, this was used as a cold climate nursery by Alfred and Effie Brunet for 30 years until it was donated to the Royal Botanic Gardens, Sydney, in the '70s.

Cave Hill

On the rockface by the cave is etched: 'The Cave Hotel by T. Shearwood', possibly an early landholder of Bilpin, Thomas Sherwood.

The walls of the cave are covered

with 'emu foot' markings made by the Aboriginal people of times long past. This cave must have been a place of religious significance as the emu was sacred to the Daruk, the people of the area.

We walked softly here, with a care for the dreamtime.

4 Mount Banks

After crossing Mount Charles, distinguishable by the trig station surmounting it, the watershed veers south-west; this perplexed Bell, who nevertheless wisely kept to the ridge, following his Aboriginal advisers. He had no need to climb Mount Banks. The turn-off to *Mount Banks* is on the left. From that point are seen the spectacular Grose Walls, which stopped Caley in his tracks.

After a km of gravel track is the *Barbecue and Picnic Area* and the MEMORIAL PLAQUE commemorating Caley's 1804 journey, donated by the Blue Mountains City Council and affixed to a large boulder. It is fitting that Caley should have appreciated his patron SIR JOSEPH BANKS by naming this mountain for him. From the picnic area there is a walking track to the top of Mount Banks and the trig station, King George. For many years Caley's name for the mountain was forgotten, and Mount King George was commonly used. Now the name Mount Banks has been reinstated in recognition of Caley's efforts.

From the top you can see the magnificent Grose Gorge across to Blackheath Walls, up the Govett's Leap Gorge, and downstream to the Mount Hay Walls. Walk along the track at the top of Explorers Range and from there you can see as far as Kolonga Walls. At one time the Blue Mountains National Park Trust had a vehicular track to the top of Mount Banks, with a picnic area there, and also a road along the top of the walls for a considerable distance towards Mount Caley, a mountain named for the explorer, but a place he did not reach. The road is now closed to vehicles at the foot of the mountain. The track is still available to walkers, and is recommended for the wonderful views of the gorge. The *Blue Gum Forest* can be seen below at the junction of Govett's Leap Creek with the Grose River.

Circling Mount Banks are **Frank Hurley Head, Edgeworth David Head** and **David Crevasse. Mount Strzelecki** is beyond Mount Caley. Return to the main road and continue westward.

Frank Hurley O.B.E. (1890-1962)

James Francis Hurley a photographer of renown, went to the south pole by sledge in 1911-14, went with Shackleton in 1914-17, was official war photographer in 1917-18, and for the British, Australian and New Zealand expeditions to Antarctica in 1932 to 1934. He did many camera studies of Australian scenery.

Professor Edgeworth David (1858-1934)

Edgeworth David Head and David Crevasse were named for this geologist of world renown. His work contributed greatly to the understanding of the geology of the Blue Mountains and it is fitting that his name should be given to features of its scenery.

The Professor had a family home at Woodford at the turn of the century.

Count Strzelecki (1797-1873)

Sir Paul Edmund de Strzelecki, geologist, mineralogist and explorer,. was born in Polish Prussia and educated in Edinburgh. He arrived in Sydney in 1838. His discovery of gold near Hartley was suppressed by Governor Gipps' order. He named Mt Kosciusko in honour of the Polish patriot.

Strzelecki recorded being trapped during a thunderstom in a cave on Mount Banks in 1839.

5 Pierce's Pass

Leaving Mount Banks, drive another km westward to Pierce's Pass turn-off. Here one can choose a walk to suit time and energy available.

The short left-hand road goes to *Walls' Lookout* car park. The track takes about 30 minutes each way to walk. The view of the gorge is spectacular and from a different angle to that seen from Mount Banks.

The road on the right takes you down to another *Car Park and barbecue area.* Toilet facilities available.

There is a choice of two walking tracks from this point. The paths are signposted. The track to *Rigby Hill* is on the left. It takes about half an hour to reach the lookout and it is well worth the effort.

The track on the right down **Pierce's Pass** leads in an hour or so to the Grose River. A further two hour walk will get you to the Blue Gum Forest. This track is the easiest one down into the Grose River Valley.

Return to the main road and turn left.

Pierce's Pass

The pass follows Pierce's Creek down to Hungerford's Gully. The track was made by Bert Pierce, of Mount Tomah, and Clarrie Hungerford, of Berambing, about 1930. The Blue Gum Forest became a reserve in 1932 and part of the Blue Mountains National Park in 1961.

The track starts off through fairly dry open forest, with a variety of sandstone country vegetation. Bird watchers will pause to look for finches, honey-eaters, treecreepers, wrens, whistlers and parrots, and with luck may see lyrebirds and whipbirds. Passing a coal seam, the track descends through dark and damp rainforest, of tall sassafras and coachwood trees. Below the rain forest is a sloping shale terrace, with its distinctive vegetation, and the ravine widens out to give a magnificent view of the Grose Valley, Blackheath Walls and the landslide scar of Burramoko Head. The layers of shale and sandstone rock, with coal

Lindfield Park (open daily), between Mount Wilson and Mount Irvine (p.170).

Steam engine at Top Points, Lithgow Zig Zag (p.178).

Blast Furnace Park, Lithgow (p.184).

View of Grose Gorge westward from the Caley monument at the foot of
Mount Banks

MOUNT BANKS

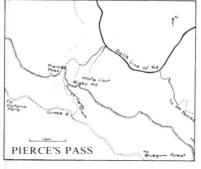

PIERCE'S PASS

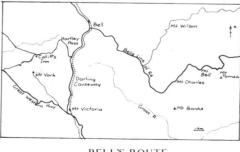

BELL'S ROUTE

seams interspersed, can be clearly seen in the cliffs. The track passes through stands of paperbark trees (*Melaleuca*) and then out onto the banks of the Grose River.

Here many deep pools are separated by huge boulders, and the marine rocks exposed are a joy to the geologist. One interesting mud stone with fossil worm tracks also contained small stones which probably fell from the bottom of glaciers and became embedded in the mud which was later pressed into rock. From this evidence it appears that the area had once been the bottom of a shallow sea, in a climate cold enough for glaciers to push down to sea level.

Crossing the river, we found the track to the Blue Gum Forest marked, a walk of five kilometres downstream, and the track leading in the other direction, upstream, to Victoria Falls and Mount Victoria.

The downstream track is open and easy for most of the way, with rougher patches as you near the Blue Gum Forest proper. There are several patches of these magnificent trees (*Eucalyptus deanei*) to be found before the main forest, which grows where Govett's Leap Creek flows into the Grose River. The forest is a lovely place, the gums tall and stately, and the forest floor covered with grass and ferns; indeed, worth the long walk.

Rules About Camping

No fires or camping are allowed at the Blue Gum Forest itself, but there is a camping area a short distance up Govett's Leap Creek at Acacia Flat. There is also a camping area in the other direction at Burra Korain Flat near Victoria Falls.

However, *NOTE WELL — A PERMIT* is required to camp. The permit is free and may be obtained by phoning or writing to the Blackheath Visitors' Centre at Govett's Leap, headquarters of the Blue Mountains National Parks and Wildlife Service.

Rubbish must be carried out, and drinking water needs to be boiled or sterilised as water in rivers and creeks may be polluted due to developments in the area.

Camping in the forest is prohibited with good reason. The future of the Blue Gum Forest depends on the conservation of an understorey which includes the Blue Gum seedlings necessary to replace the present trees when they die of old age. Unless regeneration begins now, it is likely that the forest will cease to exist in its present form within the next thirty or forty years.

Alternative Tracks Out of the Forest

From the Blue Gum Forest, the walker can climb out by way of Govett's Leap, Evans Lookout or Perry's Look-down to Blackheath, follow the track upstream to climb out near Victoria Falls, or climb out to Mount Hay Road, or even follow the Grose River itself to Faulconbridge or perhaps to Richmond. The last alternative needs much preparation and planning as the route is long and very rough and there is no track at all for much of its length. When contemplating this route, it is absolutely necessary to inform the Parks and Wildlife Service and your friends of what you have in mind. It is not a route to be taken by inexperienced bushwalkers.

6 Bell's Route Into the Vale of Clwydd

From the Pierce's Pass turn-off, the road continues north west, correcting the earlier southern diversion towards Mount Banks. The next turn-off, on the right, leads to *Mount Wilson.* Cross Flagstaff Hill and *Watertrough Hill,* and so to Bell village and the main western railway line.

Bell headed the Grose River and so, following his track, turn left and onto the road to Mount Victoria and follow it for 2 km. Then, like Bell, plunge downhill through Hartley Pass to Hartley Vale and Collits' Inn. This inn was on Cox's Road and three or four miles (about 5 km), as Bell stated, from Cox's River. He had made his crossing.

Return to Sydney may be made either through Mount Victoria and by the Great Western Highway or via Bell's Line of Road and Richmond.

Watertrough Hill (BMCC HR BL 3)

The watertrough from which the hill gets its name is beside the old road, which leads off to the left of Bell's

Watertrough, **Watertrough Hill** near Bell

Line, near Holly Lodge. This old section of the road is very overgrown; there is a walk of about a km.

The trough is only a few centimetres deep, cut out of a sandstone shelf about 60 centimetres above ground, and is filled by a continually running stream of water oozing out of the rocks above it. The date '1894' is carved into the rock.

A trough of similar design is to be seen beside the Berghofer Pass, built to assist motor traffic up Mitchell's Ridge in 1913.

Bell's Route Down Into the Vale of Clwydd

Bell's observations of the country after his party left Mount Tomah were concentrated on observing whether there was grass for his horses or not. One can understand this preoccupation. He noted that the ground was barren, as on the other road, for about five miles past Tomah. Then there began to be good grass and this continued till they joined up with Cox's Road.

Of his track into the Vale of Clwydd he writes,

'The whole of the last Day we found the Ridge on which the Bathurst Road runs on our Left Hand inclining towards us and it falls off at the Big Hill two ridges from the one which we came down.'

The road into Hartley Vale in the main follows this route.

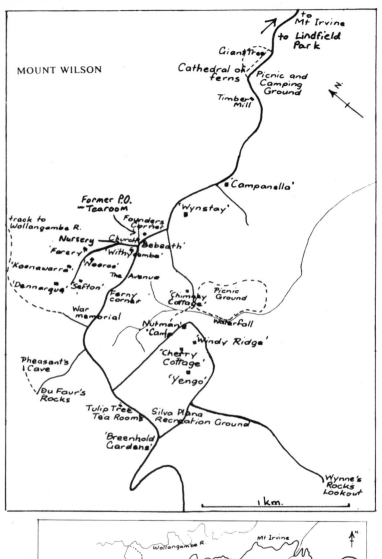

MOUNT WILSON

to Mt Irvine
to Lindfield Park

Giant Tree
Cathedral of ferns
Picnic and Camping Ground
Timber Mill

'Campanella'

Former P.O. ~Tearoom
'Wynstay'
track to Wollangambe R.
Founders Corner
Nursery
Church
'Bebeath'
'Farery'
Withycombe'
'Keenawarra'
'Neeroe'
'Dennarque'
'Sefton'
The Avenue
Ferny corner
Picnic Ground
'Chimney Cottage'
War memorial
Waterfall
Nutman's Camp
'Windy Ridge'
Pheasant's Cave
'Cherry Cottage'
'Yengo'
'Du Faur's Rocks
Tulip Tree Tea Rooms
Silva Plana Recreation Ground
'Breenhold Gardens'
Wynne's Rocks Lookout

N

1 km.

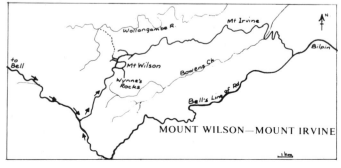

Wollangambe R.
Mt Irvine
to Bell
Bilpin
Mt Wilson
Bowens Ck
Wynne's Rocks
Bell's Line of Rd

N

MOUNT WILSON—MOUNT IRVINE

1 km

13 Mount Wilson and Mount Irvine

1 Getting to Mount Wilson

The road to Mount Wilson leads off Bell's Line of Road about eight kilometres on the eastern side of Bell Railway Station. Seven kilometres of winding road brings you to the mountain itself.

The turn-off may be reached by following Bell's Line of Road from Richmond, or along the Great Western Highway through Penrith and the mountain towns, turning off at Mount Victoria to Bell. These roads are excellent and the travelling comfortable.

Refreshments are available at weekends at the *Tulip Tearoom*, on the left after Breenhold Gardens, and at the former Post Office, in The Avenue, after the church.

The road through Mount Wilson leads on to Mount Irvine where the tar stops. The road down over Bowen's Creek is narrow and winding with a gravel surface. It is mainly a single lane with a few wider places for opposing traffic to pass. The road hugs the mountainside and the scenery is impressive. It joins Bell's Line of Road two km west of the village of Bilpin. The Bowen's Creek Road is not recommended, especially if there has been recent rain.

2 Background to Mount Wilson

Appreciation of this unique mountain is heightened by knowing a little about the **History of Mount Wilson,** its discovery by **William Romaine Govett** and **G. B. Bowen;** its development by **E. S. Wyndham** and **P. F. Adams** of the Lands Department; and finally, **Railway Access to Mount Wilson** and **Some Names at Mount Wilson.**

History of Mount Wilson

The development of Mount Wilson from the 1870s onwards was part of a movement of the well-to-do of the Australian cities to purchase summer residences in the mountains. As the British in India had retreated to the hills, to Darjeeling and Simla, to escape the heat of the plains, so their counterparts (or so they saw themselves) of Sydney migrated to the Blue Mountains.

On this basalt topped mountain the early residents found soil and climate suitable for the planting of the English-type gardens which their birth and education made desirable. At least half of the 'founders' of Mount Wilson were born in England and so perhaps they were home-sick.

There is also evidence, in the layout of Mount Wilson, of the dawning appreciation of the beauties of native Australian plants and natural bushland, noticeable in that period. Tree ferns and many eucalypts were saved and incorporated into the garden scene, and gardens were designed to be a contrast to the bush and to be formal centres in a wild setting.

Discovery

It is clear that Mount Wilson is, geographically, an out-of-the-way place. For this reason it was not settled till the latter half of the nineteenth century, when the European colony was eighty years old.

Archibald Bell makes no mention of the ridge leading off to the north nor do early travellers over Bell's Line of Road. Neither Andrew Brown, of 'Cooerwull', Lithgow, nor Count Strzelecki mention it. There is no record that the Blaxland brothers noticed it when droving their cattle through the Bell's Line route from the Hunter to their Bathurst properties.

It was at least surveyed by W. R. Govett as early as 1833, but this did not lead to settlement at that time. Govett's plan evidently lay forgotten in a drawer in the Lands Department.

Rediscovery leading to settlement came about when G. B. Bowen found his way across Bowen's Creek and up the rough eastern escarpment in 1867. Guided by him came Assistant-Surveyor E. S. Wyndham, who on his subsequent visits to the mountain used Cox's Road and the Darling Causeway to reach it. Perhaps he had hunted around in the Lands Department and found Govett's traverse!

William Romaine Govett (1809-1848)

Assistant Surveyor Govett made the first traverse of Mount Wilson in 1833, as part of a survey of the entire region. Govett was young, only twenty, and inexperienced when he joined the survey staff in 1827 on his arrival in New South Wales. In 1831 Govett surveyed the Blackheath area, finding Govett's Leap Falls, which Mitchell named after him.

He was then instructed to continue the survey made by Assistant-Surveyor Dixon of the Clarence-Wolgan valley area and to finish Assistant-Surveyor Stapylton's work at Mount Tomah. He was also to complete a survey of the country to the north as far as the Macdonald River.

When we look at a map today, we can see that this was an impossible task and that Mitchell obviously did not know what he was asking of his youthful assistant. How could he, in this unknown country, have guessed at the difficulty of the terrain? Until aerial techniques of surveying were developed, this area was never adequately mapped.

Govett eventually sent in his report six months late, after struggling with the smoke and haze of bushfires and problems created by bullocks straying, packhorses breaking down and provisions running out.

On Govett's map a red line shows Bell's Line of Road. Wollangambe Creek and Bowen's Creek are shown but not named. The main range is marked with a line of red dots along which are the words — 'High mass of range of the richest soil covered with almost impenetrable scrub'.

Mitchell complained that the work was unfinished and sent him off to complete it. On 14 August 1833 Govett produced what he described as a 'plan of the ranges terminating at the Colo River being a continuation of his former survey'. This map Mitchell regarded as 'inaccurate' and 'unfinished'. One is not surprised to find that Govett returned to England in 1834.

The talent of the young man was demonstrated a couple of years later when he had a series of articles about New South Wales published in *Saturday Magazine*. They have been described as 'very readable' and 'well-informed'.

G. B. Bowen (1846-1909)

Until 1867 Mount Wilson's lush rainforest was left to grow undisturbed. Then a European settler from a neighbouring mountain made his way across.

George Bartley Bowen was the eldest son of George Meares Countess Bowen, of Bowen Mount. In 1867 he crossed the wild and rough country between Mounts Tomah and Wilson and was impressed by the rich soil and lush growth which he found there.

G. B. Bowen's discovery was reported to the Deputy Surveyor-General of the day, P. F. Adams, who instructed one of his assistant surveyors, Edward S. Wyndham, to look into it.

E. S. Wyndham

Edward Sanford Wyndham came from Wiltshire, England, to his uncle's farm at 'Dalwood', north of Maitland. Judith Wright, one of the descendants of this uncle, George Wyndham, has written of this family in *Generations of Men*.

Edward Wyndham joined the Survey Department in 1867 and his first assignment was to go with G. B. Bowen to Mount Wilson. They crossed the deep gorges between Tomah and Wilson, and Wyndham turned in an enthusiastic if sketchy report. The excuse was that they had been unable to carry sufficient surveying equipment over such rough country. Adams instructed Wyndham to make further examination at his convenience.

There is no mention of Govett's map in any of the correspondence, but when next Wyndham set out, he went by way of Mount Victoria and marked out the road from Bell's Line to the foot of Mount Wilson. He found that the good soil on the top of the ridge varied in width, being richer on the south-eastern side and poor and sandy on the north-western side.

The land on Mount Wilson was withdrawn from conditional purchase pending further survey and Wyndham was instructed to subdivide it into sixty-two portions. Camp was pitched near Waterfall Creek, the area later called Nutman's Camp, and the work was eventually completed by 1869. Copies of the subdivisions map were available by June 1870.

P. F. Adams

Philip Francis Adams became involved with the development of Mount Wilson through his official position of Deputy Surveyor General. After assigning Assistant-Surveyor Wyndham to accompany G. B. Bowen to the mountain, and receiving his report, he sent Wyndham back to survey the mountain into sixty-two portions. At Wyndham's suggestion, he had the land reserved from conditional purchase until after survey, so allowing the job to be done efficiently.

The lots were put up for auction in 1870 but they did not sell quickly at first, as there was uncertainty about access to the mountain. After the opening of the Mount Wilson Platform (near the present Bell Station) in May 1875, all the blocks then surveyed were sold within twelve months. P. F. Adams was one of the first purchasers.

Railway Access to Mount Wilson

Development of Mount Wilson was closely connected with the extension of the railway line over the mountains.

The line was opened at Cleveland Paddocks at Redfern in 1855 and had advanced as far as Weatherboard (later called Wentworth Falls) by 1867 and to Mount Victoria by 1 May 1868. Wyndham was able to use the train to send his plans to the Lands Department. Sydney people were already buying their holiday homes in the mountain towns.

The section of the railway from Mount Victoria to Bowenfels, on the other side of Lithgow, was completed in October 1869, by way of the famous Great Zig Zag. During the course of its construction, Wyndham, who was working at Hartley Vale, found, when he had occasion to go to Mount Wilson, that the road was blocked by the railway. He pointed out that if the land he had recently surveyed was to be sold, there would need to be a level crossing. As a result Mr John Whitton, Engineer-in-Chief of the Railways and builder of the Zig Zag,

constructed a bridge over the railway. A platform was built near the bridge and opened in May 1875, under the name of Mount Wilson Platform. It retained this name until 1889, when it was changed to Bell. The platform was moved to its present site in 1910.

Once access was assured, the blocks on Mount Wilson sold rapidly and travel by train was an integral part of the mountain experience.

The railway brought mail and supplies and heavy articles to the station and took away produce. The residents took it in turns for one of them to drive in each day and pick up the mail and light supplies. Bullock teams took timber and other produce to the station and camped overnight, next day bringing back any heavy items that had arrived.

Some Names on Mount Wilson and Mount Irvine

Deputy Surveyor-General, Mr P. F. Adams, visited Wyndham's camp in 1868 and named the mountain for the Minister for Lands of the day, Mr J. Bowie Wilson.

John Bowie Wilson (1820-1883) was born in Irvine, Ayrshire, Scotland, came to Australia in 1840, and entered the Legislative Assembly of New South Wales as representative for Patrick Plains in 1859. He became Minister for Lands from 1867 to 1868, during the second ministry of Sir James Masters.

We may assume that the extension of the range, Mount Irvine, was named for Mr Wilson's birthplace.

The Five Mile and the Zigzag

The distance by road from Bell

railway station (or Mount Wilson Platform, as it was then), to the turn-off to the mountain is five miles (i.e. eight kilometres), and it is almost the same distance from that turn-off to the township of Mount Wilson. hence the name, applied both to the turn-off and the access road.

From Bell's Line the road runs along a fairly flat sandstone ridge, on which heath type vegetation flourishes. Waratahs and other species of the sandstone bloom in their season, preparing the visitor for beauties to come.

A botanist of the 1880s, Alexander Greenlaw Hamilton, wrote of the area: 'It takes no long experience of Australian plants to know that the more barren and forbidding the soil, the more lovely the flowers you may expect to find.'

Where the mountain proper begins, the zigzag in the road is impressive, both for the steepness and sharpness of the turn and for the magnificent stand of Mountain ash, tree ferns and other rainforest species.

This line of road was surveyed by E. S. Wyndham in 1868, and Richard Wynne, one of the 'founders', was responsible for the construction of the zigzag in the later 1870s.

The 'Five Mile' was maintained by the residents of Mount Wilson at their own expense for many years.

3 Interesting Features of Mount Wilson

The Gardens and Avenues of Mount Wilson, Lookouts, Picnic Areas and Walking Tracks and Development of Amenities

The Gardens of Mount Wilson

In spring and autumn some of the property owners on Mount Wilson open their gardens to the public, the proceeds going to charity. Some gardens were established 100 years ago, others are relatively new, but all are beautiful.

You will not be able to see all the gardens in one visit, but the addresses are given beside the descriptive and historical notes which follow.

Bebeah, The Avenue, near the Post Office

This is one of the older gardens and was planted by early owner, Mr E. K. Cox.

Breenhold, The Avenue, at the top of the Zigzag

This is the newest and most ambitious undertaking on the Mount and will take many years to complete.

Breenhold includes the block selected soon after the first survey by the Surveyor-General, Mr P. F. Adams.

Cherry Cottage and Windy Ridge, Queen's Avenue

These two beautiful gardens are often open to the public in spring and autumn.

Dennarque, Church Avenue

This was the home of Mr E. C. Merewether. The two-storeyed residence is built of local stone, as are 'Yengo' and 'Wynstay'.

Farcry, Church Avenue

Koonawarra, Church Avenue

Lindfield Park, Farrer Road, halfway between Mount Wilson and Mount Irvine.

Nooroo, Church Avenue

The house and garden were built and laid out by the original owner, William Hay. After passing through the hands of a number of owners, the property was taken over by Mr George Valder, former principal of the Hawkesbury Agricultural College, in 1919.

Sefton, Church Avenue

This is on the original 'Balangra' property bought by Mr J. D. Cox. The old cottage has been converted to a billiard room and the new residence is across the lawn opposite. Henry Marcus Clark named his new home after Sefton Park, near Liverpool, England, the place of his birth.

Withycombe, on the corner of The Avenue and Church Avenue

This piece of land was bought from its original buyer, Lockyer, by Mr G. H. Cox, who named his residence — 'Beowang', one of the native names for tree fern.

Wynstay, The Avenue

At the end of The Avenue are the gates and lodge of 'Wynstay', which is very much the manor house of the village.

Yengo, Queen's Avenue

This was Jesse Gregson's colonial-style home, built of stone quarried on Mount Wilson and completed in 1880. The garden is 100 years old.

The Avenues of Mount Wilson

These are glorious in spring and autumn. The early residents regarded the roads as extensions of their properties and beautified them accordingly.

The main road through the township, from Ferny Corner to 'Wynstay', was originally planted with Spanish and horse chestnuts, oriental planes, limes and elms. Unfortunately the Spanish chestnuts were affected by a fungus disease. They were replaced by beeches which have grown well and have filled the gaps. In more recent years the planting of trees has been extended along the part of The Avenue towards the Zigzag.

In 1925 Mr Fred Mann, of 'Yengo', and the Hon. W. C. Holman, one time Premier of N.S.W. and resident of Mount Wilson, planted liquidambers and pink cherries alongside the oaks of Queen's Avenue. It is a sight to be seen in spring and autumn. A rare golden Deodar was planted here to mark the coronation of Queen Elizabeth II.

An English oak was planted near the church to commemorate the coronation of King George VI in 1937. Nearby Church Avenue is shaded on one side by elm trees and bordered with stately *Eucalyptus oreades* on the other.

Look-outs, Picnic Areas and Walking Tracks

Wynne's Rocks Look-out via Queen's Avenue and Wynne's Rocks Road

This is a picnic and barbecue area. From this point on the south-eastern edge of Mount Wilson, one looks over Bowen's Creek and sees a typical Blue Mountain skyline.

The look-out is named for early settler, Richard Wynne, whose residence, 'Wynstay', is on the top of the mountain.

The deep valleys seen to separate Wilson from Tomah were crossed on foot by G. B. Bowen in 1867.

Du Faur's Rocks — Du Faur's Rocks Road leaves The Avenue near the Fire Shed

From the Rocks the view is towards the west, enclosed by the distant ranges of the Great Divide and the deep ravines of Du Faur Creek and Bell Creek, both tributaries of the Wollangambe River.

A walking track to the left leads to the curious rock formation of the 'Chinaman's Hat', below which some fake Aboriginal art has been painted by film-makers. On the right another short track takes you to the Pheasant's Cave. A track at a lower level joins these two places.

Walking Track to the Wollangambe River

A road turning off to the left at the War Memorial Park takes you to a track of about three kilometres through fairly rough terrain to the Wollangambe River.

Waterfalls Picnic Ground and Walking Track

The road from The Avenue at 'Founders Corner' and 'Wynstay' leads to a picnic and barbecue area with a distant view of Kurrajong Heights. A three kilometre walking track circles down through rain forest past the Waterfall and comes back to the picnic area.

The Cathedral of Ferns

This beautiful spot is a short distance along the Mount Irvine Road. Opposite Kirk's Timber Mill is a large picnic and camping area. The walking tracks in the Cathedral of Ferns begin at the Mount Irvine end of the picnic area. This is a good place to park your car, as the road beyond the start of the track is very narrow, leaving little room for parking.

Tree ferns, sassafras and coachwood trees and a few large eucalypts provide cover for the understorey of vines and ferns characteristic of rain forest. The 'Giant Tree' is appropriately named.

Development of Amenities for Mount Wilson Residents

Nutman's Camp

A magnificent hedge of rhododendrons lines the road where Queen's Avenue curves round into Wyndham Road. Behind these properties bordering the road is the flat and sheltered spot where Assistant-Surveyor E. S. Wyndham made his camp while surveying the mountain. Here Robert Kirk built a hut and Eccleston Du Faur and Richard Wynne camped there on their first visits to the mountain.

Nutman was a contractor for logging and building, who later used the site and whose name the area retains. Wyndham Road, of course, reminds us of the surveyor.

Silva Plana Reserve — entrance from The Avenue

This large flat area became a recreation ground for local residents owing to the generosity of Mrs Esmey Burfitt, daughter of James Elliott Mann, of Dennarque, in the early part of this century. The first owner of the 4.4 hectares of which the reserve was part was C. B. Brownrigg, a son of Captain Brownrigg, Superintendent of the Australian Agricultural Company from November 1852 to July 1856. Young Brownrigg had been an assistant-surveyor sent to work with E. S. Wyndham in the Hartley Vale area after completion of the Mount Wilson survey.

Brownrigg did not hold the land for long, selling out to E. C. Merewether, who built a cottage there while his home on the higher part of the mountain was being built. The cottage was used as a post office in the early days of settlement.

The Mann family named the cottage 'Silva Plana' after a house they had at Springwood, it also being built on a level wooded spot.

St George's Church of England

This church was built by the children of Henry Marcus Clark, of 'Sefton', to perpetuate his memory. Lieutenant Colonel R. O. Wynne, of 'Wynstay',. donated the land on which the church stands. The church was consecrated in 1916. Before that time, church services had been held in the schoolhouse, and earlier in the homes of the residents, the visiting clergyman travelling then, as now, from the Church of England at Mount Victoria.

Founders' Corner

Opposite 'Wynstay' is a small park, planted with ornamental trees and shrubs, and kept in order by the local Progress Association. In a semicircular seat of local basalt is set a plaque, which reads:

'This Park was planted in 1932 by the residents of Mount Wilson in memory of E. K. Cox, G. H. Cox, J. D. Cox, E. Du Faur, J. Gregson, W. Hay, R. Kirk, E. C. Merewether, Judge M. H. Stephen and R. Wynne, who came to Mount Wilson 1875-1880.'

A second plaque has been added more recently. It reads:

'Mount Wilson Centenary. The Mountain was first explored by William Romaine Govett in 1833. This Plaque commemorates the centenary of settlement following survey in 1878. This plaque was set by Mr S. W. Kirk, Nov. 6, 1968.'

The park is situated at one end of The Avenue, which was planted by those founders and is an even more fitting memorial to them.

4 The Founders of Mount Wilson and Mount Irvine

The Cox Family, Eccleston Du Faur, The Gregson Family, William Hay, Robert Kirk, Edward Merewether, Sir Matthew Stephen, Richard Wynne, and Charles Scrivener, of Mount Irvine.

The Cox Family

Three grandsons of William Cox, of road building fame, bought land at Mount Wilson and built summer residences there.

Edward King Cox, of 'Fernhill', Mulgoa, was a member of the Legislative Council from 1874 until his death in 1883. He built a cottage, 'Bebeah', on the south side of The Avenue and laid out its beautiful garden.

George Henry Cox, of 'Burrundulla', Mudgee, was the first Mayor of the Municipality of Cudgegong, and from 1856 to 1859 represented Wellington County in the Legislative Assembly of New South Wales, and was later a member of the Legislative Council. He built a residence which he named 'Beowang', an Aboriginal name for tree fern, on the opposite side of The Avenue from 'Bebeah'. This is now 'Withycombe'.

James Dalrymple Cox, of 'Cullenbone', Mudgee, built 'Balangra' on the western side of William Hay's 'Nooroo'. In 1910 the property passed to H. M. Clark, an able and enterprising merchant of Sydney.

The Cox family played a considerable part in the development of Mount Wilson.

Eccleston Frederick Du Faur (1832-1915)

Eccleston Du Faur was an Englishman of French descent. Born in 1832, he attended Harrow and read mathematics at Cambridge until he abandoned the course because of ill-health. He arrived in Sydney in 1863 and became Chief Draftsman with the Surveyor-General's Office, a position he held until retirement in 1881. His work was mainly settling disputes over run boundaries and in mapping the state.

Being interested in the beauties of nature and the Australian scenery, he spent time in the Blue Mountains and encouraged others to do so, and when the railway had extended as far as 'Weatherboard' (Wentworth Falls), the surge of interest in the area was called 'Du Faur's Blue Mountain Craze'.

Du Faur may have been partly responsible for the interest taken in reports of Mount Wilson in the Lands Department. As early as 1868 he visited the mountain and explored it with Robert Kirk of Windsor. He encouraged his friends, Richard Wynne, E. C. Merewether and H. Stephen, to do likewise.

Du Faur bought a block of 11.3 hectares on the poorer soil, his co-purchaser being Sir Joseph George Long-Innes, M.L.A. He built a hut and employed as caretaker Lewis Thompson. He used this hut as a base for excursions, keeping camp equipment and pack horses there.

One excursion was made into the Grose Gorge, via Engineers' Track from the Darling Causeway. He and his party penetrated to the foot of Govett's Leap. Mr Bischoff, a landscape photographer, and Mr

Piguenit, a landscape painter of distinction, were able to illustrate, as Du Faur wrote later, 'our mountain scenery from points where it can be studied to the best advantage, from the bottom of the gorges instead of the summit of the ranges'.

Du Faur's interest in science led to his selection as an observer of the 'transit of Venus' at the Surveyor-General's Observatory Camp at Woodford in 1874. His main residence was on Sydney's north shore. He brought about, through the Hon. Henry Copeland, the Minister of Lands of the day, the foundation of the Ku-ring-gai Chase National Park. A founder of the National Art Gallery, he was one of the board of five trustees, acting as Honorary Secretary and Treasurer, and later President of its Board.

The Gregson Family

Jesse Gregson came to Australia in 1856 from Essex, England. Gregson became manager of the Australian Agricultural Company, succeeding E. C. Merewether, whose friend he had become. He heard of Mount Wilson from Merewether and, in the course of a holiday at Bowenfels near Lithgow, he visited the mountain and eventually bought the land on which he built 'Yengo', on Queen's Avenue. Gregson wrote to a friend: 'We never missed a summer at "Yengo", generally going there early in December and remaining till April'. Although their main home was in Newcastle, as work with the A. A. Company required, he and his wife and children were very fond of their mountain retreat.

Edward Gregson, younger son of

Jesse Gregson, succeeded his father in the beautification and maintenance of the property, and in furthering the collection of native species, specialising in identifying, classifying and describing the eucalypts of the area. His collection reposes in the University of New England at Armidale.

William Hay

William Hay purchased nine blocks of the original survey, in all about 38.5 hectares. He built 'Nooroo' and established the garden there. His cottage is now the billiard room. 'Sefton' and 'Bebeah' are built on land which he sold to the Cox family.

Robert Kirk

Robert Kirk had been a hotel owner and farmer at Windsor. He came to Mount Wilson with Eccleston Du Faur and explored it. He moved onto the mountain in 1875, became a sawmiller and contractor for building and farming. His descendants still live on the mountain.

Two of Robert's grandsons have attained international fame S.B.W. (Tom) Kirk was world champion axeman from 1940 to 1952. In 1936 he and his brother, E. R. S. (Peter) Kirk won the world championship in double-handed sawing.

Edward Christopher Merewether (1818-93)

E. C. Merewether, came to New South Wales in 1838, where he was Civil Aide-de-Camp of governors, Sir George Gipps and Sir Charles Fitzroy.

In 1861 Merewether became General Superintendent of the Australian Agricultural Company and served two terms of seven years, resigning in 1875. While in this post, he used to take his family each summer to Lawson. In 1876 he went to Mount Wilson, explored it and was so impressed with the soil and vegetation that he bought three blocks in different parts of the mountain.

He built first on the area at the top of the Zigzag, which he had bought from its first owner, Brownrigg. He called this place Silva Plana and lived there with his family while the 'big house' was being built on the top of the mountain.

Merewether built his new house of local sandstone and called it 'Dennarque', an aboriginal name for tree fern.

The suburb of Merewether in Newcastle is called after him.

Sir Matthew Henry Stephen (1823-1920)

Matthew Henry Stephen a judge of the Supreme Court bought a block of 4.25 hectares on the Mount Irvine side of 'Wynstay'. There he built 'Campanella', one of the larger residences at the time, and a yearly dance was held there, where 'masters and mistresses mingled with their employees in ye olde English fashion'. This house burnt down, but has been rebuilt.

Richard Wynne

A lover of nature, and a friend of Eccleston Du Faur, Richard Wynne was one of the early visitors to the mountain and one of the first to take up several blocks of land.

On the top of the mountain he built a cottage which he named 'Yarrawa', an aboriginal name for tree fern and later 'Wynstay' next to it.

Richard Wynne is remembered elsewhere in Australia by art-lovers for the Wynne Prize, which is given annually on the recommendation of the Trustees of the Art Gallery of New South Wales to the Australian artist submitting the best landscape painting, in oils or in watercolours of an Australian scene, or the best example of figure sculpture.

Mount Irvine

In 1897 Charles Robert Scrivener, a staff surveyor of the Lands Department, was given the job of surveying a road to the end of the Mount Wilson spur He described the land there and located an approach across Bowen's Creek, to Bell's Line of Road near Bilpin. He suggested that it should be proclaimed a National Reserve, but instead it was thrown open for settlement.

The men who took it up were C. R. Scrivener's son, Charles P. Scrivener, and two of his friends, Harold Morley and Basil Knight-Brown. These three young men had graduated with credit from the Hawkesbury Agricultural College in 1897, the first year of Mr George Valder's principalship. They each selected 10 hectares, and developed orchards there. Their chief problem was access, and for twelve years each worked on the road to Mount Wilson for one month each year.

14 The Great Zig Zag and Lithgow District

1 Darling Causeway to the Zig Zag

Turn right off the Great Western Highway at Mount Victoria along the road to Bell. You are driving along the **Darling Causeway** discovered by **Hamilton Hume** in 1827.

About 5 km from Mount Victoria and just past the Hartley Vale Road on the left, is the **Site of the Hartley Vale Railway Station** now demolished, also **The Engineers' Track** started down into the Grose Valley from the other side of the railway line.

Continue along the road to Bell. At the T-junction turn left into **Chifley Road** which goes to Lithgow. About 5 km along notice on the left *Dargin's Creek Dam* which once provided water for steam engines at the *Clarence Siding* nearby. From this point on, the road is following or actually occupying the 1869 railway line to the Zig Zag.

About 3 km past the bridge over the present railway line, on the right is the restored CLARENCE RAILWAY STATION, from which trains running on **The Great Zig Zag** depart. The trains run at weekends and on public and school holidays, making three or four trips of about 80 minutes each. The railway is operated and maintained by the voluntary services of members of the Zig Zag Railway Co-op Ltd. For information about departure times and fares, write to P.O. Box 33, Woodford, N.S.W. 2778, or phone (047) 57 3061 in business hours.

Newnes Forest Road, near Clarence Railway Station, goes to *The Glow Worm Tunnel*. This interesting and scenic place is reached by about 20 km of gravel road which occupies the old railway track into the Wolgan Valley. The walk through the tunnel is worth while — take a torch for each person for maximum enjoyment.

Back at Chifley Road, turn right towards Lithgow. A short distance along, on the left, is an area to pull off to 'view' the Zig Zag train.

The Darling Causeway

Hamilton Hume discovered this section of the Blue Mountains Range, which divides the Grose River from tributaries of the Cox's River, when looking for a better route off the mountains than the Mount York descents. He so named it, he said, as he had 'discovered it during General Darling's Administration and my going out under His Excellency's patronage'.

This name had fallen into disuse, but has recently been revived.

Hamilton Hume (1797-1873)

Hamilton Hume is best known for his explorations to the south of Botany Bay and for his discovery, with W. H. Hovell, of the Murray River and the route to the Port Phillip area.

Hume was born at Parramatta, but

his family soon moved to Appin. From there, Hume, at the age of 17, explored as far south as the Berrima district. Later he accompanied James Meehan and Charles Throsby into the Goulburn area, and afterwards Yass and Gunning.

On 13 August 1827 Colonial Secretary Alexander MacLeay published a Government Notice offering a reward for the discovery of a better road to avoid the two difficult patches at Mounts York and Blaxland, and Hume set out soon afterwards.

In October *The Monitor* reported that Mr Hume had discovered a much better road to Bathurst, and Assistant-Surveyor White, and the Deputy Surveyor-General, Major Mitchell, and Lieutenant Shadforth accompanied Mr Hume over his track.

Mitchell objected to Hume's line on the grounds that it was too far from the Fish River where the settlers were, was not near the Vale of Clwydd, and was not shorter and was still over mountains where water and grass were scarce.

Although his line was not used by Major Mitchell, who was at that time planning his own deviation down the Pass of Victoria, Hume claimed his reward and six months later was granted 1280 acres (518 hectares) in the Yass district.

Site of Hartley Vale Railway Station — 1870-1975

A siding to serve the kerosene shale mines in the valley was opened in 1870 about 6 km along Darling Causeway. A road and a tramway down a steep cliff brought the shale to trucks at the siding. This continued till the mines closed in 1913, when the shale was exhausted.

A passenger platform was also built near the siding. Tourists from Sydney would stop there and walk down to look at the shale mines. The station was closed and removed in 1975 through lack of patronage.

Engineers' Track

In 1857 it was decided to make a trial survey of a route along the Grose Valley for the proposed railway over the Blue Mountains. There was to be a tunnel through Darling Causeway to Lithgow. After three years work, it was then decided that the route would be too expensive and difficult.

Part of this track was used by Eccleston Du Faur in the 1870s to take a party of artists and journalists to see Govett's Leap from the bottom.

Chifley Road

This road was completed in the late 1940s as part of the second strategic highway being built during World War II. It was named for Joseph Benedict (Ben) Chifley, (1885-1951), Prime Minister of Australia, 1945 to 1949. He began his working career as a locomotive driver with the N.S.W. Railways, and entered parliament in 1928. He became leader of the Labour Party and Prime Minister on the death of John Curtin.

In the early 1930s there was only a track connecting the railway formations abandoned after 1910.

A road was constructed over Scenic Hill and opened in 1939 giving access to the Zig Zag from Lithgow.

The Great Zig Zag, Lithgow

The railways of New South Wales owe much to John Whitton, Chief Engineer from 1857 to 1889, during the period when most lines were constructed. The line over the Blue Mountains and the two zigzags, were the result of his genius and vision. The Lithgow Zig Zag is recognised as one of the great engineering feats of the nineteenth century. Visitors came from all over the world to see it.

An alternative scheme to get down into the Lithgow valley from the mountains was a tunnel project which would have cost much more. In the event, no contractor could be found to undertake to build the tunnel. Therefore the Zig Zag, relatively cheaper, was the method used. 'Switchback' railways were being built in America, but these were the first constructed in Australia.

In the form of a simple Z, like the Lapstone Zig Zag, but much larger, the Lithgow Zig Zag curves round the mountain, crossing three large viaducts and passing through a tunnel and numerous cuttings. The beauty of the sandstone viaducts seen against the rugged mountain is a sight never to be forgotten.

The contract was let to Mr Patrick Higgins and after nearly three and a half years work, it was completed. On 18 October 1869 'without public ceremony' the 9.00 a.m. passenger train from Sydney steamed down the Zig Zag and arrived at Bowenfels at 2.45 p.m.

A dam to provide water for the engines, a siding to let trains cross and a platform for tourists were added.

Duplication of the line took place in 1880. Here the line descends in a 1 in 42 grade around an 8 chain curve, the sharpest mainline curve in N.S.W.

In spite of the improvements made over the years, traffic on the line became too heavy for the Zig Zag, and in 1907 it was decided to build a deviation which required 10 tunnels under Mount Sinai.

Such was the interest created by the engineering achievement and the grandeur of the Great Zig Zag that in 1881 the area was declared a public reserve. Then, after 1910 and the advent of the tunnel deviation, the top and middle roads were neglected until the opening of the Scenic Hill Road from Lithgow in 1939.

The Zig Zag Railway Co-operative Ltd was formed in the 1960s and a narrow gauge line was laid on the middle road. The first of the co-operative's engines used the track on 18 October 1975, on the 106th anniversary of the original opening.

The popularity of the Zig Zag Railway encouraged the Co-operative to extend the line to Clarence Railway Station so that the trains could operate over the whole of the Zig Zag. This new section was opened on 29 October 1988.

From the station the train enters the long Clarence tunnel. It emerges beside Chifley Road, rounds Mt Sinai and heads into the bush to the top of the Zig Zag.

The 1975 approach road followed the 'Top Road' of the original line, which had a grade of 1 in 42. It passed the site of the Edgecombe Signal Box and a crossing loop opened in 1901.

A parking area, picnic shelters and barbecue area were provided.

From *Engineers Lookout*, at No 1 viaduct, all three viaducts are visible

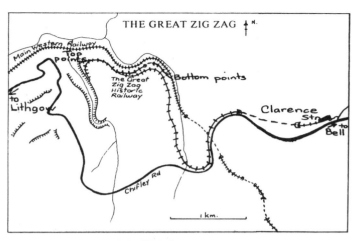

No 2 and No 3 viaducts, Great Zig Zag Railway, from Engineers Lookout.

No 1 viaduct, Great Zig Zag Railway, from Engineers Lookout

and the Z-shaped layout of the three levels can be seen. John Whitton is said to have supervised the construction from this point.

The 'Top Road' then passes over No 1 viaduct — 2 x 4.57 metres and 5 x 9.14 m (2 x 15 ft and 5 x 30 ft) arches on a ten chain curve.

A ledge cut in the cliff provided the first reversing wing at Top Points. The first Co-op trains left from a station here for their run along the Middle Road. The concrete block at the dead end of the cliff above Ida Falls Gully was placed there after an engine over-ran the stops and was balanced precariously over the edge before two engines pulled it back to safety.

The longer wing extending round the hill on a ledge cut through the rock was completed in 1908 to enable whole goods trains to be accommodated there so that trains no longer had to be divided at Clarence and Lithgow. No. 1 Car Park was in the vicinity.

Starting down the middle road, along which trains originally had to be pushed by the engines, the line crossed No 2 viaduct — 9 × 9.14 metre (9 × 30 ft) arches on a straight alignment, the highest pier being 22.86 metres (75 feet). Then there is a narrow ledge which was made by an electrically fired blast of explosive, the first to be so fired in Australia. To achieve this technically advanced method, as it was then, of setting off the charges,

Chief Engineer Whitton needed the co-operation of the Superintendent of Telegraphs for New South Wales, Edward Charles Cracknell, who had a high reputation in this field of expertise.

Next to be crossed is No 3 viaduct — 8 x 9.14 metre (8 x 30ft) arches located on a 10 chain curve. Then, at the foot of No 1 viaduct is a picnic area with shelters, named *Cockerton Place*, for H. K. Cockerton who was a Trustee of the Zig Zag Reserve for seventeen years and encouraged the development of the site.

From the broad area a ledge leads to the tunnel, 68.58 metres (225 feet) long on an 8 chain curve. The line emerges beside *Belmore Place*, the site of a projected second tunnel. This proved to be unsafe and another electrically fired blast was set off to bring down the dangerous rock. The Countess of Belmore, accompanied by the Governor and other spectators travelled by train to Mount Victoria and by carriage down Victoria Pass to Lithgow and the Zig Zag. They were all refreshed with lunch after the Countess had pressed the button to set off the blast.

The Middle Road then runs past Bottom Points. Today these old passing loops are occupied by the Co-op's engines and carriages. A short distance away in the gully is a sandstone dam which provided water for past engines and still does so for engines of the present tourist trains.

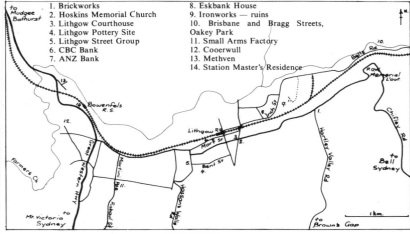

1. Brickworks
2. Hoskins Memorial Church
3. Lithgow Courthouse
4. Lithgow Pottery Site
5. Lithgow Street Group
6. CBC Bank
7. ANZ Bank
8. Eskbank House
9. Ironworks — ruins
10. Brisbane and Bragg Streets, Oakey Park
11. Small Arms Factory
12. Cooerwull
13. Methven
14. Station Master's Residence

LITHGOW

2 Lithgow

After visiting the Great Zig Zag, return to Chifley Road, turn right and drive west towards Lithgow. About 4 km on the right, on the inside of a sweeping curve, are the ruins of GUN EMPLACEMENTS from WWII.

Half way down Scenic Hill pause at the EX-P.O.W. MEMORIAL LOOKOUT to see views of the **Lithgow Valley**.

Continue down the hill towards Lithgow.

On the left, at the corner of Hartley Vale Road, is the site of the VALE OF CLWYDD BRICKWORKS built about 1912 (Nat. Tr.). Follow the signs which direct you along Mort Street as the alternative route through the town. Near the top of the hill, on the left, is the **Hoskins Memorial Uniting Church** on the corner of Bridge Street. On the right, on the diagonally opposite corner, is the LITHGOW COURTHOUSE, built in 1879 of brick in a symmetrical Federation style (Nat. Tr.).

Turn left at Eskbank Street, right into Bent Street, and left into Silcock Street, to the **Lithgow Pottery Site**. Some of the buildings still standing are being used by the coal mining company and by Mr Bob Cunningham. His art gallery and hand-made pottery works are open daily, 10 a.m. to 4.30 p.m. Visitors are welcome.

Turn left at Bent Street and right at Lithgow Street. On the left are the imposing terrace houses of Nos 8–22, the LITHGOW STREET GROUP (Nat. Tr., private property), and No. 24, LITHGOW STREET built in 1876 to the design of Edward Gell (Nat. Tr.) and now a restaurant.

Turn right into Main Street and drive east. On the left is the former **CBC Bank** (the *National Australia Bank*) on the corner of Gray Street (Nat. Tr). On the right, a block or two further on, is the ANZ BANK, built in 1888, (Nat. Tr.).

Turn left at Bridge Street and cross the railway line. Turn immediately right into Inch Street. Just past the race track turn left into Bennett Street. On the right is **Eskbank House**, period home and museum administered by the Lithgow District Historical Society. The museum houses displays of Lithgow Pottery, the history of local coal mining and other industries, a photographic collection. Larger items are to be seen in the coachhouse and the 'Possum', a steam locomotive used at the Hoskins Steel Works, is on display in the grounds. Open Thursday to Monday, 10 a.m. to 4 p.m. Admission is charged.

Return along Bennett Street and turn left into Inch Street. Soon on the right is **Blast Furnace Park**, opened as a bicentennial project on 17 December 1988. It is being redeveloped by the Greater Lithgow City Council.

Continue along Inch Street and Bell Road to **Oakey Park**.

Turn left into Island Parade and left again into Brisbane Street. Nos 1–9 and 2–12 THE BRISBANE STREET GROUP are listed by the Nat. Tr. In the next street parallel to Brisbane Street are Nos 1–13 and 2–12 THE BRAGG STREET GROUP (Nat. Tr.).

Retrace your route to Lithgow, noticing on the left the old RAIL-WAY BARRACKS built on the first BROWN'S PLATFORM (built for Thomas Brown, of Eskbank) and ESKBANK RAILWAY STATION originally to serve the nearby house and now the Lithgow Goods Yard.

Cross the railway and turn right along Main Street. At the western end of the shopping centre on the left is *Queen Elizabeth Park* named for Queen Elizabeth II on her first visit to Australia in 1954. Many beautiful trees and the rose garden make this a pleasant stopping place. Picnic, barbecue and toilet facilities.

Three blocks further on the left (285 Main Street), is the *Lithgow Tourist Information Centre* where helpful leaflets about the area are available.

Turn left at Lawrence Street, left into The Avenue, right at Wright Street and left into Hassan's Walls Road.

About 3 km of winding gravel road, very pretty, leads to the top of the hill to *HASSAN'S WALLS LOOKOUT.* There are good panoramic views from several vantage points. On a clear day Mount York is visible to the east and Mount Blaxland to the west. There are barbecaues, shelters, but no toilets. The road on the left leads to other lookouts and several km brings you to BRACEY'S LOOKOUT above the Lithgow Valley.

Return via Hassan's Walls Road to

Wrights Road. Turn left and immediately right into Methven Street. On the hill above on the left is Lithgow Reservoir. The SITE OF ANDREW BROWN'S COAL MINE was in this vicinity.

About ½ km along, on the left, is the **Lithgow Small Arms Factory.** Turn left at Martini Parade (beside the S.A. Factory) and keeping left follow the curves of Rabaul Street. On the left is **La Salle Academy.** Turn left from Rabaul Street at the highway.

Lithgow's Valley

Lithgow's Valley was named in 1826 after William Lithgow (1784-1864), first Auditor-General for the colony and later chairman of the Land Board. He had no land grants in the district, but was a personal friend of John Oxley (1783-1828), Surveyor-General from 1812 and responsible for many names on the map.

The first property in the district was Andrew Brown's *Cooerwull*, and that name was used for some time. Then the town adopted the name of Lithgow and in 1889 it was incorporated as a Municipality. In 1977 the Lithgow City Council and Blaxland Shire Council were united to form the Greater Lithgow City Council.

Hoskins Memorial Uniting Church (Nat. Tr.)

The Hoskins Memorial Church was built as a tribute to the memory of Guildford Hoskins, who died in 1916 at the age of 26. He was the eldest son of Charles Hoskins, who had taken over the Lithgow Iron and Steel Works in 1907. Built under the direction of Architect J. Barr it is set in gardens landscaped by Mr Paul Sorensen.

Lithgow Pottery Works Site (Nat. Tr., Her. Aus.)

In 1876 the Lithgow Valley Colliery Company began making pipes and bricks from clay on the site. Three years later, James Silcock came from Chesterfield, England, to make domestic pottery there. The pottery closed during the depression of 1898 although bricks and pipes were still made. Pottery was made again for twelve months by Edward Brownfield in 1906. Surviving from that period are the brick flue, brick clay store, brick warehouse and residence, designed by Edward Gell; the last is still used by the coal mining company. The large pipe kiln, "Big Ben", dating from 1875-89, collapsed on 29 May 1977. It was one of the few well-preserved surviving industrial structures of its kind of that date.

The old buggy shed and pattern store are being used as an art gallery and a hand made pottery workshop by Mr Bob Cunningham who has rented the site from the mining company.

Examples of the original pottery may be seen in Eskbank House.

CBC Bank (Nat. Tr.)

The Commercial Banking Company of Sydney set up its offices in Lithgow in 1876 but soon outgrew its temporary accommodation. In 1883 a Tudor-style building designed by

George Allen Mansfield of Mansfield Bros. was completed.

Still standing in Main Street, it is one of the few works by this architect remaining.

Eskbank House (Nat. Tr., Her. Aus.)

This elegant single-storey sandstone Georgian-style house was built in 1842 for Thomas Brown, who first established the coal industry in Lithgow. He purchased 700 acres (283.4 hectares). His land contained coal and he supplied it to the railway from 1869. Thomas Brown served as a magistrate at the Hartley Courthouse, travelling there on horseback via the Gap Road which connects the two valleys.

The house was purchased from Australian Iron and Steel by Mr Eric Bracey, well-known businessman of Lithgow, restored and handed over to the City Council for historical purposes.

The house and museum is in the care of the Lithgow District Historical Society.

Blast Furnace Park
(Her. Aus.)

This visually dramatic and industrially important site was used by the Eskbank Ironworks Company from 1875 to 1930. The company was founded by James Rutherford, N.S.W. manager of Cobb and Co., Dan Williams, a Canadian railway engineer, the Honourable John Sutherland, Minister for Public Works and Enoch Hughes, ironmaster at Mittagong.

When the company ran into difficulties, the employees formed a cooperative and leased the works. In 1886 William Sandford became the manager and finally bought the works and estate. The open hearth furnace established here is thought to have been the first in Australia. The Hoskins brothers were the next owners. Eventually they moved the company to Port Kembla.

The ruins include large scale brick structures with a network of underground tunnels, a large slag heap, the blast furnace base and foundations of other buildings.

Oakey Park

This suburb of Lithgow developed as a result of industrial growth in the late 19th century. The houses in Brisbane and Bragg Streets were built for the workers at the mines. Brisbane Street has a number of cottages built in pairs. The Bragg Street houses, except for one pair, are single cottages. The blue roofed house was the original mine manager's residence.

Parts of the brewery, built about 1912, can still be seen at the end of Brewery Lane.

Hassans Walls

There seems to be no actual record of the naming of this tremendous pile of cliffs. A number of suggestions have been made, from a bushranger named Hassan leaping over the cliff (shades of Govett!) to the *Arabian Nights,* 'Place of Hassan, stupendous ruins in the midst of solitude'.

Historians are inclined to think that Governor Macquarie named them. In India there is a large district called

Hassan, separated from the state of Madras by the towering Western Ghats. In the neighbourhood where Governor Macquarie was stationed in his early years as a soldier in India, these rugged mountains were known as the *Walls of Hassan*. It would seem likely that Macquarie had named these rugged walls for a possible similarity to this part of India. The name appears on maps as early as 1823.

Lithgow Small Arms Factory

Opened in 1912, the plant was based on the manufacture of Lee-Enfield .303 Rifle No. Mk III. Pratt and Whitney, an American firm, managed it, training Australians in their American factory.

Work was extended during both World Wars. The factory was able to convert to peacetime manufacture because of the high standard of its equipment and tradesmen.

The streets in the adjoining suburb of Littleton are named for battlefields of World War I and various small arms made by the factory. The houses nearby were constructed for the influx of workers during both wars, each period having its own distinctive style.

La Salle College (formerly Cooerwull Academy) (Nat. Tr.)

This two-storey Victorian Gothic building, of dressed local stone, was designed by Andrew Brown and built by George Donald and James Kirkwood about 1882.

Andrew Brown took up land at the western end of the Lithgow valley in 1824. As well as farming his own property, he also managed James Walker's Wallerawang property, and his name appears in the register of Hartley Courthouse as Deponent against runaway convicts from the Walker estate. Later he hired Chinese to fill the gap after the end of transportation, but the lure of gold was too much for them, and it did not solve Brown's labour problems.

3 Old Bowenfels

From Lithgow, turn left onto the highway, drive about 6 km towards Sydney to **Fernhill** (right) (private property). Turn where the road widens.

A km back along the highway towards Lithgow, on the left, **Forty Bends Road** begins. There are several workmen's cottages and an old homestead, now a poll hereford stud (private property). The winding road was part of Mitchell's Bathurst Road. Continue along the highway. Beyond

the Jenolan Caves Road is the village of **Old Bowenfels** which spreads for a km or more along the road. The village consists of **Former Emu Store** (private property), **Umera** (private property), **Ben Avon** (private property), **Former National School Group** (private property), **Somerset House** (private property), **Presbyterian Church and Cemetery** (opposite) and the site of the Old Glasgow Arms and outbuildings, demolished in the 1980s.

After Rydal Road turn left next at Kirkley Street. Half a km along is AIRDIE (private property, Nat. Tr.) formerly the Presbyterian Manse, built 1860 and additions in 1880s.

Return to the highway and turn left. A short distance along, on the left is SWEET BRIAR HOUSE (private property, Nat. Tr.).

Continue along the highway for a further 2 km and turn left at the lights into Caroline Avenue. Drive down to **Farmer's Creek**. Nearby is the **Site of the Woollen Mill** and **Cooerwull** (private property).

Return to the lights and turn left. A short distance along turn right. Stop at the **Former Station Master's Residence** now *Caddie's Restaurant* and **Bowenfels Railway Station** now an art and crafts gallery.

Turn left onto the highway; on the left is COOERWULL PRESBY-TERIAN CHURCH, 1875. Turn left at the lights and drive through Lithgow to turn right at Hartley Vale Road. This becomes the Gap Road, going through *Brown's Gap* to Hartley Vale. Think of Thomas Brown travelling to Hartley Court House, along this road, to attend to his duties as magistrate there.

Keep left to Little Hartley, and, via Collits' Inn, up Hartley Vale Road to the Darling Causeway. Note the old coal mine on the left as you drive up the hill. At the top a left turn will take you to Bell's Line of Road; a right turn leads to Mount Victoria and the Great Western Highway.

Fernhill (Nat. Tr., Her. Aus.)

This single storeyed building was built

as an inn about 1858 by John Blackman. It was called the *Australian Arms Inn.* It was an important link in the chain of roadside inns.

Forty Bends (Nat. Tr.)

Formerly called *Monte Vista,* this sprawling single storey house, built about 1890, is surrounded by verandahs and is set in a large garden of lawns, trees and shrubs. There are several workmen's cottages on the estate.

Michael Keenan had his *Travellers' Arms Inn* nearby. He was appointed Deputy postmaster in succession to Collits at the foot of Mount York.

The winding road, now no longer part of the highway, was the original Bathurst Road.

Village of Bowenfels

The village was named for George Mears Countess Bowen by Surveyor-General Mitchell. Bowen had been a surveyor in Mitchell's department; then he had resigned and taken up land at Berambing and Bowen Mount. There had been some clash of personalities between the two men. When they met later, Mitchell decided that Bowen was not so bad after all and named the small township after him.

Mitchell's new line of road to Bathurst, constructed in 1832, passed close to Hassan's Walls. Bowenfels developed to serve travellers, as did Hartley.

Former Emu Store (Nat. Tr.)

Built as a private home in 1840, it was

converted to a shop by the addition of an extra room on the front about the 1850s.

Ulmera (Nat. Tr.)

This was formerly the *Bowenfels Inn,* built of sandstone in 1850. James Connors held the licence until 1869, when he returned to his trade as a stonemason.

The Australian Joint Stock Bank opened a branch in this building. After several years, in the early 1870s, the bank moved to Lithgow.

Ben Avon (Nat. Tr., Her. Aus.)

This single-storey dressed sandstone dwelling with attic was built about 1845 by John McLennan as a store and residence. It was later bought by George Lee and converted to a hotel. At one time it was the *Royal Hotel* and was a Cobb and Co. changing station.

The eight bay verandah runs the full length of the house, its roof being supported by fluted timber posts.

Former National School Group (Nat. Tr.)

The school residence was built by H. Robertson in 1851 and the school in 1858.

Somerset House (Nat. Tr., Her. Aus.)

This two storey brick and sandstone house has an attic and was originally built as an inn about 1840. Additions were made about 1870 in brick, with scalloped bargeboards, linked to the stone section by a five-bay timber verandah.

Presbyterian Church (Nat. Tr., Her. Aus.)

This was the first Presbyterian church built west of the Blue Mountains and forms the nucleus of the Bowenfels settlement. The oldest part was financed and built by Andrew Brown about 1842. The vestry at the front and the large hall at the rear were added in 1885 by the Reverend W. McKenzie.

The walls are of local dressed sandstone, the floors of pit sawn Mountain Ash boards laid on hardwood log bearers, and the original cedar joinery may still be seen in the pulpit, wall panelling and pews.

Farmer's Creek

Thomas Mitchell named Farmer's Creek near Lithgow after his horse *Farmer* which fell and broke its neck in the creek. Mitchell had another horse named *Farmer,* which drowned

'Ben Avon', Old Bowenfels

in the Murrumbidgee. After this, he decided that it was an 'unfortunate appellation' for a surveying horse!

Andrew Brown called the creek *Cooerwull Brook,* after his property, but Mitchell's name has survived.

Site of Woollen Mill (Nat. Tr.)

Behind his residence Andrew Brown built a water-powered flour mill, and later converted it to a steam powered woollen mill, using coal mined from his property, the mine being located near the junction of Wrights and Hassans Walls Roads.

Cooerwull (Nat. Tr., Her. Aus.)

Andrew Brown built this house in the 1840s on his 200 acre (about 81 hectares) property, which had been marked out by G. M. C. Bowen. Brown named it for a small flowering plant called by the Aborigines *Cooerwull.*

Station Master's Residence, Bowenfels (Nat. Tr., Her. Aus.)

This charming Gothic Revival sandstone cottage, designed by John Clifton and built in 1869, is now in use as *Caddie's Restaurant.* The coursed random rock face walls are surmounted by a steeply pitched slate roof with large chimneys and curved iron roofed verandahs. The timber bargeboards are ornately carved. A small stone privy is connected to the laundry.

Bowenfels Railway Station (Nat. Tr., Her. Aus.)

The station and the nearby station master's residence were built as components of the Penrith to Bathurst railway extension.

The symmetrical Victorian station, also designed by John Clifton and built in 1869, is of dressed sandstone.

Caddie's Restaurant, former station master's residence, Bowenfels

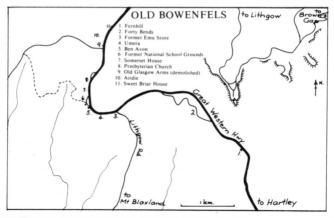

OLD BOWENFELS   to Lithgow   to Brown's Gap

1. Fernhill
2. Forty Bends
3. Former Emu Store
4. Umera
5. Ben Avon
6. Former National School Grounds
7. Somerset House
8. Presbyterian Church
9. Old Glasgow Arms (demolished)
10. Airdie
11. Sweet Briar House

Great Western Hwy

Lithgow Rd

to Mt Blaxland   1 km.   to Hartley

Bibliography

Local

ATKINSON, Louisa: A Voice from the Country, Mulini Press, 1978.

BATES, Geoff: Centenary of the Carrington Hotel 1880-1980.

BATES, Geoff: Gardners Inn, Blackheath, Blue Mountains, N.S.W. Sesqui-centenary 1831-1981.

BAYLEY, William A.: Blue Mountains Railways, Austrail Publications, 1980.

BAYLEY, William A.: Lapstone Zig Zag Railway Blue Mountains — New South Wales, Austrail Publications, 1975.

BAYLEY, William A.: The Great Zig Zag Railway at Lithgow, Austrail Publications, 1977.

BAYLEY, William A.: Lithgow Zig Zag Railway Blue Mountains — New South Wales, Zig Zag Press.

BLUE MOUNTAINS HISTORICAL SOCIETY, with Joseph BENNETT & Sons: Excursion into history, rev. ed., 1982.

CITY OF LITHGOW: Greater Lithgow Information Booklet, City of Lithgow, and N.S.W. Dept. of Tourism, 1980.

CURREY, C. H.: Mount Wilson New South Wales, Angus & Robertson, 1968.

DUNLOP, B. T. & N.S.W. Government Tourist Bureau: Jenolan Caves, New South Wales, Australia, 1964.

DYSON, R. T.: Kurrajong North Public School Centenary, 1878-1978.

FOSTER, W. C., HAVARD, W. L. & DOWD, B. T.: The Story of Hartley and Its Historic Court-house, Blaxland Shire Council, 1937.

HUGHES, Gilbert: The Story of Mount Wilson in the Blue Mountains of New South Wales, Rev. ed., Mt. Wilson Progress Association, 1974.

McKENZIE, E. J.: Hassan's Walls, Lithgow, 3723ft, Lithgow District Historical Society.

MARTIN, Thomas: The Belmont Park Story, St John of God Hospital, Richmond.

N.S.W. Dept. of Railways: The Little Lapstone Zig Zag. (sheet).

ROACH, Steve, and PARIDAENS, Iris: Lithgow and Hartley Valley Sketchbook, Rigby, 1978.

ROTARY CLUB OF BLACKHEATH: Historic Blackheath, edited by John Yeaman, 1975-76.

SEARLE, Allan E.: Faulconbridge, Springwood Historical Society, 1977.

SEARLE, Allan E.: Historic Woodford and Linden, Springwood Historical Society, 1981.

SEARLE, Allan E.: Springwood Notebook 1788-1977, Springwood Historical Society, 1978.

SMAIL, J. M.: Louisa Atkinson of the Kurrajong, Kurrajong Heights Garden Club, 1979.

SPRINGWOOD HISTORICAL SOCIETY, and SEARLE, Allan E.: Places of historic interest on the Lower Blue Mountains, 1977.

WEBB, Vivienne: *Kurrajong; an early history*, 1980.

THE ZIG ZAG TRUST AND THE ZIG ZAG RAILWAY CO-OP LTD: *The Lithgow Zig Zag Railway*, 3rd ed., 1976; and 4th ed., 1982.

General

Australian Dictionary of Biography. The Australian Encyclopaedia. Various editions.

BECHERVAISE, John, and WHITE, Unk: *Blue Mountains Sketchbook*, Rigby, 1971.

BLUE MOUNTAINS CITY COUNCIL: *City of Blue Mountains Historical Register Catalogue.*

Blue Mountains National Park Visitor Guide, National Parks and Wildlife Service.

BLUE MOUNTAINS TOURIST ASSOCIATION: Guides, pamphlets, maps.

BOOKER, Jo: *A Pictorial History of the Blue Mountains*, Blue Mountains City Council, 1978.

BOWD, D. G.: *Macquarie Country*, F. W. Cheshire 1969.

COLLINS, David: *An Account of the English Colony in New South Wales*, (Vol. 1. ed. by Brian J. Fletcher), The Royal Australian Historical Society and A. H. & A. W. Reed, 1975. (Originally published 1798).

CENTRAL MAPPING AUTHORITY: *Tourist Map of Blue Mountains-Burragorang*, 1981.

CENTRAL MAPPING AUTHORITY: Topographic maps. 1:25 000 series Penrith; Springwood; Katoomba; Jamison; Kurrajong; Mount Wilson; Hampton; Jenolan; Kanangra; Yerranderie; Hartley; Lithgow.

CURREY, J. E. B. *ed.*: *Reflections on the Colony of New South Wales by George Caley*, Lansdowne Press, 1966.

The Heritage of Australia, Macmillan, 1981.

Historical Records of New South Wales. Vol I, Part 2. Phillip 1783-1792, Lansdown Slattery, 1978. (facsimile reprint, originally published 1892).

GREGORY'S: *Blue Mountains Street Map.*

MACKANESS, George, ed.: *Fourteen journeys over the Blue Mountains of New South Wales 1813-1841*, Horwitz-Grahame, 1965.

NATIONAL PARKS AND WILD-LIFE SERVICE: Leaflets.

THE NATIONAL TRUST OF AUSTRALIA (NEW SOUTH WALES): *National Trust Register as at December 31, 1976*, and *Supplement No. 1*, January 1, 1977 to December 31, 1977.

POWELL, Greg: *Bushwalking in the Blue Mountains*, Rigby, 1980.

POWELL, Greg: *Ghost Roads of the Blue Mountains*, Blue Mountains Tourist Association (leaflet).

RICHARDS, Joanna Armour, *ed.*: *Blaxland-Lawson-Wentworth 1813*, Blubberhead Press.

ROYAL AUSTRALIAN HISTORICAL SOCIETY: *Journal.* Various references.

SPRIGGS, P. W.: *Our Blue Mountains Yesterdays.*

SPRINGWOOD HISTORICAL SOCIETY: *Bulletin.*

TENCH, Capt. Watkin: *Sydney's First Four Years*, Royal Australian Historical Society and Library of Australian History, 1979. (Originally published 1789).

TAYLOR, Griffith: *Sydneyside Scenery*, Angus & Robertson, 1970.